D1551352

Belleville, Ottawa,
and Galesburg

Kay J. Carr

Belleville, Ottawa, and Galesburg

Community and Democracy on the Illinois Frontier

JUN

1998

Southern Illinois University Press

Carbondale and Edwardsville

Library of Congress Cataloging-in-Publication Data

Carr, Kay J.
    Belleville, Ottawa, and Galesburg : community and democracy on the
Illinois frontier / Kay J. Carr.
        p.   cm.
    Includes bibliographical references (p.   ) and index.
    1. Belleville (Ill.)—Politics and government.   2. Political
culture—Illinois—Belleville—History—19th century.   3. Belleville
(Ill.)—Social conditions.   4. Ottawa (Ill.)—Politics and
government.   5. Political culture—Illinois—Ottawa—History—19th
century.   6. Ottawa (Ill.)—Social conditions.   7. Galesburg (Ill.)—
Politics and government.   8. Political culture—Illinois—
Galesburg—History—19th century.   9. Galesburg (Ill.)—Social
conditions.   I. Title.
    F549.B3C37   1996
    977.3'89—dc20   95-30743
    ISBN 0-8093-2017-7   CIP

For my mother and my father

Contents

Maps

Acknowledgments

Throughout the course of this project, I have been fortunate to have worked with many thoughtful and generous people. From the beginning, my fellow graduate students at the University of Chicago aided me in ways that only they can appreciate, especially Winstanley Briggs, Ellen Eslinger, Susan Gray, and Jean O'Brien. My graduate advisor, Kathleen Neils Conzen, was always helpful and encouraging, as were the other members of my dissertation committee, Edward M. Cook Jr. and Michael Conzen. I also thank Rodney Davis, Keith Sculle, Valerie Martin, and John Hoffmann for their suggestions and encouragement. David Werlich, the chair of the history department at Southern Illinois University at Carbondale, has been of tremendous help during the preparation of the book, and I thank him for his guidance. Other colleagues at Southern Illinois University—Marji Morgan, Michael Batinski, Arnold Barton, Jim Allen, Robbie Lieberman, Howard Allen, Bill Ferraro, David Wilson, John Simon, and Susan Neel—read and commented on portions of the book manuscript, and I thank them for their time and recommendations. Special thanks go to Angela Calcaterra, Beth Haas, and Jan Griffith for five years of office support. I was also given valuable suggestions by participants in the Social History Workshop at the University of Chicago and the History Workshop at Southern Illinois University, where portions of the manuscript were read and critiqued. Parts of chapters were also read to meetings of the Illinois History Symposium, the Social Science History Association, the Knox College History Club, and the Symposium on the Occasion of the Twenty-fifth Anniversary of the John F. Kennedy-Institut für Nordamerikastudien at the Freie Universität in Berlin, and I thank the various chairs and commentators for their useful suggestions.

This work could not have been produced without the monetary support that I received. The initial research was financed by a Bessie Louis Pierce Fellowship at the University of Chicago. The Stifftung Volkswagenwerk provided money for parts of the Belleville research through a grant to the German-American Assimilation project, directed by Willi Paul Adams and Kathleen N.

Conzen. I was able to research the history of Ottawa with a Newberry Library Short-Term Research grant during the summer of
1990 and with a Southern Illinois University Summer Research
Fellowship during the summer of 1992. I thank Pamela Vaughan
and Randall Gonzales for their work with the computer analysis.
Of course, I owe a huge debt of gratitude to the staff members at
libraries all over the state of Illinois: the Regenstein Library at the
University of Chicago (especially the Interlibrary Loan Department), the Center for Research Libraries, the John Crerar Library,
the Newberry Library, the Chicago Historical Society Library, the
Federal Archives and Records Center of Chicago, the Belleville
Public Library, the Ottawa Reddick Library, the Galesburg Public
Library, the Knox College Archives, Morris Library at Southern Il-
linois University at Carbondale (including the Illinois Regional Ar-
chives Depository), the Archives of the State of Illinois, the Illinois
State Historical Library, the Illinois Historical Survey Library at the
University of Illinois. I thank Rick Stetter, Susan Wilson, Carol
Burns (all of the Southern Illinois University Press), and Ruth Kis-
sell (a wonderful copy editor) for their expertise and patience.

Special thanks go to my friends and family outside the history world for debts both intellectual and emotional. The women's
pedagogy group that meets at various times and places in Carbondale remains a source of support and stimulation. G. P., T. I., B.
W., P. H., M. M.,and L. P. have lived with this project all of their
lives. And, of course, thanks to Allen, Joyce, Glenn, Sue, Daryl,
Peggy, Diane, Winn, Stuart, Jenny, Steve, Laura, Brad, Sean,
Joseph, and Heidi—all Carrs of various years and models—for
their understanding.

A previous version of chapter 5 appeared in the *Illinois Historical
Journal* as "Community Dynamics and Educational Decisions: Establishing Public Schools in Belleville and Galesburg," vol. 84,
1991.

One Introduction

When the voters of Illinois went to the polls on June 4, 1855, in a special election to decide whether the sale and consumption of liquor would be outlawed in the state, they responded with a resounding "no," voting against the Illinois version of the "Maine law" by a majority of 14,447.[1]

Opposition to prohibition was strongest in the southern counties of the state and was particularly acute in the German communities in St. Clair County. In Belleville, the center of early German migration in Illinois, political leaders spoke out against the temperance movement because it threatened their cultural understanding of the role of alcohol in daily life. The newly incorporated city of three thousand had forty licensed liquor establishments in 1850, including grogshops, saloons, and beer gardens.[2]

Support for prohibition in Illinois came mainly from the northern counties where the majority of voters were migrants from New England and New York. In Galesburg, in Knox County, the sale of intoxicating beverages had been officially forbidden since 1842 when the village Board of Trustees decided that the Knox College rule against liquor did, indeed, apply to all of the inhabitants of the young college town.[3]

The people of Ottawa, in LaSalle County, where the majority of voters were either German or Irish immigrants, licensed liquor establishments in 1853, outlawed them in 1855, and then allowed them again in 1857.[4]

The reactions of the people of Belleville, Ottawa, and Galesburg to prohibition illustrate the variety of early Illinois communities. Newly settled towns that appeared much alike on the surface could be very different from one another at a more fundamental, cultural level. This book is about the processes of decision making in Belleville, Ottawa, and Galesburg and about the different types of political cultures that were formed by the people in each of the communities. Soon after their settlement by various ethnic groups in the 1830s and 1840s, the three towns were faced with a series of problems that demanded the immediate attention of their leaders. They became acutely aware that, in addition to the social problems caused by the swelling consumption of alcohol in America in the first half of the nineteenth century, they would have to meet the economic, cultural, and political challenges brought by a rapidly expanding and increasingly diverse nation. They would have to attract the new railroad technology to their towns, or they would become geographically isolated from the ever-expanding national economy. They also realized that they would have to build and administer comprehensive public school systems so that young couples would choose to settle and raise children in their towns. And, finally, they became aware that they would have to work out their local philosophical and cultural differences and construct local governmental systems within a complex national climate of political realignment. The manner in which the leaders and people of Belleville, Ottawa, and Galesburg responded to these and other challenges would go a long way toward determining the nature of their local community cultures.

The United States was changing drastically during the period in which much of the Illinois frontier was settled. At the dawn of the nineteenth century, the nation's local political leaders relied on traditional notions of power to rule their communities; in such a *deferential democracy*, government remained in the hands of a few individuals who were thought, by their natural or inherited superior status, best able to make decisions for the entire populace. By the middle of the century, however, new ideas about local government were beginning to emerge within the communities of the United States. By the Civil War, officeholders were beholden to a much larger electorate of adult white men than they were earlier; in such a *competitive democracy*, leaders were limited in their actions by the opinion of the majority of voters.

This transition in the expectations of those who participated in the American democratic process can be traced to a variety of causes and factors. First, the nation's economy was changing in the first half of the nineteenth century from one based upon the fruits of rural agriculture to one more involved with the products of urban industry; manufacturers and factory workers became a substantial minority of the population and demanded and received voting rights even though they did not own property. Second, the ideal American family changed during the period from one in which a powerful patriarch was the official public representative to the outside world to one in which a husband and wife were engaged in a private partnership of mutual responsibility. Third, the geographical boundaries of the country widened from a small group of states along the Atlantic seaboard to a nation that stretched all the way to the Pacific Ocean. Fourth, the ethnic composition of the United States changed from one that was overwhelmingly Anglo-Saxon but contained substantial minorities of African Americans and Europeans of various origins to one that contained growing numbers of immigrants. Finally, qualifications for political participation were transformed from voting rights based upon the ownership of real property to universal, white, manhood suffrage.

Americans have long sought the historic origins of their modern democratic traditions, and historians of the United States have usually characterized the early years of the Republic as the era in which those traditions solidified into our current system. They have also generally agreed that a majoritarian democratic political culture—that is, a widespread acceptance that political decisions ought to be made by peoples of differing classes, ages, ethnic groups, and religions—had developed by the middle decades of the 1800s. Even though past scholars have obviously ignored the alien status of women, African Americans, and Native Americans during the same period in which the majority of European-American men began to flex their political muscles, at least three different historical traditions have converged to agree that the early nineteenth century was the era in which American democracy matured into one that recognized the legitimacy of the majority to make decisions.

Historians of the imperial and revolutionary periods have contended that the modern democratic way of life was formed in the cauldron of American colonial politics. They argue that the special social and economic circumstances of Puritanism, classical republicanism, and mercantilism created a new nation whose people were ripe for democracy and eventually transformed their government with revolutionary action.[5] Building on the work of their colonial forebears, historians of Jacksonian America pointed to the personalities and events of their own period to show how the nation's democratic culture had matured and then had grown to fruition by the eve of the Civil War.[6] Historians of American political culture in the 1850s agree that voters and parties identified with and set a new social agenda for the nation. They argue that former Whigs, northern Democrats, Free-Soilers, and nativists were troubled by the social consequences of intemperance, industrialism, slavery, and immigration and eventually joined with one another to form new political parties during the decade. When the dust finally cleared in 1860, a new party system that pitted the Democrats against the Republicans had emerged in the United States. This realignment, the historians contend, signaled the first time in which political loyalties matched sectional ones and the animosity within politics set the table for the crisis that resulted in the Civil War.[7]

The recent historical treatments of the realignment of the 1850s have clearly demonstrated the fervor with which Americans of the mid-nineteenth century approached political contests. But most of the studies concentrate upon the actions and influence of national political leaders to explain the transformation within the American democratic process. They do not usually examine the relationship between political affiliation and ethnicity because their national perspective makes the analysis of voting patterns unwieldy and difficult.[8] The examination of politics in the 1850s at the local level has been left to the third and most familiar historical tradition concerning the origins of American democracy. In his *frontier thesis*, first outlined in "The Significance of the Frontier in American History" of 1893, Frederick Jackson Turner argued that the interaction of European-American settlers with the environment of the western lands made the American people a most democratic lot. To this day, his thesis continues to spur arguments, both pro and con. Generations of Turnerians, anti-Turnerians, and neo-Turnerians have come and gone, yet historians still look to the frontier past to explain the development of American democratic political institutions.[9]

Over the last three decades, the local approach of the Turner school has been imitated by the large group of new social historians. Working with the vital records of individual communities, they have given a local explanation for the emergence of a democratic political culture in the United States. Local colonial historians have examined seventeenth- and eighteenth-century New England communities and have shown that the residents' ideological viewpoint was evolving into one that accepted diversity and, at the same time, rejected authority. Social historians have also examined community life during the Jacksonian period and have proven that a relatively egalitarian class identity was emerging on the local scene at the same time that the franchise was widening to include all adult white males.

Given the large number of books on towns in the eastern section of the United States, it is surprising that the Turnerian school of American democratic development has not led to more studies of frontier communities. There are, of course, some notable exceptions to this rule. Don Harrison Doyle's *Social Order of a Frontier Community* examines the community dynamics of Jacksonville, Illinois, and Ralph Mann's *After the Gold Rush* looks at social relationships in three California gold towns. Richard Hogan's recent *Class and Community in Frontier Colorado* examines six Colorado towns during the second half of the nineteenth century and shows that traditions of class-tainted social interaction within the towns resulted in the establishment of lasting political structures that were also based upon class identity. But Hogan's reliance upon class-based antagonisms to explain the development of political structures does not take into account other important factors, such as ethnic and religious identities.[10]

With the exception of Mann and Hogan, the authors of the local studies in the East and in the West have not been able to compare the social dynamics of individual towns with those of other communities because each examines a unique set of historical circumstances and uses a different type of historiographical methodology.[11] And while the studies of Mann and Hogan are brilliantly written and exceptionally informative, they profile towns in the Far West that were settled and populated long after the era when democratic political processes had been established in the East. In fact, today's most influential frontier historians limit themselves to the Far West—the Great Plains, the Rocky Mountains, and the Pacific Coast. These "New Western Historians" argue that the settlement of the West was motivated by the greedy impulses of European Americans and that the results have been environmentally catastrophic and economically despotic.[12]

The American Midwest has received a fair amount of attention from historians over the last century, but its towns have rarely been seen for their variety or the people in them for their diversity. Depending upon the motives behind and purposes for their tracts, lay historians and boosters of the nineteenth and early twentieth centuries often wrote of the opportunities, events, and virtues extolled by the subjects in midwestern towns. But they did so in a systematic manner that dwelled on a similar, successful community-building formula rather than on the variety of different strategies employed by separate towns. Authors of more recent historical works on midwestern communities in the nineteenth century have placed greater emphasis on the significance of their subject cities to the development of United States history in general but have continued to deal in stereotypes, often stressing the negative aspects of life in the small-town Midwest. Lewis Atherton, for example, wrote that "every town sought and still seeks unobtainable goals, and perhaps even false goals. The result has been disillusionment and lethargy."[13] We know from Doyle's work on Jacksonville and from John Mack Faragher's wonderful 1986 work, *Sugar Creek: Life on the Illinois Prairie*, that life in frontier Illinois was not the same for all of the people, nor was it necessarily boring or pathological.[14] The settlement of Illinois and the other midwestern states coincided with the emergence of democracy in America; and the people in the towns of Illinois experienced lives that were full of the excitement and drama that came with living in a transitional age.

I contend that there is a link between frontier community building and the acceptance of particular types of democratic political processes in the United States. This study of three Illinois communities—Belleville, Ottawa, and Galesburg—in the first half of the nineteenth century illustrates that connection. It compares and contrasts the decision-making processes (and the resultant political cultures) of the three communities, where settlers were challenged by the same historical circumstances. All of the towns were planned communities: Belleville as the new seat of St. Clair County in 1814; Ottawa, in LaSalle County, as the western terminus of the Illinois and Michigan Canal in 1831; and Galesburg, in Knox County, as the home of church-affiliated Knox Manual Labor College in 1837. Belleville's earlier founding date does not mean that its community was more advanced than the others, however, since its most influential ethnic group, the Germans, did not arrive until the 1830s. All of the towns were incorporated as cities in the 1850s and had roughly equal total populations throughout the remainder of the nineteenth century. The towns were all demograhically dominated by surrounding counties whose inhabitants differed ethnically from the majority of the town dwellers. And, finally, the residents of all three towns had to make decisions about similar economic, social, and political problems while building their communities.

But the towns were very different from one another in their economies and in their ethnic compositions. From its founding, Belleville, located in the southwest part of the state, was overshadowed economically by neighboring St. Louis. Ottawa, in the north-central portion of Illinois, depended upon the business of the Illinois and Michigan Canal for its survival and competed continually with LaSalle (the eventual terminus of the canal) for dominance of the county. Galesburg, in the northwest, was and remains a geographically isolated city; its people relied upon the business from the surrounding farm economy for their livelihoods. Belleville's residents were mostly foreign-born until the end of the century. Ottawa's population was evenly split between the native-born and the foreign-born. Galesburg's citizens have been overwhelmingly native-born throughout its history. Belleville's native-born residents were descended from southerners, whereas those of Ottawa were from the New England and the Middle Atlantic states of the East. Galesburg's natives were mostly New Englanders or were second-generation New Yorkers whose families came from New England.

Nineteenth-century Belleville, Ottawa, and Galesburg, then, are ideal subjects for a study of decision making and political culture on the Illinois frontier. They were comparable in size and age and were faced with the same set of challenges to community building. Yet they contrasted enough in their economic and social structures to make it possible to account for any differences in their development. By looking at the reactions of the people to similar problems—attracting railroads, establishing public schools, and choosing political leaders—we see that the type of democratic decision making that developed in each town depended upon the economic, cultural, and political structures with which each was founded. Belleville's German population was not as cohesive as one might expect. The immigrants had come to the American Midwest from many of the German states of central Europe, and the settlers in Belleville varied tremendously by class, religion, and social philosophy. This variety caused Belleville's elites to be extremely competitive with one another, and the town's politics were wildly factious. As a result, at the end of its settlement period, the town's residents had developed an extremely competitive democratic culture that relied upon simple majorities to settle political disputes.

During its settlement period, Ottawa's decision-making process was dominated by an elite group of Yankee business and professional men. However, this dominant group was divided along philosophical and political lines. The result was a frontier political culture that recognized the legitimacy of a traditional leadership but was highly inefficient; the Democrats and the Republicans traded political control of the town so often that it was impossible for either to build a viable infrastructure. The political leaders appealed to the large Irish and German populations of Ottawa to fill out the ranks of their parties. Eventually, patronage and party affiliation became more important than ability or ethnicity, and the town's residents developed a democratic culture that relied upon the political contests between local leaders to solve local disputes.

In Galesburg, where the Yankee population held an overwhelming numerical advantage over the Swedish and Irish minorities, the political culture remained consensual and traditional. The cultural elites who were affiliated with Knox College conferred among themselves concerning any and all decisions about their community. When they had decided on the best course of action, they submitted their findings to the populace who either confirmed the wisdom of the leadership or kept their objections to themselves. In Galesburg, there was very efficient local government, but there was also little room for dissension.

Two The Towns

Small cities and towns were integral to the development of Illinois during the state's frontier period, and the existence of the frontier was an essential factor in the early history of the state's small cities and towns. Places such as Belleville, Ottawa, and Galesburg were created by people who were attuned to the rhythms of their time, including the effects of the tremendous economic and geographic expansion of the United States during the first half of the nineteenth century (see map 1). When each of the communities was planned, platted, sold, and settled, the United States was a simple, but perplexing, country. It was full of opportunity, but it was fraught with inequality. The War of 1812 had finally freed the old Northwest (later, the Midwest) from foreign interference, and Americans from the East poured across the Appalachians and into its territories. The great hardwood forests of Ohio, Indiana, Michigan, and Illinois fell before the onslaught of settlers who were anxious to reap the rewards of frontier farming. If a poor eastern family could scrape together one thousand dollars or so, its members could move west and begin life again, either on a new farm or in a new town. To many Americans, the Northwest was the land of milk and honey and they struck toward it with a religious fervor. And when they got to their promised land, the pioneers set about to extract as much from it as they possibly could. There was no conservation ethic among the early midwestern settlers. They did not worship nature; they cursed it. The resources of the frontier were there, in their view, to be exploited. Their only questions concerned the identity of the rightful exploiters. By the second and third decades of the nineteenth century, the government of the United States had given them some answers. Any European-American man who could afford to do so could go to the frontier and take a share of the wealth. The four million European-American women, the two million African Americans, and the half million Native Americans who lived in the United States were not eli-

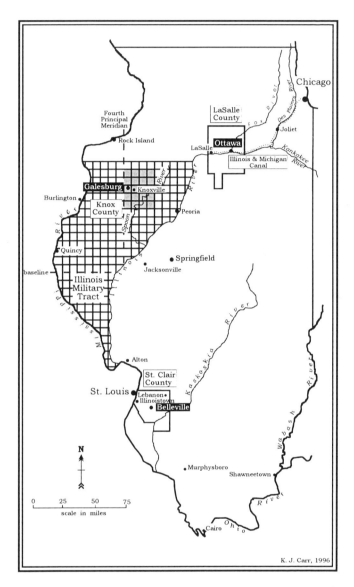

Map 1. Belleville, Ottawa, and Galesburg in Nineteenth-Century Illinois

gible to profit from the exploitation of the frontier, even though their labor and their lands helped to make it all possible.

European-American men could not and would not go off to the frontier as individuals, harvesting its resources, willy-nilly. During the decades in which Belleville, Ottawa, and Galesburg were settled, Americans developed a complex set of economic rules by which pioneers had to play if they and their loved ones were to profit from the settlement of the Northwest. One of those rules involved the role of towns on the frontier. A hierarchy of urban centers, from small villages to large cities, grew up with the Northwest. Towns were a necessary component of settlement because they provided the services that made settlement and profit possible. They were the transportation centers in which farmers traded their harvested crops. They were the manufacturing centers from which farmers bought their tools and equipment. They were the social centers in which farmers were entertained and went to worship. And they were the political centers to which farmers traveled to hear candidates and to cast their ballots. Without towns and cities there could not have been an American frontier.

Each frontier town was different from another. Each played a unique role in the urban services that it provided to the rural population in its hinterland, and each competed with its neighbors to serve a wider area. Some, such as Chicago, began to serve other towns, in addition to its surrounding farmers, and grew larger and larger. Others, such as Springfield, specialized—as educational, medical, manufacturing, or governmental centers—and drew people from farther and farther away. Still others competed with nearby towns for the business of farmers but finally failed, lost population, and disappeared utterly into the mists of time. Some towns, such as Belleville, Ottawa, and Galesburg, came to occupy a middling position in this urban hierarchy and became regional centers, larger than the villages that surrounded them but smaller than the national cities around which they orbited.

The ultimate position of a town in the system of cities that developed in the Northwest was not preordained. The settlers in each worked to secure a particular role for their towns, but their efforts were not always successful. As a general rule, the residents of frontier towns wanted theirs to be as large and to serve as many functions as possible. And with the possible exception of the settlers in Chicago, they were all ultimately disappointed. But they would eventually come to terms with the positions of their towns and would even come to embrace them as their fates. We can look back at that period in history when towns struggled to reach their loftiest goals, before they became resigned to their urban positions, as a time when their fate was still up for grabs. We can also look back at the people in those towns to see how they reacted to the possibilities and disappointments of their urban dreams. If we do, we can begin to see how the people of the old Northwest created unique communities in their individual towns.

The reactions of the people of Belleville, Ottawa, and Galesburg to the challenges of community building during their frontier periods were colored both by the physical environment in which they settled and by the historical milieu in which they developed. Belleville, along with most of southern Illinois, was inhabited by European Americans and African Americans at least a half century before the northern part of the state, in which Ottawa and Galesburg are located. The domain of the peoples of the Illinois Indian alliance in the seventeenth and eighteenth centuries, the southern portion of the state, along the Mississippi River, was settled and farmed by small communities of Frenchmen, French Canadians, and Native Americans as early as the seventeenth century. English colonial authorities claimed the French settlements in 1763 following the French and Indian War. Americans did not arrive in large numbers until the United States took over jurisdiction from the British in 1788. During the half century following the Revolutionary War, small groups of Americans—most of whose families had moved from the backcountry of Virginia and the Carolinas, through Kentucky, Tennessee, and southern Ohio and Indiana—stopped off in the wooded, southern portion of Illinois, squatting on public lands that would not officially be sold by the federal government until 1814.[1]

The Illinois River valley and the present site of Ottawa was occupied by the Peoria and Kaskaskia peoples—groups of the Illinois confederacy—in the late seventeenth century. A hunting and farming people, the Illinois had suffered a post-Columbian population decline and could offer little resistance to the invasions into their territory in the eighteenth and nineteenth centuries, and they left little physical impact on the northern Illinois landscape. French-Canadian Louis Jolliet and Frenchman Jacques Marquette found a village of seventy-four cabins on the north bank of the river when they explored the region in 1673. In 1674 Marquette, a Jesuit priest, returned to the village, called "Kaskaskia" by the Native Americans and "LaVantum" by the French, to found the Mission of the Immaculate Conception of the Blessed Virgin. By 1677 the village contained four to five thousand people, many seeking refuge from the invading Iroquois. The mission and village were destroyed in 1680 by a group of Iroquois, and most of the survivors fled to the western bank of the Mississippi River. In 1682 French explorer Robert Cavelier, sieur de La Salle, built and occupied Fort St. Louis, on the southern bluffs overlooking the Illinois River. The fort was abandoned in 1691 when the French and their Illinois allies realized that the site would not allow access to wood or water if it were attacked. Groups of the aboriginal Illinois people remained in the area of the abandoned fort for the following century, but they were constantly under pressure from groups of Pottawatomi, Kickapoo, and Miami who, pressed by the encroachment of their lands to the east by the Iroquois, had moved into the northern part of the state. Fighting intensified in the 1760s and culminated in the 1769 siege, starvation, and massacre of the remaining Illinois on the top of "Starved Rock." Between 1776 and 1833, when all Native American claims to Illinois were ceded, groups of Ottawa, Chippewa, Kickapoo, and Winnebago had all moved into the Illinois River valley from the north. European Americans slowly made their way into the area during the early nineteenth century.[2]

The northwestern part of the state, where Galesburg is located, was not inhabited by Americans in great numbers until the 1830s. Before then settlement was precluded both by the negative perception held by Americans of the mostly prairie environment (which would become positive by the 1830s) and by the persistence of Native American settlement in the area. The Indian claims to the land resulted in the infamous Black Hawk War of 1832, which finally eliminated the Sauk and Fox people's occupation of northwestern Illinois. The timing of the Black Hawk War was far from coincidental since it occurred at the very time that pressures for settlement of the northern prairies were becoming more intense after the opening of the Erie Canal and the drawing of plans for an Illinois and Michigan Canal to connect the waters of the Great Lakes with the Mississippi River. So when Americans did finally begin to inhabit the northern prairies, they came not only from the South but from the farms of New England, New York, and Pennsylvania.[3]

During the summer of 1813, the five thousand inhabitants of St. Clair County, Illinois, were up in arms. The English-American majority desperately wanted to move their seat of justice from French-dominated Cahokia, a small town on the Illinois side of the Mississippi River just south and east of St. Louis, to a place that would be closer to the geographical center of the county. So a vote was taken, and the residents of the county decided to petition the territorial legislature to take whatever means were necessary to relocate the county seat. In December 1813 the St. Clair County Court of Common Pleas notified "John Hay, James Lemen, Isaac Enochs, Wm. Scott, Jun., Nathan Chambers, Jacob Short and Caldwell Cains, commissioners appointed by the legislature, to fix upon a place for the seat of justice of this county . . . on the 25th of January next" and to make a report on their findings by February. The commission did indeed return to the court, but not until early April, with a report of its initial difficulties in coming to any conclusions. They had met but had chosen not to make any decisions because there was no officer present to swear them to their duties. They agreed to try again on April 14, in Cahokia. Even though they had straightened out the legal technicalities, the commission members again postponed their decision, this time because they could not find suitable land. They agreed to meet once more on March 10, this time at the home of George Blair, who owned some land on the eastern bluffs of the Mississippi River. In the meantime, the commissioners were able to strike a deal with Blair when, eventually, a majority of the commissioners agreed to fix the county seat for St. Clair County on his land. Blair agreed to donate one acre of land for a public square and every fifth lot in a twenty-five-acre plot around the square to the county. Blair also suggested that the new town be called "Belleville" (beautiful city).[4]

Belleville's subsequent founding by an act of the Illinois Territorial Legislature was the result of a desire by St. Clair County residents to solve two separate but related problems that would continue to plague the inhabitants throughout the community's frontier period. First, the town was founded specifically to undermine the economic and cultural dominance of the French-descended farmers and merchants of Cahokia. And second, Belleville was established as an American-controlled Illinois alternative to the all-around urban hegemony of the prosperous, French-dominated, west-bank, Missouri city of St. Louis. The new St. Clair

County seat was platted in the summer of 1814 on a ridge (also known as Compton Hill) in what had been Blair's cornfield. The ridge extended north and west all the way to the bluffs overlooking the Mississippi River floodplain (also known as the American Bottom) and was drained by unnavigable Richland Creek (see map 2). Blair realized immediate profits from the transaction when he constructed a hotel to provide temporary shelter for the new town's first residents. He eventually benefited even more from the sale of four out of every five town lots. However, George Blair is not usually credited with having been Belleville's founder. He was seen in his time as something of a conniver who had simply been lucky enough to purchase the rights to two hundred acres of militia land in 1796 that accidentally ended up in the middle of the newly platted St. Clair County in 1814. The new county seat was not incorporated as a village by the state of Illinois until 1819. By then, French-American Etienne Pensoneau, who had built the town's new courthouse, had managed to purchase most of the house lots from Blair. Pensoneau then resold the village to Ninian Edwards, a longtime Illinois resident from Kentucky and the territorial governor from 1809 until 1818. (He would also serve as Illinois governor from 1826 to 1830.) Edwards resurveyed Belleville and renamed the main streets.[5]

The first ethnic American settlers of St. Clair County must have felt that the world had truly been turned upside down when they arrived in the late eighteenth century. Expecting to find a semi-wild frontier on the outermost edge of American territory, they discovered a comparatively civilized agricultural community on the east bank of the Mississippi River. Frenchmen from Quebec, Europe, and New Orleans had been living on and cultivating the rich alluvial soil of the American Bottom since 1699 when the village of Cahokia was founded. Although Cahokia was something of a backwater to the Illinois French whose settlements were centered further south in Kaskaskia, it had grown after the Spanish took over the Louisiana territory in 1763. Many of the Illinois Frenchmen, fearing the English authorities on the eastern bank of the Mississippi, then moved to the west and founded St. Louis. Cahokia, just east of St. Louis, thus became the locus of the French population that did remain in Illinois. So by the early nineteenth century, individual settlers and town builders of both French and American descent knew that immediate economic success was dependent upon locating as close to St. Louis as possible

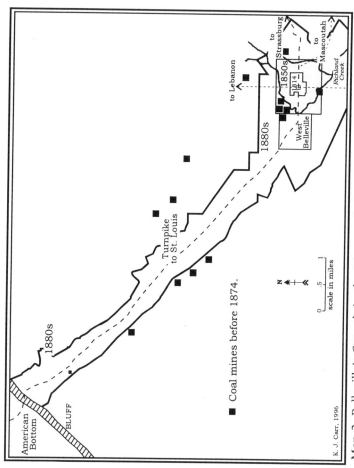

Map 2. Belleville's Growth in the Nineteenth Century

since its services could guarantee access to markets along the Mississippi River and in New Orleans. By the time Americans began to arrive in large numbers after the Revolutionary War, all of the lands in St. Clair County in the fertile floodplain across from St. Louis—except for a small strip on the border with Monroe County to the south where the Americans established Piggot's Fort—were already claimed and controlled by the surviving French population.[6]

Unlike Etienne Pensoneau and Ninian Edwards, most of Belleville's earliest pioneers were not connected with the old French settlements below the bluffs but began their midwestern lives as farmers on St. Clair County's rolling woodlands above the alluvial floodplain. They had been born in Virginia and other states of the American South and settled in the county with their families or as young single men seeking their fortunes. They and their immediate descendants were the people who had petitioned the legislature to move the county seat to Belleville in 1813, but they do not appear to have been very influential in the new town during its first decade. There is little doubt that the French-occupied bottomlands opposite St. Louis continued to be more attractive to the Americans who belatedly chose to settle in the area. Writing in 1834, J. M. Peck described the area as "the most extensive and fertile tract . . . in this state. . . . Opposite St. Louis, in St. Clair county, the bluffs are seven miles from the river, and filled with inexhaustible beds of coal."[7]

The Americans who did choose to settle in the area in the 1790s continually tried to wrestle the bottomlands away from the French inhabitants. In an effort to protect the French from American avarice, the United States Congress, in 1791, decided that every family that had made improvements to a claim in Illinois prior to 1788 (the French inhabitants) would be granted four hundred acres of land as long as the family could show legal ownership under the old regime and could pay for the services of a surveyor. However, the requirements were soon revamped because there were so many complaints by the French that they could neither prove ownership—so many of the French documents had been destroyed or lost—nor afford to pay for a survey. Eventually, a French Illinoisan needed only to produce a witness who would swear that occupation had begun before 1788 to qualify for his four hundred acres. By 1810 it was common knowledge that the improvement rights of the Frenchmen (as well as the rights to land earned from service in the Virginia militia) were the subjects of tremendous speculation and corruption in a highly competitive land market. When the Americans took over the jurisdiction of French Illinois in 1788, it was estimated that there were 150 families who would qualify for land claims as French settlers—80 in Kaskaskia, 12 in Prairie du Rocher, 50 in Cahokia, and 4 or 5 in Fort de Chartres and St. Philipe. By 1810, however, 1,544 claims for land had been filed (including land for "ancient grant" [Indians], "improvements" [longtime squatters], "militia rights" [Virginia veterans], and "donations of families resident before 1788" [Frenchmen]). A special commission was appointed in 1812 to investigate the allegations of misdeeds. Fourteen men, both American and French, were found to have been willing to claim intimate knowledge of the land status of any individual for a small fee. One of these men, a Frenchmen from Prairie du Rocher, admitted to giving two hundred false depositions. In January 1813 the Commission recommended that the United States Congress accept 27 ancient grants, 143 improvement grants, 207 resident-before-1788 grants, and 214 militia grants.[8]

Until the federal land office could make a decision about the status of the various land claims in St. Clair County, settlers were left in a state of legal limbo. The Congress did finally pass a special preemption act in 1813 that both accepted the Commission's recommendations and allowed further claims of no more than 160 acres of land by squatters who had made improvements up to two weeks before the commencement of sales at the Kaskaskia Land District Office in August 1814. The record of claims made before August 1814, however, shows how desirable the American Bottom lands were and, conversely, how undesirable the lands on top of the bluffs were to the early American settlers. Very little of the preempted land, in any of the categories, was located above the floodplain. And even then, most of the preempted land was in and around the town of Belleville, which had been platted just before the opening of the land office. The timing of the founding of Belleville, therefore, was far from accidental. It appears as though the formation of an isolated settlement above the bluffs was viewed as too uncertain to sink real money into the venture. But it was worth the effort if the financial risk was removed through the securing of preemption claims surrounding the new settlement. In other words, speculation in land above the bluffs was still undesirable, compared with that on the American Bottom, unless it was funded by the government and was close to a town that appeared to have some sort of commercial promise.[9]

By 1813, when the first rumblings were heard to move the county seat, American settlers already outnumbered the French descendants in St. Clair County. Even so, those same Americans do not appear to have been living in great numbers above the bluffs. They, in fact, had been largely successful in taking control of much of the bottomlands from the French inhabitants. It also appears that they had not been able to control enough land to satisfy the demand brought by the rush of American immigrants. The Americans were not able to compete with the French because the French had been given an economic advantage by the territorial and state legislatures of Illinois. The French were permitted to keep their slaves even though the Northwest Ordinance of 1787 and the Illinois Constitution of 1818 prohibited the introduction of new slaves into the territory. In fact, many of the early settlers from Virginia had brought slaves with them to the Illinois country and later moved to Missouri where they could maintain their "possessions." In any case, the Americans would have been in a disadvantageous position since they were forced to pay for labor, whereas the French could hold and work slaves both in the bottomlands and in and around the new town of Belleville. Frenchman Etienne Pensoneau, for example, purchased huge tracts of land in the new county seat and ran a dry goods store and mill on Richland Creek along with his "negro slaves." He was later chastised by American early arrivals for paying too much attention to his own accumulation of wealth and not enough to the aspirations of the town. He was the object of a number of rhetorical attacks by Americans, and in 1816, a preacher named Taylor observed in his sermon that where there were two servants, one would be taken. Pensoneau took the pronouncement as a personal threat and rushed the pulpit and Taylor "with the double tree of a Wagon."[10]

Even though the founders of Belleville assumed that their village would quickly become the primary metropolis in the area, it stagnated until 1825 when Ninian Edwards took over its proprietorship. St. Clair County only grew from 5,248 to 7,078 between 1820 and 1830. Belleville grew at about the same rate as the county, so its population was probably about 200, up from 150 in 1820. But its inability to stand out from the other small towns of southern Illinois was caused by more than the economic challenge imposed by the surviving French population with their slaves. From its very inception as the new county seat, Belleville had to deal with another chronic problem that would continually dampen its aspirations. The American founders of Belleville quickly found that physical isolation from the established Frenchmen of the bottomlands was not enough to guarantee success as long as the Illinois side of the Mississippi River was held in economic orbit by the financial gravity of St. Louis.[11]

Unlike his predecessors, Ninian Edwards offered house lots to businessmen and artisans on "liberal terms." He was most successful in persuading French-connected St. Louis and Cahokia businessmen to move to the top of the bluffs and set up shop in the young village. Commission member John Hay, for example, lived in Cahokia and ran a thriving law practice there before moving to Belleville. He was the son of the English governor of Upper Canada and made a respectable career for himself after moving to French Illinois in the early nineteenth century by writing English-language wills and other legal documents for the local French population that had suddenly found itself in the new United States in 1788. Edwards was also able to convince another early Belleville resident, Joseph Kerr, to open a much needed dry goods store that Kerr stocked from his brother's store in St. Louis. The other new settlers to the village in the late 1820s came directly from Virginia, including the Halberts, Samuel Chandler of Rockbridge County, and Lucius Don Turner of Nelson County. But no matter how much they wanted or tried to establish themselves as a separate entity, Belleville residents were always confronted with the reality of their economic dependence on the Missouri city, not only for the origin of their earliest businessmen but also as a market and transportation hub for their raw materials and manufactured goods.[12]

Regardless of how Belleville saw itself in its pioneer days or what its aspirations might have been, it remained an appendage to St. Louis throughout the nineteenth century. Unbeknownst to its three successive proprietors, the new town was seated on top of a huge coal deposit and that fact was to seal Belleville's fate; it became the supplier of energy to the larger city. In 1825, the first coal mine in St. Clair County was opened just six miles south of Belleville with St. Louis capital. By 1834, huge amounts of the bituminous coal that "burns well, and appears to be inexhaustible . . . [were being] taken to St. Louis annually, and the demand for it [was] rapidly increasing."[13]

Despite the small increase in the populations of St. Clair County and Belleville during the 1820s, by 1830 the American residents of St. Clair County greatly outnumbered the remaining French inhabitants, and their numerical dominance eventually made it possible to gain economic control. Then, during the 1830s, the populations of both the county and the village began to mushroom. The county nearly doubled (from 7,078 to 13,634), making the largest percentage gain since the 1800s. Belleville itself grew by a factor of ten, from about 200 in 1830 to 2,000 by 1840. But before this new population could consolidate, the ethnic American citizens of Belleville were faced with the appearance of another ethnic minority whose existence would soon again make it impossible for the young town to formulate a unified set of economic, cultural, and political goals. By 1840, about 20 percent of the county residents lived in households whose heads were of probable foreign (i.e., nonethnic American) birth, almost all of whom seem to have been German. Already, it appears as if most of the Germans were residing in or close to Belleville, especially to the northeast near the village of Shiloh and southeast of the town on Turkey Hill.[14]

Belleville quickly became the capital of the German settlements of St. Clair County. By 1850, the year in which Belleville was incorporated as a city and the year of the first census in which accurate nativity statistics are available, there were 1,199 German-born residents in the city. Before 1830, there were only two German families in all of St. Clair County, the heads of which, Jacob Maurer and Conrad Bornmann, were both blacksmiths. The increase over the next few years was due, in part, to events taking place in Europe. Students from Hesse-Darmstadt, Württemburg, Frankfurt, Rhenish Bavaria, upper Baden, and the Black Forest plotted in 1833 to unite the various German states into a single confederacy. The revolution failed and many of the leaders of the movement fled Germany, first for France. A large group of the refugees, including the Abends, the Engelmanns, the Knoebels, the Scheels, and Gustave Körner (all of whom would eventually settle in St. Clair County), then sailed from Havre to New York. The group traveled to Missouri—via the Erie and Ohio Canals— where Theodore J. Krafft, an acquaintance of Körner during his

student days in Heidelberg, and other Germans had planned to
settle when they had emigrated in 1832 as part of a back-to-the-
land movement among German intellectuals. Krafft and Dr. Theodore Hilgard, however, had instead purchased and settled on four
hundred acres of land in St. Clair County, Illinois, near Turkey
Hill. Körner and the other German families followed Krafft and
Hilgard to Illinois and purchased farms around Belleville that
would then form the nucleus of further German settlement.[15]

But the Germans were divided from the start into two groups.
One, composed of Körner and his acquaintances and joined after
1848 by latter-day revolutionaries, had left Germany for political
reasons and were more highly educated than the bulk of the later
immigrants. The second group, which also arrived in the United
States during the 1830s and 1840s but who settled in Belleville in
the largest numbers during the 1850s, was motivated to emigrate
for various economic reasons, including overpopulation, land con-
solidation, and potato blight. In 1836 sixteen of the political immigrants met in Belleville to form the St. Clair Library Society.
The signatures on its constitution—composed in 1838 and written in both English and German—read like a Who's Who of what
were to become the leading families of the city: E. Hilgard, J. C.
Hildebrandt, J. Lederberger, Th. Hilgard, J. Hilgard, A. Berchelmann, George Bunsen, Dr. Anton Schott, J. Engelmann, E. W.
Decker, Hermann Augthusen, Henrich Denzen, E. Kruger, C. Ser-
ini, Herrmann Wolf, F. A. Wolf, Franz Köhler, Cornelius Schu-
bert, Carl Runnwitz, Gustav Körner, Theod. J. Krafft, Theod.
Engelmann, Fritz Wolf, Fritz Hilgard, Fr. Th. Englemann, Gustav
Heimberger, Dr. Edward Franz, A. Cunrad, A. Trapp, N. Lippen,
William Friedanken, Edward Klinckhardt, A. Voegle. These early
St. Clair Germans had a deserved reputation as highly educated
"Latin Peasants" and formed the group who would later become
known as the *Dreissiger,* or "Grays," who would challenge the
later-arriving *Achtundvierziger,* or "Greens," in the mid-nine-
teenth-century struggle over the leadership of the German element in the United States.[16]

The eventual numerical dominance of Belleville by a German-
born majority did not automatically spell economic defeat for the
ethnic Americans within the town. On the contrary, the native-
born residents—along with some of the earliest German arrivals—were able to wield a disproportionate amount of economic
power within the young city, which was quickly developing an in-

dustrial base. The mere presence of yet another foreign element and the social disorientation that came with it made it difficult for Belleville to compete for cultural, economic, and political dominance with the other towns in the region, but the quickly developing industrial economy—with the expansion of the coal mines and the building of the railroads—was able to absorb the new immigrants in great numbers. By 1846, the citizens of Belleville were resigned to their position as a St. Louis adjunct. The editor of the weekly English-language newspaper, the *Belleville Advocate*, recognized that "St. Louis is destined soon to be one of the great cities of our continent. . . . From Galena to Cairo, Illinois can never build up a rival to St. Louis." He urged his readers to temper their own town's aspirations and begin thinking in terms of taking advantage of the propinquity of the larger city. By 1862 the "coal trade of Belleville to St. Louis, and the consumption of coal in [that] city, [was] almost beyond belief." There were twenty-three coal mines located either within the city or on its outskirts, and 16,500 bushels were being transported daily. Beer soon followed coal as a major export to St. Louis to the tune of 30,500 barrels per year by the early 1860s. During its frontier period Belleville thus moved from a position of deliberate isolation to one of acceptance of the economic hegemony of St. Louis, a city that also had a substantial German immigrant population. The editor of the *Advocate*, writing in 1849, declared, "We have a fine market at St. Louis, such a one as answers our every purpose. What more do we want?"[17]

So Belleville's early difficulty in attracting settlers, despite its designation as the St. Clair county seat, was due in part to the inability of the Americans to compete for the premium bottomlands with the entrenched French minority and for the economic control of the town with St. Louis.[18] Their attempt to take control of the county by switching the seat of justice away from French Cahokia and into the isolated center of the county did nothing to remedy the economic hegemony of the earliest settlers. Later, beginning in the 1830s, the Americans were again stymied by the presence of an ethnic minority, this time the Germans, who would quickly gain numerical dominance. Belleville's immediate success was also hampered by the fact that, despite being located in what must have seemed at the time to be a stark wilderness, it was actually too close to St. Louis to escape from the western city's social and economic orbit. As a consequence, Belleville's growth from the beginning depended more upon the larger city's trade networks than the 1814 founders would have liked to admit.

It was a "Most Melancholy Accident," according to the headline in the *Illinois Free Trader* of April 2, 1841. Dr. Aaron Bain of Ottawa had traveled to South Ottawa to treat a patient. On his return trip, across the Illinois River on a ferryboat, he lost his balance, fell into the icy water, and drowned.[19] He was not the first person, nor would he be the last, to lose his life in the cold waters off Ottawa. In fact, accidents that caused death and injuries were a common occurrence in the early nineteenth century. On a monthly basis, the town's newspapers reported that somebody, usually a resident child or an unwary visitor, had lost his footing on an Illinois and Michigan Canal swing bridge, or had become entangled with some driftwood while swimming in the Fox River, or, like Dr. Bain, had fallen from the ferry on the Illinois River. The people of Ottawa incessantly badgered their local and state representatives to improve the situation by building more and safer bridges over the canal and the rivers, but they never complained about the waterways themselves. For Ottawa *was* the Illinois and Michigan Canal and the Illinois River and the Fox River. Its residents owed the canal and the rivers for their collective existence and for their individual livelihoods. But this intimate connection was to prove both a blessing and a curse to the people of Ottawa over the nineteenth century.

Even before there was any place called Ottawa, Illinois, Native Americans and Europeans had become very familiar with its site. Because it was situated at the confluence of the Illinois and Fox Rivers and was easily accessible by canoe, Native Americans and early Europeans saw and used it as a convenient place to trade goods. Groups of the aboriginal Illinois used it as a seasonal village site as late as the eighteenth century. And since it is located just downriver from a fall of eighteen feet on the Illinois River, Europeans and Americans also settled in the area because it was the northernmost spot to which keelboats could be brought in the summer. In the fall of 1825, Wilbur Walker, a young man from Rockingham County, Virginia, by way of southern Illinois, brought a small keelboat up to the southern side of the Illinois River near the present site of Ottawa. There he was soon joined by a man who was probably his uncle, the Reverend Jesse Walker, a Methodist preacher who had moved to a farm on the southern side of the Illinois in 1825. The Reverend Mr. Walker had traveled to the southern part of the state in 1824 to arrange for the transportation of provisions and had then returned to his farm on the Illinois River the next year. On his second trip to the north he brought six more men with him. About the same time, Enos Pembrook of New York (by way of Alton, Illinois) and a man named Bailey moved into the area. The next spring, James Walker, also from Rockingham County and most probably a relative of the preacher, arrived with his family and settled on a farm on the northern side of the Illinois, east of the Fox River. Meanwhile, Jesse Walker had also moved to the northern bank of the river where he established a farm and a mission school for the local Ottawa children. His school, which he hoped to finance with the sale of goods produced on the farm by the children, failed completely. However, the Walker relatives continued to move into the Illinois River valley; in 1826, Dr. David Walker, a practicing physician who was also from Rockingham County and who was the father of Wilbur, arrived with at least five of his other seven children. David Walker settled on the northern bank of the Illinois on the west side of the Fox and is usually reckoned as the first settler in Ottawa. By 1830, when the state of Illinois platted the town of Ottawa, about twenty families were living on farms in the area, mostly on the southern side of the Illinois River. Unlike the Walkers, however, most of the other early settlers were from New York. And once the town was founded, that trend toward settlers from the northeastern states was to continue.[20]

Ottawa was born as Chicago's twin. In 1827 the United States Congress gave the state of Illinois a ten-mile-wide stretch of land for the purpose of "opening a canal to unite the waters of the Illinois river with those of Lake Michigan." The sale of the odd-numbered sections of land in the grant, stretching five miles on each side of the proposed canal, was to finance the state's construction of the canal. In 1829 the Illinois General Assembly approved the appointment of a Board of Canal Commissioners that began to choose the land to be included in the grant and to lay out towns along the proposed route of the canal. Chicago was established as the obvious eastern terminus of the canal. State surveyor James Thompson platted the town of Ottawa in Township 33 North of the baseline and Range 3 East of the Third Principal Meridian in December 1830 as the presumed western terminus of the canal. In his plan, the town was located primarily south of the

Illinois River but also included a narrow strip of land on the northern side, where the Fox River fed into the Illinois River. In 1831 the state created LaSalle, Cook, and Putnam Counties out of a larger Peoria County and platted the northern portion of Ottawa, in Section 11 of the township, as the new county seat.[21]

Meanwhile, initial sales of lots in Ottawa and Chicago had been disappointing so the canal commission proposed that the state build a railroad in place of the canal. The General Assembly balked at the suggestion and dismissed the commission in 1833. In 1835 the General Assembly passed a law that appointed a new commission and authorized the governor of Illinois to borrow $500,000 to construct the canal. The act also called for the lengthening of the canal closer to the big bend of the Illinois River, some fifteen miles downstream from Ottawa; more modern estimates of navigation possibilities suggested that navigation all the way to Ottawa would be problematic during the low waters of summer, and the commission did not want to risk a chronic slowdown in navigation on the canal. Ottawa would never be the metropolis that the earlier plans had promised.[22]

In fact, the town of Ottawa, on the northern bank of the Illinois River, was a town only in name until 1835. In that year, it contained two houses, a tavern, and a general store. But with the construction of the canal finally assured, sales of land in Chicago and in Ottawa picked up. On July 4, 1836, ground was broken just east of Chicago for the hundred-mile-long Illinois and Michigan Canal. Even before the canal construction reached Ottawa, the town was growing somewhat from the increased services that its residents provided to the surrounding farmers. In 1835 the federal government offered a large part of LaSalle County outside the canal corridor for sale at $1.25 per acre. Eastern speculators quickly bought up much of the land and then offered it for sale to settlers at $5 to $10 per acre. In 1839 the town was incorporated as a village by the state of Illinois. The settlers of Ottawa in the 1830s and early 1840s came from the northeastern and the middle sections of the United States. One large group—including the families of P. A. and George Dunavan, David Letts, James McFadden, William Parr, Samuel Millikin, David Shaver, and Anna Pitzer—moved from Licking County, Ohio, in 1830. Others arrived from Pennsylvania, Kentucky, Vermont, Connecticut, Massachusetts, New Hampshire, and Illinois and from Canada and England, but most were migrants from the counties of northern

New York. These early arrivals—including the families of Joseph Avery, Washington Bushnell, John Dean Caton, Christopher Champlin, Burton C. Cook, William H. W. Cushman, Lucien Delano, Abner S. Fisher, Joseph O. Glover, William Hickling, John Hise, Daniel F. Hitt, John V. A. Hoes, Edwin and Lorenzo Leland, George H. Norris, William Osman, David Strawn, Milton H. Swift, William True, William H. L. Wallace, and Alson Woodruff—were to be the economic and political leaders in Ottawa for the next twenty-five years.[23]

The 1830s would also see the arrival of another group of settlers, about whom little is recorded but whose presence would affect Ottawa's development. Irish Americans and immigrants from Europe arrived with the Illinois and Michigan Canal. They were hired from the eastern cities and from Canada by construction contractors who seemed never to be satisfied with the number or quality of their laborers. By 1838, some two thousand Irish, French, and German Catholics were living in the area of Ottawa and LaSalle-Peru, working on the canal by day and sleeping in makeshift tents and shanties along the canal and against the river bluffs. In that year a small Catholic mission, soon to become St. Columba's Catholic Church, was founded in Ottawa. The majority of its attendants were Irish and Irish-American canal workers and their families. The mission was initially staffed by a priest, Aloysius Parodi, who had been sent by the bishop of St. Louis to begin a parish in LaSalle. He celebrated mass every second Sunday in Ottawa.[24]

The immigrant workers on the canal brought Ottawa much needed capital and labor during the town's infancy. Working for independent contractors who set their own pay scales, they earned $20 to $26 a month and were charged $2 per week for food. That left a fair number of young men with extra spending money for socializing and entertainment. But then in late 1837 the State Bank of Illinois, which had been providing specie for the workers, suspended all payments, and work along the project was spotty for the next ten years. When laborers were convinced to continue working, they were often paid less than they were promised or with bank bills that were not worth their face value. The canal directors issued their own "canal scrip" to pay the laborers, but the new bills also deteriorated in value. When the Illinois General Assembly agreed to accept the bills as payment for state land, many of the Irish contractors and laborers bought lots along the canal and in Ottawa. Others of the Irish stayed in the shanties at the edge of town and competed with one another for work on the canal.[25]

In the summer of 1838, two groups of laborers fought with one another in a series of incidents all along the canal. The Catholic Irish, called "Corkonians" by the European Americans of Ottawa, were the majority of the Irish workers. The presence of the small number of Protestant Irish, referred to as "Fardowners," was not appreciated by the Catholics who often saw the Protestants receive special consideration in hiring by the American contractors. Beginning in Chicago, a gang of Catholic ruffians made their way down the length of the canal, beating any Protestants who got in their way. The Catholics made their way to Ottawa where they forcibly commandeered the ferryboat across the Fox River. They then marched to LaSalle where a large group of workers remained idle from the financial troubles. The Catholics cornered a Protestant contractor by the name of Durgan in the camp near LaSalle before they turned and began marching back to Chicago. In the meantime, Sheriff Alson Woodruff of Ottawa called on the American settlers of the county to muster with their arms. About eighty men turned up and met the Catholics near Buffalo Rock and marched them back to South Ottawa. There the sheriff supposedly read the riot act and ordered the Catholics to disperse. It is not clear what happened next, but a volley of gunfire was leveled at the crowd and the Catholics ran in all directions. Some fled west, back toward Buffalo Rock. Others ran northward, toward the Illinois River, and tried to swim to the other side. Shots were fired at the fleeing men, but there is no record of the number of deaths or injuries. Sixty men were arrested by the sheriff but were later released because the county did not have the facilities to hold or to try so many.[26]

In 1840, when the first LaSalle County courthouse was completed in Ottawa, the village contained about one thousand people, "exclusive of the laborers on the canal." The town's ethnic American population clearly did not appreciate the presence of the large number of Irish among them, but it is also clear that the laborers brought a level of prosperity that had not been seen before. Ottawans could boast of twenty-two stores, two bakeries, three tailor shops, four hotels, five blacksmith shops, a chair factory, two churches, and two schools. The young town also had three ministers, seven doctors, and fourteen lawyers. Some of the Irish were even welcomed into the leadership ranks of Ottawa by the late 1830s and early 1840s. William Reddick, an Irish Presbyterian whose family had immigrated to America in 1816 when he was only four years old, moved to Illinois in 1835 and was elected sheriff of LaSalle County in 1838. He had been a glassmaker in Ohio, Pennsylvania, and the District of Columbia before moving to the Northwest where he became a farmer and a merchant. He would go on to become a state senator in 1847 and would found the Ottawa Glass Company in 1865. In the 1850s, Reddick was Ottawa's wealthiest citizen. Another Irishman, Thomas Larkin, emigrated in 1837. He was hired as a contractor on the canal in 1839 and was an early member of the Ottawa Catholic church. He was elected a justice of the peace in 1841 and a probate judge in 1843.[27]

Financial difficulties caused the complete cessation of work on the Illinois and Michigan Canal in 1842. The state of Illinois had already spent close to five million dollars on the project, and the chief engineer reported that its completion would cost three million more. Canal workers began to drift away. In 1843 the General Assembly passed a law that permitted the governor to borrow $1.6 million to complete the project by offering, for collateral, 230,476 acres of land along the canal and 3,493 lots on state-owned land in Chicago, Lockport, LaSalle, and Ottawa. One letter writer to the *Ottawa Free Trader* on January 19, 1844, lamented the economic stagnation of Ottawa and urged the legislature to convene "for the purpose of acting on the arrangement with the foreign landholders to complete our canal." But creditors in London and New York would not lend the state any money unless it agreed to a tax, which the legislature levied in 1845. The state was also required to dismiss the old commission, which it did, and accepted a three-member board of trustees to supervise the completion of the canal. Work began anew with Irish laborers recruited out of the cities of the East, especially New York, Boston, and Montreal. In fact, many more laborers than were needed made their way to Chicago and were forced to return. There were so many workers competing for jobs that wages were pushed down to as low as $1.00, for a day's work that began as early as 4:30 in the morning and ended at 7:45 in the evening. Some workers struck for better pay ($1.25) and shorter hours (6 A.M. to

7 P.M.) for two weeks in 1847, but to no avail. More laborers were easily found to replace the strikers and work continued on the canal.[28]

The Illinois and Michigan Canal was finally completed in early February 1848, but the icy winter did not allow the first canal boat to be towed through Ottawa until April. The little town had grown during the two decades it had taken to build the canal, from zero population in 1830 to nearly two thousand inhabitants in 1848. It was now surrounded by waterways whose use would permit the shipping of Illinois products through Ottawa and out to the markets of the world; the Illinois and Michigan Canal ran straight through town, from east to west; the Fox River ran under the canal from north to south and emptied into the Illinois River; the Illinois River ran south of town, from east to west; and the "side cut" and the "feeder canal" ran north and south into the canal and into the Illinois (see map 3). And now that the canal was finally opened, the town would also attract manufacturers who wanted to take advantage of the shipping facilities along its waterways. When that first canal boat arrived in April 1848, it was met by a cheering crowd of happy Ottawans. The people in the crowd were aware that their town had suffered, through the long delays in the construction of the canal and with the continued animosity between the canal laborers and the townspeople. But now, they thought, they could relax a bit because life with a completed canal would be easier and more prosperous. Little did they know that they would have to work even harder, now that they had become a water town.[29]

Isaac Robertson walked east along a straight line through the tall dry grass. He looked up and scanned the countryside from horizon to horizon. He bent down and felt the soil beneath his feet. Finally, he stood up and began to write in the notebook with which he always traveled: "This mile prairie [has] thin soil [and is] not fit for cultivation."[30]

It was December 1816 and Robertson was surveying the Military Tract of west-central Illinois for the United States Land Office. He had secured a federal contract to mark plots of land in the 7,500-square-mile reserve so that they could be awarded in a lottery to veterans of the War of 1812.[31] When he pronounced the surrounding prairie "unfit for cultivation" and kept it out of the lottery, he was surveying the line that separated Sections 10–11

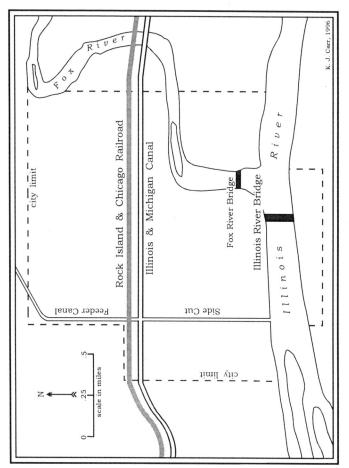

Map 3. Ottawa, Illinois: Waterways and Railways, 1855

from Sections 14–15 of Township 11 North of the baseline, Range 1 East of the Fourth Principal Meridian and where, twenty years later, the founders of Galesburg, Illinois, would lay out their Main Street. The town would eventually prosper as the Knox County center of a productive agricultural economy made possible, in part, by the fertility of the very soil that Robertson claimed too "thin" for farming.

Historians have long recognized the midwestern settlement period as one in which the people of the nation were working out land policies and settlement strategies that were continued into areas farther to the west. Officials of the federal government were often ambivalent about whether they wanted most to make money from the sale of large areas of federal lands to investors at high prices or to promote the number of family farms from the sale of small plots of land to settlers at low prices. The trend throughout the antebellum period was the decline of both the price and the acreage requirement of land sales. In 1820 federal law made it possible for individuals—either settler-farmers or absentee-speculators—to buy as little as 80 acres of government land for $1.25 per acre, down from a minimum of 160 acres at $2.00 per acre. As a result of this liberalization of federal purchasing laws and the ready availability of credit from private and state banks, thousands of land buyers participated in an unprecedented speculative land boom during the 1830s. Most historians now agree that local settlers and absentee purchasers were equally involved in the speculation.

But the historical consensus concerning the federal government's increasing accommodation of settlers at the expense of investors and the individual settler's emerging role as a speculator has ignored the fact that representatives of corporate settlements also participated in the land rush of the 1830s. At least twenty-three group-communities were founded in Illinois during the first half of the nineteenth century by people intent on preserving either their religious or their ethnic identities, including the northern towns of Andover, Bishop Hill, Geneseo, Princeton, Wethersfield (now Kewanee), and Galesburg. Those settlements were usually small and were headed by very influential and often charismatic leaders. They were generally ethnically and religiously homogeneous and were often intolerant of people who did not share the founders' moral philosophies. The corporate settlements were established at the very time that federal land laws made it

easier for individuals to buy homesteads from the federal government, a system that made speedy action an important element in
the successful purchase of land. Within such a speculative atmosphere, the complicated workings of corporate bodies, by their very
nature slow and deliberate creations, could be a hindrance in the
race to buy prime midwestern land.

It is obvious that groups could and did acquire land even though
their representatives moved comparatively slowly. Indeed, some
groups such as the one that settled Galesburg in 1836 were even
able to purchase large areas of very fertile land. It does not turn
out, however, that the early corporate settlers were able to purchase land because they successfully competed with individuals:
they were able to do so because of the systematic nature of the
original federal land survey. Once begun, the land office surveyors
marched continually westward with little concern for obstacles
of human or geographic origin. Townships and sections were
marked and established according to precise measurements and
were usually not altered to suit the whims of individual purchasers. This unyielding nature of the federal land survey occasionally resulted in the creation of large plots of land that individual settlers avoided and that groups could and did later purchase.

When the United States government hired surveyors to mark
the Illinois Military Tract in 1816, large numbers of European
Americans and African Americans had not yet encountered the
open prairies of the Midwest. After nearly two hundred years of
agriculture based on the continual clearing of the wooded lands
in the East, the people of the United States were understandably
leery of the stark emptiness of the western plains. Popular convention held that any land that did not support a natural growth
of trees would not be fertile enough to grow corn or wheat. With
the end of the Black Hawk War in 1832, the Illinois Military Tract
became available for general sale. As settlement went on, opinions
about the productivity of prairie soil shifted considerably.

By the early 1830s, then, the northern Illinois environment was
seen as generally healthy and productive, although farmers still
avoided the open prairie for want of timber and transportation.
After that, buyers sought land with five principal characteristics.
First, purchasers preferred land away from the disease-laden lowlands of river floodplains. Second, although buyers by the 1830s
were aware of the fertility of prairie soil, they preferred land that
had some timber for fuel, housing, and fencing. Third, purchasers

preferred holdings along or close to existing transportation routes, either over land or on water. Fourth, buyers preferred locations near existing towns or near spots where a town was likely to be established to have access to supplies and markets. And fifth, if a buyer was already a settler in an area and chose to buy more land, he invariably did so in his home county.[32]

The United States government used the information gathered by their federal surveyors about the agricultural capabilities of particular tracts of land to ease the sale and settlement of much of the country's public lands—its "national domain." First, to speed sales, midwestern surveyors such as Isaac Robertson sent their field notes to government offices in St. Louis where cartographers would compose maps of all of the thirty-six sections in each township. Federal employees in various districts throughout the settlement area would, in turn, use the maps to prepare tract books in which they would record bounty claims or individual sales of land. Second, prospective settlers would use the surveyor's judgments about its agricultural potential in deciding whether to purchase one parcel of land over another. Finally, when the settler actually began improving and farming his holdings, he would separate his own fields from those of his neighbors by noting the wooden posts, sod mounds, or marked trees that the surveyor had left on the corners of each 160-acre quarter section.[33] The purchasers of the land that would eventually become the site of Galesburg, Illinois, were some of the many settlers who took advantage of the aid given to them by the United States Land Office. But because these settlers were interested in buying as a group and could not act as quickly as individuals, they had to take advantage of an unanticipated result of the survey system.

Galesburg was named for the Reverend George Washington Gale, a minister from Oneida County, New York. In the early 1830s, his intention was to establish a village and manual labor college in Michigan or Indiana as a training ground for western ministers. The Presbyterian church of which he was a member had joined the Congregationalists in 1801, in part to organize better their missionary activities in the American West where adherents of more "primitive" religions—Baptists and Methodists— were gaining converts. Gale's plan was one of many similar ones that were formulated by residents of upstate New York's "Burned Over District" during the perfectionist reforms and revivals of the "Second Great Awakening." He planned to solicit subscriptions for purchase of an entire township—23,040 acres—at the government minimum price of $1.25 per acre. The plan called for setting aside three sections—1,920 acres—for the town and college and the sale of the remainder to settlers at $5.00 per acre. Sales of town lots were to finance the establishment of precollege academies for students of both sexes, and the profits from the sale of farmland were to be used to build the college and to set up its endowment. The actual business of selecting and buying land was to commence when forty thousand dollars in subscriptions had been recorded.[34]

By 1835, Gale had convinced forty-five families in upstate New York to pledge twenty-one thousand dollars to the venture. While these subscribers to the plan were probably willing to consider moving west for the altruistic purposes emphasized by Gale, many were just as anxious to exchange their exhausted New York farms for the economic windfall that the frontier promised. But by the time subscriptions to the venture were large enough to make its success probable, sales in the federal land offices of the old Northwest were already brisk, and desirable land was becoming scarcer. Realizing the need to speed up the process, Gale called a meeting of subscribers on May 6, 1835, in Rome, New York, though the original forty-thousand-dollar target had not been reached. Also anxious to begin the acquisition of land, the subscribers at the meeting appointed a Prudential Committee to handle the business details. The Prudential Committee immediately decided to send an Exploring Committee to the West to look for, but not purchase, suitable land. Although Gale had originally planned to settle in Michigan or in Indiana, the Exploring Committee of the New York Society for Establishing a Colony and Literary Institution in the Valley of the Mississippi (from now on called the Society) was directed to prospect in six different locations: northern Indiana; southern Michigan; and northern Illinois, in southern Cook County, LaSalle, McLean, and Putnam Counties, along the Fox River Valley, between the Fox and the Illinois Rivers, and in the northern part of the Military Tract.[35]

As the three-man Exploring Committee made its way west, the possible locations began to disappear before the members' very eyes. "We saw no prospect of locating in Michigan," wrote committee member Timothy Jervis from Chicago on June 15, 1835. "In Indiana," he reported, "we were rather disappointed with the country." Jervis continued his observations by proclaiming that "the only land east of the Military Tract that is or will be in market this season is the canal lands along the Illinois. . . . If we are to be restricted to lands in the market . . . my opinion is that the [canal] tract land mentioned and the Military Tract afford altogether the best opportunities for us." The other two committee members, Nehemiah West and Thomas Gilbert, left Jervis in Chicago where he was to review the trends in land sales at the Northeastern Land Office. Gilbert went to the Quincy, Illinois, Land Office to do the same, while West traveled to Ottawa, Illinois, along the path of the Illinois and Michigan Canal. All three met eventually in Knox County where Gilbert had purchased a farm for himself while he was in Quincy. Jervis soon fell ill and returned to New York. Gilbert stayed on his new farm, and West returned to New York where he and Jervis reported to the Prudential Committee. They recommended four sites in Illinois for possible settlement: near the Robinson River in Putnam County, near the Vermillion River in LaSalle County, in Union Grove in Putnam County, and on the Military Tract in Knox County.[36]

Two months passed before the Prudential Committee organized and sent another committee to the west. Meanwhile, land was being sold at the Quincy Land Office at the rate of one township every three days. The Society delayed the purchase of land because the subscribers were unable to meet their pledges without selling their New York farms, and they were unwilling to do so without some further assurance that Gale's venture would be successful. The reports of the Exploring Committee did not immediately cause subscribers to join the western venture. Gale was only able to collect about seven thousand of the forty thousand dollars that his original plan required. Finally, Sylvanus Ferris, a wealthy dairy farmer and cheese merchant from Herkimer County, New York, personally endorsed a note that permitted the Society to negotiate a loan of ten thousand dollars from the Bank of Michigan. The Prudential Committee then sent a newly formed Purchasing Committee to Illinois to buy land for the colony. The Purchasing Committee members were Gale, West, Ferris, and Thomas Simmons. Subscribers Samuel Tompkins and the Reverend John Waters, as well as Waters's son James and Ferris's son Western, accompanied the committee. Tompkins replaced Gale as a member when the latter fell ill in Detroit on the way to Illinois.[37]

During September 1835, the Purchasing Committee made its way across Illinois. The members eliminated the first three of the

Exploring Committee's recommended sites because they were unable to find enough suitable land. Finally, in Knox County, they found what Gale later described as "the finest prairie, lying in a body, rolling, well watered, surrounded with groves of the finest timber, with ravines yielding an abundance of mineral coal." The committee immediately bought 260 acres of improved land just to the north of the prairie for a temporary settlement; this initial purchase cost $1,500. At the Quincy Land Office, Gale discovered that the entire township containing the prairie was still available for the minimum price of $1.25 per acre. On October 20, 1835, the Purchasing Committee bought 8,978 acres of the township— spending $11,222.50 of the money entrusted to them by the Society. On the same day, Sylvanus Ferris purchased close to 3,000 acres in the same township for himself.[38]

Apparently someone outside the colony thought that the college-town plan had some economic potential since, ten days later, Richard F. Barrett of Sangamon County, Illinois, bought 1,428 acres in the township in alternate eighth-sections. Barrett's optimism was apparently infectious, even among the members of the Society, because, on November 5, six days after Barrett's purchases, the committee returned to Quincy where its members bought another 5,128 acres in the names of West, Sylvanus Ferris, Gale, and Henry Ferris. Meanwhile, the committee paid a surveyor $15.00 to fix exact locations for the college and the village on the colony lands. All together then, the Purchasing Committee spent $13,823.70 for about 10,000 acres of Society land (including $636.20 for travel expenses.) The entourage returned via the Ohio River to New York where the entire Society met to plan and name their new "Prairie College" (later, Knox College) and to plat their new town of Galesburg.[39]

In their plat, the town's founders placed Main Street along the line between Sections 10–11 and 14–15 of Township 11 North of the baseline, Range 1 East of the Fourth Principal Meridian. Their surveyor took advantage of Isaac Robertson's earlier work and used the section markers to fix the locations of Galesburg's streets. But this was not the only way that the land survey helped in the settlement of Gale's colony. When the Exploring Committee prospected during the summer of 1835, they were looking for lands with the same attributes as those sought by individual settlers and speculators. Everybody wanted fertile land that would promote a healthy environment, contained a supply of available timber, was along an existing transportation line, and was close to a place to market their goods. The Exploring Committee, however, required that their land exhibit one additional characteristic: it needed to contain a large amount of contiguous, unalienated land so that the group members could settle together. Or, as Gale put it, the Society needed land that was "lying in a body." However, because corporate settlement was also a slow process, any sizable tract of land that was still not alienated by the time a group wanted to buy had probably already been labeled "not fit" by individual purchasers. Therefore, groups faced a dilemma: they sought land that had not been bought piecemeal by local or absentee speculators, but if such a tract existed, it was probably not good enough to buy.[40]

The alienation histories of the townships of Knox County, Illinois, show how individual and group needs affected the speed and order with which people bought federal land (see map 4). The Purchasing Committee bought improved land for their temporary settlement in Township 12 North, Range 1 East (Henderson Township);[41] it was the only totally alienated township in the county by the end of 1835 but was largely claimed with military bounties during the 1810s because it was heavily wooded. Knoxville, the only established town in the county before the 1830s land boom, was located in Township 11 North, Range 2 East (Knox Township). It can be used to illustrate the fact that settlers began to reevaluate the fertility of the treeless prairie during the 1830s; only 25 percent of the township was taken by military bounties in the 1810s, but it was 60 percent alienated by 1836—and nearly 35 percent of the township's land had been bought in the Quincy Land Office between its opening in 1831 and the Society purchases in late 1835.

Knox Township is one tier removed from the Spoon River bottomlands and is located on the border of the timber-prairie line that bisected Knox County from northeast to southwest. The Galena Road, the major overland route from Peoria to Galena, went straight through the township. Knox Township was thought to be such a desirable location by the 1830s—with its prairie and accessible timber—that the county's residents voted to purchase and plat its seat of justice in Knoxville in 1831.[42] In fact, the location of Knoxville only added to the desirability of the township for land purchasers since its market services attracted even more people to the surrounding area. The majority of Knox Township land purchasers during the 1830s were already Knox County resi-

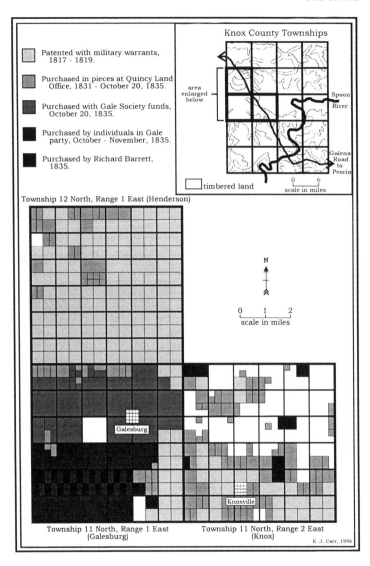

Map 4. The Alienation of Three Illinois Townships, 1817–1835

dents; only seven were from outside the county and only four were from outside the state. The out-of-county buyers, however, were true speculators who recognized the choice location of the township; they bought 37 percent of the land that was sold between 1831 and 1836.

Galesburg would eventually be located in Township 11 North, Range 1 East (Galesburg Township). Unlike the more timbered tracts to the north and to the east, Galesburg's prairie township was not alienated with military warrants; surveyor Robertson had deemed it "not fit for cultivation" in 1816 and had kept it out of the bounty lottery. Only 12 percent of the land in the township was warranted in the 1810s, compared with 96 percent in Henderson Township and 25 percent in Knox Township. The lack of timber in Galesburg Township accounts for the early rejection of the area by settlers. But even in the 1830s when settlement took off in the other parts of Knox County, Galesburg Township remained essentially empty—only 20 percent of the land was alienated before the New Yorkers arrived in 1835; this compares with a minimum of 42 percent in each of the five surrounding townships.[43]

Galesburg Township was not attractive to either local or absentee speculators because it met only one of the criteria for ideal land purchase during the 1830s; it did not contain bottomland and was, therefore, considered a healthy place. But the township was most notable for its extreme undesirability in an area of the state and during a time when almost any land was being snapped up by local and absentee speculators. The systematic nature of Isaac Robertson's original land survey of the Military Tract had created a township that was almost without desirable land; it had very little timber, was as far away from a navigable waterway as one could be in northern Illinois, and was off the beaten track of any existing land transportation routes.

Although Galesburg's founders bought up a large portion of the prairie in Galesburg Township (that they quickly described as full of positive attributes), even they did not originally view the tract as desirable. The directions given by the Prudential Committee to the Exploring Committee of the Society charged the prospectors with finding land that included a good supply of timber, had facilities for easy communication with the East, contained enough waterpower for a mill, and, if possible, was "on some great thoroughfare such as a canal or navigable water . . . it should however be on some important road or where it is probable such road would be opened."[44]

The lands of Galesburg Township were simply undesirable for settlement, although its soils were certainly fertile. The Purchasing Committee bought the tract anyway because it possessed the one quality that was essential for the town and college; it contained a large amount of unalienated, cheap, contiguous land. Yet the very fact that the land was available for government purchase so late in 1835 meant that individual buyers had already found it wanting. Despite its deficiencies, the land that the group-settlers of Galesburg purchased was really their only choice and it was theirs by default.

Therefore, from the very first the settlers of Galesburg were confronted with the need to make up for their land's deficiencies. To guarantee themselves a supply of timber, they were compelled to buy land from private holders, spending nearly two thousand dollars of their limited money. The township's other deficiencies were to be handled over a longer period. In fact, for at least two decades after its founding, the survival and success of the colony depended on the group's ability to make up for the original undesirability of their land. At the same time, this undesirability assured the continued existence of the colony since only group action could improve its isolated situation. Galesburg's settlers were compelled to spend their collective energies in a continuous attempt to wrest the county's economic and political center away from the people of Knoxville, their neighbors to the east who had clearly been dealt the winning hand. And the fact that the people of Galesburg were ultimately successful in doing so—evident by the 1870s when they had acquired both the junction of the Chicago, Burlington and Quincy Railroad and the county seat—owed as much to Galesburg's continued existence as a group venture as had the original purchase of the land.

Galesburg remained an ethnically homogeneous town until the 1850s. In 1840, the village contained 324 people in fifty-six families. Only twelve of the families were members of the forty-five who had subscribed to the Society's venture during the planning stages in New York. However, only six of the subscribers placed family members in the township outside the village and only one of these did not have relatives in the village itself. So from the beginning, the town of Galesburg was seen as important to the Society's plans for a successful outcome to the venture. Galesburg's future was most immediately tied to that of Knox College since the town's relative isolation meant that future settlers would be attracted for other than economic reasons. During the 1840s, however, the college went through one crisis after another. Four-year scholarships to the college were given as premiums to anybody who purchased an eighty-acre plot of Society land around the village. By the time Knox College opened in 1841, it owed a total of 2,050 years of schooling to 512 students. The Presbyterian-Congregational "Society for the Promotion of Collegiate and Theological Education at the West" gave Knox an emergency grant in 1845 after poor management dashed hopes of a financial windfall from a land speculation deal. In 1848, the same organization again bailed out the college with a grant of two thousand dollars to help it survive another rough year.[45]

By 1850, the town held 800 people and 150 families, nearly half of whom had been born in either New England or New York. Galesburg Township contained 634 people, the majority of whom were Yankees. However, with the exception of Hendersonville, the site of the original improved land that was purchased by the settlers, the surrounding towns and townships of Knox County contained mostly people from either southern Illinois or from the states along the southern migration route. So by 1850 the Yankee founders of Galesburg had retreated into their village and township and were concentrating on establishing them as an important economic and cultural center in western Illinois. However, only 12 percent of the 1850 inhabitants were foreign-born. In 1860, the city of Galesburg contained 4,953 people, 77 percent native-born and 23 percent foreign-born.[46]

While the populations of Belleville, Ottawa, and Galesburg were large enough by 1850 to ensure that none of the towns would disappear altogether, their inhabitants had not yet had the time or the opportunity to make decisions about the shapes of their ultimate economic, cultural, and political social structures. Yet the towns were already very different in their compositions. Belleville had attracted large numbers of immigrants from its founding because of its location close to St. Louis and its early designation as a refuge for Germans. Ottawa had initially attracted settlers from the northeastern United States but had also become the home of a large group of immigrants. Galesburg remained relatively isolated in its prairie location, and its exclusively northern American group-founding did not readily attract outsiders of either American or foreign birth. But the residents of all three towns had not yet fixed their towns in the regional and national economy, established permanent institutions for the education of their children, or worked out the methods for distributing leadership positions in town and county politics. However, the historical and geographical development of Belleville, Ottawa, and Galesburg before 1850 would partly determine how their residents would make decisions about their structures. Bellevillians, with their persistent history of economic ambivalence toward St. Louis and their long experience with ethnic diversity, would continue to find it difficult to reach decisions reflecting common objectives and values. Ottawans, with their legacies of ethnic animosity and reliance upon water transportation as the key to their prosperity, would find it difficult to develop a different identity. Galesburgers, with their comparatively short history of geographic isolation and ethnic homogeneity, would continue to be dominated by a small clique of men who were connected with Knox College. But the leaders in the three towns were facing a future that would demand thoughtfulness and innovation. All three towns would emerge from the 1850s as viable entities, assured of a continued existence as small urban centers, but they would look different from one another and from their previous selves.

Three The People

The pioneers of Belleville, Ottawa, and Galesburg were all winners in the game of town building. The founders of each had left the eastern United States and the western parts of Europe with dreams of establishing new homes on the American frontier; there they hoped to achieve personal financial success and, at the same time, live in a community where they could be sure that their families would be surrounded by others who shared their same sense of social morality. In so doing, the early settlers to each place had built three unique towns on the Illinois frontier. Belleville, founded as the seat of St. Clair County in 1814, had grown to become a small city whose survival depended upon its status as an economic satellite of St. Louis in 1850. Ottawa, founded in 1830 as the western terminus of the Illinois and Michigan Canal, had become an important shipping and manu-facturing center by the middle of the century. Galesburg, founded in 1835 as the home of a manual labor college, had grown, by 1850, into a small but prosperous shipping center for the farm produce of western Illinois. But even though each had found its own niche in the midwestern economy of the nineteenth century, none of the towns was yet a complete community.

A visitor to Belleville or Ottawa or Galesburg in 1850 would have sensed a tentativeness to his or her surroundings. The people in each town were in the process of establishing and implement-ing the rules that would govern their economic, social, and politi-cal relationships. That is, they were still building their communi-ties. They knew that they needed to trade with one another on a daily basis, gather in the churches together on Sundays, and at-tend lectures and political rallies with each other in the evenings. But by mid-century the dynamics of these activities were not en-tirely clear. The people in the three towns would spend the next decade working out, by trial and error, how each of their town's occupational, ethnic, and religious groups would interact with the others. And, in doing so, they would choose the leaders who would, in their turn, guide the towns through a decade of tremendous economic, social, and political changes. By the Civil War, each of the communities' social structures would be complete. The people had worked out their differences and had established methods of decision making that would permit continued development.

The 1850s were, after all, a time when all Americans, whether on the frontier or in the established communities of the East, confronted a series of challenges to their traditional lives. An industrial revolution was taking place throughout the nation, and factory workers were churning out products for mass distribution and consumption throughout the nation and in Illinois. The new telegraph and railroad technologies encouraged people in all sections of the state and country to communicate and visit with others in all parts of the nation. In 1850, there were only 111 miles of railroad tracks in Illinois; by the end of the decade, the state contained 2,270 miles of track and no community was more than 50 miles from a railroad.[1] And the establishment of railroad connections went right along with the construction of telegraph lines. In fact, the construction of railroads and telegraphs in the state paralleled one another, both figuratively and literally. Telegraph wires were routinely strung on poles along railroad rights-of-way to form what one commentator has labeled the "Siamese twins of commerce."[2] Industrialization and improvements in communication brought with them many of the trappings of modern society, including an increase in population, larger and more cities, and a redefinition of the ideal family.

In traditional agricultural America, men and women worked together on farms, each with his or her own sex-defined tasks but all with the well-being of the family in mind. In the new industrial and urban America, men and women were said to occupy "separate spheres" of human life, and it was thought best for husbands to go off to work in factories and offices while wives stayed at home and raised children. While far from the reality for most, this new family lifestyle allowed some middle-class women the opportunity to become involved in reform movements that purported to correct the ills of the changing society.[3] Social reformers, particularly those in the North, advocated the establishment of institutions that would assure the continuation of a virtuous nation, even though the traditional fixtures of American society—family, church, and community—were in the process of evolving with the new industrial economy; this was a particularly problematical task for most reformers because so many immigrants—many of whom were not familiar with traditional American values—were making their way into the United States from western Europe. Many of the immigrants, particularly those from Germany and Ireland, were Roman Catholics, and the mostly Protestant reformers were suspicious of the new immigrants' moral literacy. Beginning with the 1820s and the religious revival movement that has become known as the "Second Great Awakening," Protestant activists worked to reform prisons, insane asylums, and schools so that the nation's social institutions might be used to inculcate ethical behavior in its urban and industrial citizens. The reformers also agitated to eliminate behaviors that, they argued, contributed to immorality; they worked to make the consumption of alcohol illegal and tried to stamp out prostitution and juvenile delinquency.

The reform movement spilled over into politics when religious leaders began, in the 1830s, to insist that the practice of slavery was, by its very nature, a sin. Such abolitionist sentiment was not very popular in the North and was clearly condemned in the South. But increasing numbers of northerners did not support the extension of slavery into the western territories because their republican philosophy relied upon free and independent labor to provide the nation with a continuous source of virtuous citizens; in their minds, slavery fostered dependence among the slaves and poor whites of the South and allowed the large plantation owners to monopolize the nation's wealth. The fear among northerners that the practice of slavery would spread into the newly acquired lands of the Southwest—New Mexico, Utah, and California, all gained at the conclusion of the Mexican War in 1848—came to a head with the Civil War. But before then, Americans realigned their political sensibilities during the 1850s, forming the modern Republican and Democratic Parties.[4]

The transformation of the United States in the first half of the nineteenth century—in the economic, social, and political lives of their citizens—was doubly troublesome for the inhabitants of frontier towns; people in the newly settled regions of the nation had to deal with the consequences of the national changes while simultaneously establishing their own local rules of interaction and choosing their own leaders. The inhabitants of Belleville, Ottawa, and Galesburg were faced with this daunting task. And, in the end, they established three distinctive communities, each with its own infrastructure, institutions, and leaders. Each town began the chore of community building with relatively small numbers of people. In 1850, Galesburg's population lagged behind those of Belleville and Ottawa since its region of the state was settled last (see table A-1). By 1860, Belleville and Ottawa were almost exactly the same size while Galesburg remained smaller. Then, by 1870, Galesburg had caught and passed both of the other towns, but all three remained moderately sized small cities. During the period in which the residents were establishing their communities, each of the towns was particularly frontierlike in that its population was extremely volatile. People were moving in and out of the towns at a dizzying rate. Americans have traditionally been a mobile people, and most established communities in the middle of the nineteenth century experienced turnover rates of between 40 and 50 percent over a ten-year period.[5] That is, between forty and fifty families out of every hundred remained in a community for the entire decade between federal censuses. Frontier communities, however, typically experienced much lower rates of persistence. Don Harrison Doyle found that only one-quarter of the nondependent population of 1850 Jacksonville, Illinois, remained in 1860, while John Mack Faragher could find only 22 percent of rural Sugar Creek's residents who stayed from 1850 to 1860.[6]

Frontier towns were also notable for the larger than normal numbers of young people. Frontier demographer Jack E. Eblen found that newly settled areas of the country were populated by folks of both sexes and of all ages but that there was a preponderance of people under the age of ten and between the ages of twenty and forty.[7] Also, there were usually more men than women between the ages of twenty and forty. This shows that many young couples migrated to the frontier in search of economic opportunity and that many young men traveled to the West to establish themselves before they married. It also meant that young communities on the frontier would have to spend an unusual amount of time answering questions about the education of their large numbers of children.

The three towns were also similar during the 1850s in that they were all populated by both immigrants and the native-born. But there the similarity ends: Belleville was dominated by the foreign-born (particularly the Germans), whereas Galesburg and Ottawa were both controlled by native-born people. By 1860, Belleville was the home of 3,881 foreign-born and 3,614 native-born people, while Ottawa had 2,547 and Galesburg had 1,141 of the former and Ottawa had 5,020 and Galesburg had 3,773 of the latter. These figures are misleading, however, since the totals include children, many of whom were born in the United States regardless of the birthplaces of their parents. The adult totals more accurately reflect the actual ethnic division in the towns. A survey of heads of households or males of at least twenty-one years in 1850 and 1860—the independent population—show an even greater number of immigrants in all of the towns. Belleville was overwhelmingly foreign: 70 percent in 1850 and 82 percent in 1860. In Ottawa, the foreign-born were 46 percent of the adult male population in 1850 and 53 percent in 1860. The Galesburg foreignborn were more visible among the independent population than in the total population; there were 16 percent foreign-born in 1850 and 34 percent in 1860 (see tables A-2 and A-3). These basic differences between the populations of the three towns would help to determine the unique social structures that they would eventually develop in their communities.

By 1850, the year in which Belleville was incorporated as a city and the year of the first census in which accurate birthplace records are available, 35 percent of St. Clair County's residents were foreign-born, the vast majority of whom were from the various states of Germany. Forty-one percent of Belleville's population in 1850 was German-born (see table A-4). In 1860, the population of German-born residents in Belleville was 43 percent, and 52 percent were foreign-born (see table A-5).[8] However, it is even easier to see the dominance of Belleville by Germans if one looks at its independent population; almost two-thirds in 1850 and more than three-quarters of the town's 1860 heads of household or males of voting age were German-speaking. The people from the southwestern Catholic states of Bavaria and Baden formed the largest German contingent, but there were also sizable groups from the central Protestant Reformed provinces of Hesse-Darmstadt, Hesse-Kassel, and Nassau and from the Lutheran northeastern states of Prussia and Saxony. The only other notable immigrant groups were the English and the Irish. Belleville's native-born also hailed from varied locations, although the largest number was born in Illinois.

Besides the state's own natives who were mostly the young sons of early arrivals, there were large contingents from the middle and southern regions of the United States. There were also small numbers from New England and from other states of the Midwest. As far as race goes, very few African Americans chose to live in Belleville. Since the town was so close to the border with Missouri, a slave state to which they might be kidnapped, and since southern Illinoisans were not welcoming toward free blacks, it is not surprising that the census taker recorded no African-American families in Belleville in 1850; by 1860, there were only about twenty-five African-American families. Five percent and 7 percent of the households in 1850 and 1860 Belleville, respectively, were headed by single women, usually widows with children. About 5 percent of Belleville's families had live-in servants during the decade. However, the typical Belleville family in the 1850s was composed of a husband and wife with two or three children.

In 1860, Belleville closely resembled the average United States county in its age distribution. But, according to the number of bachelors in the town, Belleville was frontierlike: nearly one-third of the men who were twenty-one or older were single. Eblen estimated that on the ordinary frontier only one-quarter of the adult males were single. Perhaps the time of the year in which the census was taken—summer—and the nature of Belleville's economy attracted large numbers of single men. Young men might have been drawn to work temporarily in the surrounding coal mines or in the town's construction trades. The coal mines were operating at least as early as the 1840s when tons of the bituminous ore were transported for use in St. Louis. Seventy percent of the 1860 independent inhabitants were heads of households, and 23 percent were boarders, mostly the young single men.[9]

While the internal economies of Belleville, Ottawa, and Galesburg during their frontier periods were largely commercial in orientation, they differed markedly in their degrees of industrialization and in their position in the hierarchy of urban functions. Belleville and Ottawa were more involved in bona fide manufacturing and craft production, whereas Galesburg functioned as a traditional entrepôt for a booming agricultural hinterland. Belleville's occupational structure during the 1850s shows the presence of both a commercial and an industrial group of workers.[10] Almost one-half of its employed population in 1850 and one-fourth of its employed population in 1860 worked in traditional crafts, reflecting the heavily German origins of its workers (see tables A-6 and A-7). However, many of those employed in the crafts may have been contributing to the production or support of large-scale marketable products. For example, 120 of the 579 craftsmen in 1860 were carpenters; this figure may have been inflated by the timing of the summer census, but, clearly, many men were involved in the production of mass-produced wood products. There were also 23 brewers in the city by 1860 who were, no doubt, satisfying the thirsts of the local German population but were also producing for export to St. Louis. The 60 coopers were probably making barrels for the 23 brewers. So while Belleville was the home of many craftsmen and traditional manufacturers, its commercial economy was geared toward connections with an outside trade network as well as toward its services to the local population.

Another large group of Belleville workers in 1860 also shows that the town's workers were participating in an industrializing economy. A quarter of the workforce were engaged as unskilled workers or were listed as day laborers on the census manuscripts. The major industrial pursuit was that carried on by the numerous coal mines near the bluffs to the west of the city where many of the skilled craftsmen worked as miners. Most of the coal was carted across the Mississippi River for consumption in St. Louis, but some was used in the steam engines of Belleville's own industrial establishments. By 1860, Belleville was the home of at least three flour mills (where some of the coopers worked), a threshing machine works, two carriage factories, a sash factory, and numerous cigar works. There was also at least one marble quarry just outside the town.[11]

The numerical dominance of Belleville by a German-born majority did not automatically spell economic defeat for the ethnic Americans within the town. On the contrary, the native-born residents—along with some of the earliest German arrivals—were able to wield a disproportionate amount of economic power within the young city. The continued arrival during the 1850s of Germans—and the social disorientation that came with it—certainly made it difficult for Bellevillians to compete for political dominance with the other towns in the region, but the quickly developing industrial economy was able to absorb the newcomers in great numbers.

Belleville's workforce was divided ethnically in the 1850s. Certain groups of residents were generally connected with particular types of employment. While nearly every occupation contained workers from nearly every section of the United States and from nearly every nativity group within the town, there were certainly some ethnic patterns. The German-born and the native-born were clearly the economic leaders of Belleville. German immigrants from Hesse and Prussia and the native-born held a greater proportion of the professional and commercial positions in town—doctors, lawyers, editors, clergymen, teachers, students, artists, bankers, and merchants—than their numbers would suggest. The Hessians, along with their fellow Germans from Bavaria and Baden, were more likely than other immigrants to be proprietors of local specialty stores. And the Hessians, the Prussians, and the Bavarians controlled the manufacturing sector of the community; the only exception was in the mining industry in which nearly one-half of the English immigrants worked. On the opposite end of the economic ladder, Belleville's unskilled and laboring jobs were disproportionately held by immigrants from Switzerland, France, and Ireland; they appeared on the 1860 census as unskilled workers or laborers nearly 20 percent of the time even though they only made up 10 percent of the population. (Most of the Swiss immigrants to Belleville were German-speaking and had been attracted to the town because of its large German element; a large portion of the French immigrants were Alsatians and were also German-speaking.) The Swiss population must have been particularly associated with the laboring class since nearly half of them worked for daily wages. On the other hand, the Hessians were able to almost completely avoid working as laborers.

Another occupation that shows the leadership structure of a town is that of paid professional government worker. Fifty-eight percent of the Belleville residents who were paid county officials in 1860—clerk, treasurer, judge, sheriff and deputy, censor, school commissioner, justices of the peace, constables, and notary publics—were native-born Americans. Only one-quarter were Germans, three out of five of whom were from the Hessian states. The remainder were English and Russian. The paid state and federal employees who resided in Belleville—U.S. representative, post office master and clerk, circuit court clerk and deputies, circuit court judge, and prison keeper—were also mostly native-born. Five of the eight posts were held by Americans. The remaining three were held by Germans, two of whom were from the central

German states. However, the nonelected local city offices—city surveyor, registrar, street inspector, collector, and marshal—were dominated by a wide-ranging group of the foreign-born. They were from Hanover, Brunswick, Bohemia, and Bavaria.

So Belleville's occupational structure in the 1850s was one in which the native-born, though numerically in the minority, exercised a large measure of power and control over the economic and political functions of the city. But their power had mostly to do with their ability to communicate with people outside the town. However, the Germans as a whole were able to fill many of the professional, commercial, and political positions within the town itself. The Hessian Germans were able to wield the most disproportional economic power within the city, particularly in government and industrial pursuits.

The estimates of real property holdings of the 1860 census manuscripts allow us to look at wealth structures. Over one-half of the independent population of Belleville held no real property. However, the foreign-born were nearly one and one-half times more likely to own property than the native-born, and the Germans were the most likely of all to own real estate. Within the German group, however, those from Bavaria and from Baden were slightly more apt to own real estate than any others. Other immigrants, however, were less likely to own real property; only 35 percent of the Swiss, 36 percent of the English, and 9 percent of the Irish owned any land. Although some groups in Belleville were more likely to own property, they did not necessarily own the largest amounts. In fact, while the native-born were less likely than immigrants to own property at all, those who did, owned larger amounts than the foreign-born. This shows that the ethnic Americans were more involved in land speculation than the immigrants. The native-born made up more than one-quarter of those who owned over $2,000 worth of real property—or the top 11 percent of the landowners—even though they were only 16 percent of the general population. And although the foreign-born were generally less wealthy than the natives, some were better off than others. The Hessians and Bavarians were the most likely among the Germans to be wealthy, whereas the Swiss, the English, and the Irish were the least likely. Another approximate measure of wealth confirms Belleville's economic structure. Even though only 121 households in the city in 1860 employed one or more servants, the native-born were nearly two and one-half

times more likely than the foreign-born to have them. But among
the German immigrants, the Hessians were the most likely. Belleville's servants, mostly young and female, were members of all
ethnic groups.

A person's accumulation of wealth had much to do with his age
in Belleville. However, when one examines the ages of members
of ethnic groups, it is evident that an individual's age also correlated with his birthplace. Except for southerners, the native-born
were the youngest group of residents in 1860; most of them were
Illinois natives. As one would expect of an area that was just
emerging from its frontier, the native-state population dropped off
dramatically as age increased. The oldest people in town were the
southerners, who were the very earliest settlers in the area.
Bavarians and Hessians, the immigrants with the highest percentages of property holders, had the lowest percentage of thirty-year-
olds, showing that they either immigrated to the United States as
older men with more capital or they arrived earlier than the other
immigrants and had had more time to acquire holdings. Other
than the fact that the German-born groups dominated all but the
very youngest age decile, there appear to be no other noticeable
patterns of age distribution. So older age did indeed correlate with
wealth, but age did not explain the difference in wealth among
the various immigrant groups in Belleville. Neither, it seems, did
time of arrival. Using the age of the oldest child born to a couple
in Illinois as an estimate of the years in the state, there is no clear
indication that any immigrant group arrived earlier than others.
All of the large groups of foreigners averaged between five and
eight years in the state while the native-born—especially the
southerners—averaged between ten and twenty years.

Belleville's 1850s wealth structure, then, as measured by occupations and real estate holdings, shows a community in which the
native-born minority was able to take advantage of more opportunities for advancement than were the foreign-born residents.
The immigrants, however, were able to use their demographic
dominance and compete effectively for economic control, at least
within the city itself. Among the foreign-born, the Germans
dominated both numerically and economically, whereas the
Swiss, English, and Irish remained on the lower rungs of the
wealth ladder. But within the German group, it appears as if the
people from the central states were able to take advantage of their
earlier arrival to accumulate wealth more effectively than the

others. The town's industrial and commercial connections with the regional and national market were in the hands of the native-born Americans and, to some extent, the early arriving Germans from Hesse. However, Belleville's internal trade was controlled by other Germans, namely, the Bavarians and the Badenese.

Church membership offers some insight into social relationships among the inhabitants in the towns.[12] Belleville's religious structure in the 1850s showed a general division between American and foreign church membership. There were at least nine separate religious groups in Belleville by 1860. Information on some of the members could be found for the Catholic, the Lutheran, the Methodist Episcopal, the Presbyterian, the Baptist, the German Protestant, and the German Methodist congregations. There is no available membership information on the African Methodist or the African Baptist churches, but one would assume that their presence meant that Belleville's few African Americans were segregated into separate congregations. Its American churches, mostly southern and fundamental in origin, allowed foreign membership, though they remained distinctly American. Only one of the churches, the First Baptist (founded 1831), appears to have been exclusively American—all seven identifiable members were native-born, three southerners and four Illinoisans. But the Methodist Episcopal congregation (founded around 1826) appears to have been mostly native—twelve out of the fifteen identifiable members in the 1850s were southern or Illinois natives; and of the Methodists who were foreign-born, two were English and one was German. In the Presbyterian church (founded 1833), three of the six identifiable members were natives and three were foreigners—one Prussian, one Alsatian, and one Englishman.

The major foreign churches in Belleville were more exclusive than the American ones: the Catholic, Lutheran, and Free Protestant churches all enjoyed large constituencies among the Bavarian and the Badenese, the Prussian, and the Hessian populations, respectively. The Catholic St. Peter's (founded 1842) was mostly foreign-born but had at least three native-born members—two from Illinois and one from the South; the foreign-born Catholics were from Bavaria, Baden, Hesse, and France. The remaining white churches appear to have been exclusively German. Only four 1850s members of the United Evangelical Lutheran Church (Missouri Synod, founding date unknown) were identifiable, but three were from Prussia and one was from Hesse. The Free

German Protestant Church's (founded 1839) eight known members came from Hesse, Bavaria, and northern Germany. The two identifiable German Methodist Church (founded 1850) members came from Bavaria and Hesse. So while Belleville's religious relationships showed a general pattern of American versus foreign church membership, it appears not to have been completely polarized. The native-born denominations allowed foreign membership, though they remained distinctly American. But the larger churches were more exclusive. The Catholic, Free Protestant, and Lutheran churches all enjoyed large memberships but were divided by the differing German origins of their members, and none was numerically dominant.

All three cities had an abundance of literary, fraternal, musical, moral, and military organizations during the 1850s, and their membership rolls also displayed ethnic divisions. Belleville was the home of two Masonic lodges (one English-speaking and one German-speaking), a group of Good Templars, an Equality Lodge, a band of Druids, a physical fitness *Turnverein*, a Working Men's Association, a Philharmonic orchestra, a Bible Society, a Saxe-Band, a Library Society, a *Sängerbund*, two competing fire companies, and a hook and ladder company.[13] Belleville's Library Society (founded 1836) and the Belleville *Sängerbund* combined in 1861 to form *Der Belleviller Sängerbund und die Bibliothek Gesellschaft*. The combined group's charter, approved by the state of Illinois, was printed in 1870 with a list of members from which it is possible to see some of the patterns of the town's mid-century social life.[14]

The new singing and literary society attracted members from nearly every ethnic group in town—all parts of the United States except New England, all parts of Germany, France, Austria, Bohemia, Poland, Switzerland, England, and Russia—but 81 percent of the 116 identifiable members were from Germany. However, a disproportionate number of the members were from the Hessian states, 36, and from Baden, 35. At the same time, the list shows that there was very little occupational diversity among the members: 92 percent were professionals, commercial men, craftsmen, or government officials. There were just six unskilled workers or laborers in the society, only one of whom—young Frenchman Adolph Reutz—was from the usual laboring groups of French, Swiss, or Irish workers. In fact, the one Swiss member, Lewis Abegg, was a soda factor. So, the *Sängerbund* membership was a fairly close reflection of Belleville society at large; it was led by the

Hessian Germans, although it welcomed the wealthy elites of the other groups. Belleville's social relationships, then, were the same as its externally oriented economic structure; both were defined and controlled by the wealthier native-born Americans and the Hessians, while the poorer but more numerous Bavarians, Badenese, and Prussians looked out from their own clubs and churches and controlled the internal economy.

As in Belleville, Ottawa's frontier population was split between the foreign-born and the native-born. In both the 1850 and the 1860 censuses, 34 percent of the city was foreign-born; and 20 percent in 1850 and 18 percent in 1860 were listed as having been born in Ireland. No other immigrant group in town was over 4 percent of the population (see tables A-8 and A-9).[15] However, among the independent population of heads of households and men over the age of twenty, one sees that something of a demographic revolution took place in Ottawa during the decade between the two censuses. By 1860, immigrants were a majority (53 percent) of the independent population, and the Irish were nearly a third. In fact, the Irish community of Ottawa was nearly the same size as the native-born Yankees. There were also small groups of people from Norway and Sweden; England, Scotland, and Wales; Germany; and France. Among the native-born, the people from New England and New York made up the largest contingent of Ottawa families. The early southern influence remained in some of the very oldest LaSalle county families, but, by the 1850s, they had been overwhelmed by the influx of settlers from the North. Only 2 percent in 1850 and 4 percent in 1860 of the independent population were midwestern natives. There were only three African-American families living in Ottawa in 1850, none of whom was still living in the town in 1860. Four percent of the households in 1850, and 7 percent in 1860, were headed by women. Ten percent of the households in 1860 had live-in servants.

Ottawa's more recent founding than Belleville's is reflected in the ages of its independent residents in 1860. Almost 40 percent of the heads of household were between the ages of twenty and thirty. Another 30 percent were between thirty and forty years. But Ottawa was less frontierlike than Belleville in that only 24 percent of the adult men were single, very close to Eblen's typical frontier, but much lower than Belleville's one-third. Seventy-four percent of the 1860 independent population in 1860 Ottawa were heads of households, while 19 percent were boarders and 7 percent were young men living with their families.

Ottawa's unique position on the Illinois and Michigan Canal and the Illinois River made its economy one in which both trade and industry were highly profitable ventures. Fully one-third of its employed population in both 1850 and 1860 worked as craftsmen who produced goods—blacksmiths, carpenters, molders, brewers, millers, shoemakers, plasterers, painters, bakers, cabinetmakers, masons, butchers—to trade within the city and with the people of the region (see tables A-10 and A-11). Another 23 percent were employed as day laborers or unskilled workers, and 7 percent held jobs as manufacturers. Ottawa's manufacturing and marketing enterprises were located close to the canal, where their products could be most efficiently shipped in the barges, from spring to fall, east to Chicago and the rest of the Northeast. The canal, the Illinois and Fox Rivers, and especially the ninety-foot-wide side-cut constructed by the state to connect the canal and the Illinois River, provided waterpower with which the city's millers could grind the corn and wheat that were brought in from the surrounding farms. By 1877, 12,500,000 bushels of grain and flour were being shipped from Ottawa.

In 1860, Ottawa was the home of various stores and shops and was becoming known throughout the Midwest for its mills and factories. Cogswell and Company's Foundry and Reaper Manufactory made reapers, sugar mills, mill gearing equipment, and steam engines and employed as many as 150 men; owner William Cogswell also ran a sugar mill and evaporator that made sugar and molasses from Chinese sugar cane. Patrick McGinnis managed the Ottawa Starch Factory, which used three hundred bushels of corn each day to make six thousand pounds of starch, and employed 50 men. The Ottawa Gas Works converted Illinois coal into gas for lighting the homes and streets of the town. William Gilman began manufacturing farm implements in Ottawa—corn shellers and cultivators—in 1859. The South Ottawa Water Works, founded in 1859 by John Dean Caton, the chief justice of the Illinois Supreme Court and resident of Ottawa, was designed to bring sweet water from the springs on the south side of the Illinois River; but when construction was begun, workers discovered a large gravel bed from which stone was quarried and shipped on the canal. Ottawa's most important factory in the nineteenth century,

William Reddick's Ottawa Glass Company, opened in 1868 and, by 1877, was producing $150,000 worth of glass made from the sand that was mined from large silica deposits near the city.[16] Economic fortunes were clearly tied to the town's position on the major transportation corridor through the Midwest. But few of the town's residents actually made their living directly in the transportation industry; only 3 percent in 1850 and 4 percent in 1860 of the town's workforce were employed by the canal, river, or railroad companies. Those who did work to transport goods were either boatmen or teamsters.

While Ottawans participated in a rather diverse economy during the 1850s, their employment structure showed a division along ethnic lines. There were workers from every ethnic group in nearly every occupation, but some people were clearly stigmatized by their origins. The Irish made up 65 percent of the laborers and 42 percent of the unskilled workers in town in 1860 even though they were only 28 percent of the independent population. On the other hand, the native-born from New England and New York made up 68 percent of the professionals and commercial men in Ottawa even though they were only 40 percent of the population. The small German community—13 percent of the population—controlled nearly a third of the manufacturing in the town, making beer, shoes, wagons, cabinets, soap, and other products for sale to the people in the town. But, unlike in Belleville where the Catholic Bavarians and Badenese were able to balance the economic power of the Hessians, the Irish in Ottawa were not able to wield much economic power, at least as small shop owners. They filled only 8 percent of the proprietary positions. Again, the Germans owned more shops than their numbers in the population would suggest; they filled 20 percent of the positions. The Irish were also underrepresented among the skilled craftsmen in Ottawa: only 17 percent.

There were sixteen county, state, and federal employees living in Ottawa in 1860. Only one was an Irishman, Justice of the Peace Thomas Larkin, who was listed as an Englishman on the 1860 census even though he was born in Kings County, Ireland, in 1817.[17] All of the remaining government workers—canal collectors, clerks, and tollgate keepers, post office clerk and master, county clerk and deputy, county jailer, sheriff, three more justices of the peace, and Chief Justice Caton—were from New England, New York, or Pennsylvania. The city's paid workers—a city marshal and three constables—were also from either New England or New York, except for Constable Francis Blunt, who was from Germany.

So Ottawa's employment profile in the 1850s was one in which the native-born, and particularly those from New England and the Middle states, dominated both the commercial and the manufacturing sectors of the economy. While the Irish made up the largest immigrant group, they were nearly excluded from participating in the economic workings of the town, except as laborers and unskilled workers. The small German community, on the other hand, wielded disproportionate power in the economy, having the most effect in the area of small manufacturing and in shopkeeping.

The wealth structure of the city in 1860 confirms this ethnic division. As in Belleville, over one-half of the population owned no real estate. But in Ottawa, the native-born were slightly more likely to own land than the immigrants; a little over one-half of the native-born families held some real estate, whereas only 40 percent of the Irish and the Germans did so. But while each of the ethnic groups in Ottawa owned property at about the same rate as the others, they did not all share in the wealth. Three hundred one families owned real estate that was listed in the 1860 census as worth over two thousand dollars and were, therefore, the wealthiest 15 percent of the population. And the wealthy families were overwhelmingly native-born: 75 percent were born in the United States.

There was, however, one very important exception: glass merchant and farmer William Reddick, the Presbyterian native of Ireland who had immigrated to the United States as a four-year-old in 1816, was the wealthiest man in town. He owned nearly a half million dollars in real estate in 1860 and listed the remainder of his wealth to total forty thousand dollars.[18] If one measures by servants in the households, it is again apparent that the native-born in Ottawa were wealthier than most of the immigrants; 16 percent of native-born families employed servants, while only 5 percent of immigrant households had live-in help.

Of course, the accumulation of wealth might have had much to do with a person's age, as it did in Belleville. However, Ottawa's later founding date can be seen in the fact that more than one-half of the town's twenty-to-forty-year-old independent population was foreign-born; and the number of immigrants in the older age groups was also nearly half. Age accounted less for the accumulation of wealth in Ottawa than it did in Belleville. Neither did time of arrival account for the discrepancies in wealth between the native-born and the immigrants; the ages of children born to Ottawa couples in Illinois show that the native-born arrived only slightly earlier than the foreign-born. The people from New England and the Middle states averaged seven years in the state, while the Irish averaged nearly six years and the Germans averaged four years. The distribution of wealth in Ottawa, then, shows that the native-born residents could more easily accumulate large amounts of capital and property than could the immigrants. Therefore, the native-born were able to amass more money to invest in the commercial and industrial ventures in the town.

The town's church and fraternal organizations in the 1860s were also divided along ethnic lines. There were at least ten churches in Ottawa in the 1850s.[19] The native-born divided themselves into seven different churches, while the foreign-born generally attended their own churches. The largest immigrant groups, the Irish and the Germans, formed their own churches and remained segregated from the rest of the town. The Irish generally attended St. Columba's Catholic Church (founded 1838). The German Catholics may have attended St. Columba's early in the decade but then formed their own church, St. Francis (founded 1859). The Protestant Germans attended either the German Evangelical Lutheran Zion Church (founded 1860) or, later on, the German Methodist Episcopal Church (founding date unknown). Some people in the French community founded and began attending the French Congregational Church in 1863.

Ottawa's remaining churches were American in foundation and in membership, although some of the immigrant population did attend them. The Methodist Episcopal Church (sometimes called the First Methodist) was the first church in Ottawa, founded in 1833; membership information in the 1850s is not clear, but at least one of its members, hardware dealer Joseph Dow, was a native of Massachusetts. The Epworth Methodist (or Second Methodist) Church (founded 1853) attracted mostly American families but also included at least one foreign family, that of German laborer Frederich Rane. The Protestant Episcopal (or Christ Episcopal) Church (founded 1838) was attended mostly by New Englanders in the 1850s; its members included machinery manufacturer William Cogswell, who was born in Massachusetts, and editor and publisher William Osman, who hailed from Pennsylvania. The First Baptist Church (founded 1841) appeared to be exclusively native-born in the 1850s. The First Congregational Church (also referred to as the Old First Church) was founded in 1839 with thirteen members from New England and New York.

In 1848, seventeen members of the First Congregational Church, including minister and New York native G. W. Bassett, broke away and organized the First Presbyterian Church when the congregation argued over whether to support Presbyterians in the South who owned slaves. Bassett and ten others split from the new church in 1849 to form the South Ottawa Presbyterian Church. The original breakaway church, the First Presbyterian, changed its name to the Free Church in 1851 when the South Ottawa group rejoined the original rebels. Then, in 1857 and 1858, the combined church changed its name two more times, first to the Second Congregational Church and then to the Plymouth Congregational Church. Finally, in 1870, the two congregations that remained from the Old First Church joined to form the First Congregational Church. In the 1850s, members of the various Congregational and Presbyterian churches were mostly from the United States, but there were also families from Scotland (merchant W. B. Fyfe), Germany (merchant John Nattinger), and France (gardener Andrew Rochelle).

As was the case in Belleville and Galesburg and towns and cities throughout the United States in the first half of the nineteenth century, Ottawa had a plethora of fraternal and voluntary organizations that also show that the town was socially divided into ethnic enclaves. During the 1850s there was a Young Men's Christian Association, a French Mutual Society, a German Benevolent Society, a gymnastic *Turnverein*, a German Singing Society, a Hibernian Benevolent Society, an Old Settler's Society, a Public Library Association, a volunteer fire department, two competing fire engine companies, a Phrenological and Physiological Society, the Friends of Prohibition, the Sons of Temperance, the Washington Light Guards, the City Guards, a Base Ball and Wicket Club, three Odd Fellows' lodges (two English-speaking and one German-speaking), a Knights Templars commandery, and three Masonic lodges (two English-speaking and one German-speaking).[20]

The bylaws and membership list of the Shabbona Chapter, No. 37, of the Royal Arch Masons (organized 1856) were printed in 1875.[21] Forty-six of the members from 1856 to 1862 can be identified in the 1860 census of Ottawa. Only four of the forty-six were immigrants: three Englishmen and one Canadian. Two of the foreign members, Englishman Azro C. Putnam and Canadian John B. Peckham, were physicians. The other Englishmen were a gas fitter (George J. Burgess) and a laborer (Samuel C. Walker). None of the members was born in Ireland. However, of the remaining members, all native-born and mostly from New England or New York, none were from the laboring or unskilled ranks of the masses. In fact, twenty-four were doctors, lawyers, merchants, or government employees. So Ottawa's social life was circumscribed by the same ethnic constraints as its residents' economic and religious relationships. The native-born and the foreign-born lived, worshiped, and socialized apart. If there was any integration, it took place in the workplace, when members of all of the ethnic groups had to labor side by side to foster the town's economic development. But in the social realm, the American-born population and, to some degree, the immigrants from England and Canada, kept their distance from the Irish and from the other groups of foreign-born residents. These informal rules of interaction would have consequences for community building and the development of a democratic political culture in Ottawa. The Yankee leaders would not view the Irish as equal partners in the effort to construct the town's institutions even though the immigrants were a sizable part of the population and would come to wield a substantial amount of political power.

In sharp contrast to Belleville and Ottawa, Galesburg contained a majority of native-born adults in the 1850s, and no immigrant group could claim to be a majority of the foreign population (see tables A-12 and A-13).[22] The largest number of the town's immigrants was Swedish, but there were also sizable groups of Irishmen and Germans. There were small numbers of people from England, Scotland, Canada, France, Poland, Turkey (probably ethnic Greeks), and Luxembourg. But Galesburg was largely an American-born town, and it is in the native population where one sees the emergence of a dominant leadership group. Over half of the 1860 native independent population was born in the Middle states, mostly in New York. Most of the New Yorkers, though, were descended from New England parents and grandparents. Half as many Galesburgers came directly from New England. The rest were from the southern states, from other parts of the Midwest, or were natives of Illinois. As in Ottawa, the relative youth of Galesburg was reflected in the fact that only 3 percent of the independent population of 1860 was Illinois-born. There were no African Americans in town in 1850 and only seven families in 1860. Nine percent of the households in 1850 and 7 percent of the households in 1860 were headed by single women. Ten percent of Galesburg's households in 1860 had live-in servants. The town's recent founding was reflected in its frontierlike age frequency distribution in 1860. Its under-thirty population mirrored Eblen's findings for frontier agricultural counties. However, Galesburg fell in between Belleville and Ottawa in its number of bachelors: its single male population was 28 percent of the independent total. Galesburg had about the same number of boarders in its 1860 population as Ottawa, 19 percent.

Galesburg was primarily a commercial service center for an agricultural economy. Most of its craftsmen were involved in intracity construction projects as masons, painters, plasterers, printers, blacksmiths, and carpenters (see tables A-14 and A-15). And the town's laborers were employed more often as farm laborers than as day laborers. More than one-fourth of the laborers in 1860 were young midwesterners, probably working on farms until they could strike out on their own. Even Galesburg's early industries were oriented toward agriculture; by 1860, the town had a foundry for the repair of farm machinery, a corn-planter works, and a planing mill and sash and blind factory, which later manufactured hay presses.[23] Another indication of Galesburg's position as an entrepôt was the presence of a large number of men employed in various aspects of the transportation business. In 1860 these men were employed as teamsters, hostlers, and draymen and moved agricultural products to the new railroad yards or serviced the trains themselves.

Galesburg's occupational structure in the 1850s was neatly divided along ethnic lines. The native-born dominated the town's largely commercial economy by controlling the transportation industry. The only foreign group that would claim an undue portion of the commercial sector in Galesburg by 1860 was the small German colony with its penchant for the small manufactures of shoemaking, tailoring, carpentry, and cigar-making. A German also ran the sash and blind factory, and two men from Darmstadt kept saloons.[24] The rest of the foreign-born, particularly the large Irish and Swedish groups, congregated in the unskilled and laboring positions. The two groups made up more than one-half of the laborers even though they were only about one-quarter of the population. Most of Galesburg's few African Americans were laborers, although they also served as the town's sole barbering staff.

Knox county, state, and federal officials seem not to have resided in Galesburg as often as St. Clair and LaSalle county officials did in Belleville and Ottawa. But it is the very absence of officeholders of this sort that may be the most revealing. Since only the county treasurer, an Irishman, and two justices of the peace, both Yankees, lived in Galesburg and since the remaining county, state, and federal officials did not reside there, it is clear that the city did not enjoy much political or economic control over the countryside of Knox County. Within the city itself, however, the numerically dominant Yankees held almost complete sway over the few paid city positions—as city marshal, city sexton, and city clerk. The only exception was the office of street commissioner, which was held by Swedish-born P. L. Hawkinson.

As in both Belleville and Ottawa, over one-half of Galesburg's independent population in 1860 held no real property.[25] But, except for the young midwesterners, the native-born were slightly more likely to own property than not. The Germans were the least likely of the foreign-born to own land, followed by the Swedish and the Irish. Over 16 percent of Galesburg's residents would have qualified as wealthy—owning at least $2,000 worth of land. Of these wealthy individuals, the overwhelming majority, 95 percent, were natives. And of these native wealthy, nearly all were from either New England or New York. Wealth as measured by servants in the household shows 1860 Galesburg to have the same polarized structure. While only 11 percent of all households employed servants, the native-born were much more likely to do so than the foreign-born, and New Englanders and New Yorkers were the most likely employers of servants. But when one looks at the ethnicity of the servants themselves, it is apparent that the poorer segments of society waited on the wealthier. More than two-thirds of the servants—again, mostly young and female—were foreign-born and were mostly Irish and Swedish.

Finally, age and wealth correlated in Galesburg as in Belleville. The older people were increasingly more likely to be native-born and from either New England or New York. So age was a definite advantage for the accumulation of wealth, but an early arrival as reflected in age was most important. Using the age of the oldest child born in Illinois as an estimate of time of arrival shows that the native-born of Galesburg came earlier than the immigrants. Those from New England and New York averaged eight years. The Irish, who often stopped in other states before settling in Illinois, had resided in the state for an average of four years in 1860. The Swedish appear to have traveled directly from Sweden to Illinois and had been in the state for an average of three years.

Galesburg's wealth structure, then, closely resembled its occupational structure. The city had a numerically and economically dominant native-born population that was able to take advantage of its familiarity with American society to accumulate wealth more quickly than its smaller immigrant population. And one group in particular, that from New England and New York, was able to use its dominance and early arrival to nearly monopolize the real estate and commercial markets within the city.

Galesburg's church relationships during the 1850s matched the divided nature of its economy.[26] There were fourteen churches in town by 1860, representing seven denominations. The white native-born divided their loyalties among nine different churches of five denominations—Baptist, Episcopalian, Universalist, Presbyterian, and Congregational—while the foreign-born were generally Lutherans, Methodists, or Baptists. The sole African-American church in town was the African Methodist Episcopal, also known as the "Colored" church. A black Baptist church (the Second Baptist) was organized in 1864. The two large groups of immigrants, the Swedish and the Irish, were the most segregated from the native-born in the realm of religion. Out of the 24 Swedes for whom membership information in the 1850s is available, 23 were members either of the Swedish Evangelical Lutheran Church (Augustana Synod, founded 1852) or the Swedish Baptist Church (founded 1852). There was also a Swedish Methodist Episcopal congregation, but no information on membership is available for the 1850s. Only one Irishman appears in the list of 188 total church members—a Congregationalist; the Irish were mostly Catholics, but there were no organized Catholic services in the town until 1863. The Congregationalists also could claim the only identifiable German church member. The English, Scottish, and Canadian residents were Baptists, Congregationalists, Methodists, or Episcopalians.

While Galesburg's native white population does not appear to have been as tightly constricted in church membership as the immigrant Irish and Swedes, regional differences are apparent among them. The Baptist Church (founded 1847) and the Methodist Episcopal Church (founded 1847) were the most receptive to ethnic diversity among their members and were closely connected with other congregations in Knox County. Both were offshoots of earlier southern-oriented Knoxville churches, and both had welcomed the Swedish into their fold. The Swedes of both congregations, however, eventually formed their own churches. The Baptists were initially able to attract at least a few northern Baptists, but the congregation split in 1852 when a group led by Maine-born S. A. Kingsbury formed the Cherry Street Baptist Church. The reason for the split is not clear, but one might speculate that regional differences were at least part of the cause since the two Baptist congregations stayed separated until 1864.

Galesburg's Yankees were members of fairly exclusive Episcopalian, Universalist, Presbyterian, and Congregational churches. The Episcopalian Grace Church (founded 1859) was separate from its southern neighboring congregation in Knoxville; twenty-two of its twenty-three 1850s members were either from New York or New England—the remaining member was from England—and its minister, William T. Smithett, was from Boston. The Universalist Church (founded 1860), whose constitution proclaimed that anyone of good moral and religious character who promised to follow a "Profession of Faith" could become a member, was 100 percent native-born and 92 percent Yankee.

During the 1850s, the two Presbyterian and the two Congregational churches in Galesburg, though all dominated by the native-born from New England and New York, were philosophically separated from one another. Three of the churches were descended from the original Presbyterian church that was formed in New York in 1836 but whose membership was composed of both Congregationalists and Presbyterians under the "Plan of Union." This agreement between the two groups, in 1801, was an effort to eliminate duplicate ministerial services in the American West by their leaders. The churches were temporarily more concerned with the competition for the number of frontier souls brought by the Methodists and Baptists than they were with their doctrinal differences. The founding church in Galesburg eventually split in 1851 when its members began to disagree over doctrinal issues and over the church's stand on the question of support for Presbyterians in the southern states who owned slaves. Thirty-seven members withdrew to form the Second Presbyterian (or the "New School" Presbyterian) Church. Its members were willing to compromise with their southern brethren, whereas the remaining members of the original church were not. All but one of the second church's 1860 members, however, was a Yankee or a midwesterner.[27]

Meanwhile, another group had split from the original church in 1855 to form the First Congregational Church. This split appears to have been completely amicable and a result of overcrowding. Its 1860 membership was completely Yankee, except for a sole Canadian. The original Presbyterian Church, by 1860, had withdrawn from membership in the Peoria Presbytery, changed its name to the First Church of Christ, espoused total Congregationalism, and was 92 percent native-born. Its foreign-born members were mostly English, but there was also one Irishman and one German. Finally, a separate Presbyterian congregation, calling itself "Old School," had formed in 1854. Its membership was mostly Yankee.[28]

Galesburg's social organizations also show that the town was dominated by the native-born from New England and New York. During the 1850s, the town could boast of a Library Association, two Masonic lodges, an Oddfellows Hall, a Good Templars organization, an orchestra, a Cornet Band, a Bible Society, a Mission, a Total Abstinence Society, a fire company, a hook and ladder company, the Light Guards, and an artillery company.[29] The social relationships in town can be seen in a dues ledger from 1862 to 1878 for Alpha Lodge, No. 155, of the Galesburg Freemasons from which eighty-one 1860s members can be identified by ethnicity.[30] Seventy-two were native-born, all but six of whom were Yankees. The foreign-born members were mostly English-speaking and skilled workers—three Scotsmen, two Englishmen, and one Canadian—but there were also one German locomotive engineer and one Swiss laborer. There were Freemasons from all six of the Yankee churches, and all but one of the native-born members was either a professional or a commercial man—there was also one brick mason—while all but one of the foreign-born was a skilled worker. So Galesburg's social life was circumscribed by the same ethnic divisions that dictated its religious structure. The native-born worshiped and socialized separately from most of the foreign-born. But the wall of social segregation within the town was beginning to crack by the late 1850s. The few English, Scottish, and Canadian inhabitants were accepted into the Yankee churches. The same groups, along with some of the Swedes and Germans, were invited to participate with the natives in an exclusive fraternal organization. However, even with the beginnings of social integration, Galesburg was dominated by wealthy, commercially oriented Yankees.

On the eve of the Civil War in 1860, the three towns were young communities. During the previous decade, the people of Belleville, Ottawa, and Galesburg had related with one another long enough to set up informal rules of interaction that were unique to each of the towns. They had established their transportation linkages with the other towns of the Midwest and had found their places in the regional economy. They had founded public school systems that would be used by the communities to inculcate in the many youngsters in the towns the values that their elders held dear. And they had worked out their local governmental systems amidst the social and political turmoil of the 1850s.

But each of the towns had formed a community that was unique unto itself because its leaders emerged from the fray of the frontier with different roles and expectations. The leadership of Belleville was divided among several groups. The native-born and the early arriving Hessians controlled the town's economic linkages with the rest of the region, but they were not able to dominate the community's internal commercial and manufacturing trade. The Bavarians, the Badenese, and the Prussians had enough economic power to prevent the total dominance of the Hessians and the Americans. But the various groups of Germans and the native-born in Belleville, while willing to share in the town's financial success, did not socialize with one another or agree about politics. They all went to their own national churches and joined their own voluntary organizations. And all of the ethnic groups made sure that their points of view were represented at city hall.

In Ottawa, the native-born Americans held economic sway. They owned and ran the young city's mills and factories and controlled many of the stores and shops in town. However, the immigrants were a large part of the population, and they were, by 1860, beginning to drive a wedge into the native-born hegemony. Members of the German community had the financial wherewithal to set up small-scale manufacturing establishments and specialty shops that catered to the entire populace. The Irish immigrants, however, were relegated to the bottom of the economic ladder in Ottawa. Their initial status as canal and railroad workers did not bring them the luxuries or power that often come with accumulated capital. They were usually forced to take the low-paying unskilled and laboring positions in the community and were not welcome to socialize with those who occupied more lucrative positions. But the Irish were a force with which the native-born would have to reckon. They were a large portion of the population and were competing, during the 1850s, with the native-born to become the largest ethnic group in Ottawa. Their sheer numbers—and the fact that the wealthiest man in town was one of their own—meant that the Irish would be able to challenge the Americans on the political front to change the economic and social relationships in town.

Galesburg's economic, social, and political relationships during the 1850s were the simplest of the three towns. The native-born Yankees controlled the burgeoning economy, owning both the means to trade with the other towns of the region and the disposable capital to set up shops and small factories within the city. Members of the small Irish and Swedish enclaves occupied positions at the bottom of the economic ladder. The Irish also remained separated from the Yankees in their religious and social pursuits and were not large enough to challenge the native-born in the political arena. Members of the Swedish community of Galesburg, on the other hand, were beginning to edge their way into the social and political leadership and were, by 1860, an important influence in the young community.

Four The Railroads

> Act on a grand and liberal scale, and Belleville will be second to
> no town in the State. But if you assume the grounds of stupid
> stool pigeons, Belleville will be a village for many years to come.
>> —*Belleville Advocate, 1849*
>
> What is Ottawa doing? . . . It is a notorious fact that there is
> more enterprise in a half dozen men in Peru than in the whole
> of Ottawa put together.
>> —*Ottawa Free Trader, 1850*
>
> Once more [Galesburg] ask[s] your aid. . . . True, we are a young
> community, and cannot command large sums of money, but
> though individually we are able to do little, yet collectively we
> can accomplish much.
>> —*Report of the Board of Directors,*
>> *Central Military Tract Railroad, 1851*

Once Belleville, Ottawa, and Galesburg were founded and established to the point where their survival was assured, the towns'
inhabitants had to make a series of important decisions that would
determine their eventual positions in the economic, cultural, and
political hierarchies of the Midwest. The procedures employed by
the people in making these vital judgments about the future of
their towns varied, however, according to their earlier encounters
with decision-making practices, both at home before they migrated to the frontier and in Illinois where they met and formed
more complex ethnic relationships. Afterwards, the mechanisms
that they developed to meet the frontier challenges—their political
cultures—were used again and again in their post-frontier towns,
even when the people only faced more mundane problems.

One of the first tasks that confronted the people of Belleville,
Ottawa, and Galesburg during the late 1840s and the early 1850s
can be traced to 1828 when the first American railroad company,
the Baltimore and Ohio, was chartered to connect the city of Baltimore with the rich market settlements of the Ohio River valley.
Until the late 1830s, however, railroads in the United States remained mostly small, isolated, feeder lines that connected water
transportation centers. Eastern and midwestern states continued
70 to lobby Congress for funds to build canals and to improve roads

and rivers rather than to construct whole railway networks; and the earliest railroads, relying upon huge steam engines for power, often proved to be terribly dangerous and were incredibly unpredictable. Then, in the late 1830s when the technological know-how of manufacturers had progressed to the point of reliability and relative safety, state governments pushed hard for railroad construction. In January 1837 the Illinois General Assembly passed a comprehensive Internal Improvement Act. After at least eight years of bombastic talk and piecemeal support of private ventures, the government was ready to endorse and fund a statewide system of railroads. One of the many provisions of the law added to an 1835 bill that had incorporated the Central Railroad Company. Not only would the company still build its main line from the mouth of the Ohio River at Cairo to Galena, but it would now also construct a new branch road to Belleville at a cost of $150,000 to the state. Other portions of the 1837 act provided $1,850,000 of Illinois moneys for the construction of the Northern Cross Railroad from Quincy, on the Mississippi River, to Indiana via Springfield, and $700,000 for a line from Peoria to Warsaw, Illinois, a town on the Mississippi River between Burlington and Quincy.[1]

Construction of the internal improvement projects authorized in the 1837 bill—including increased funding for the Illinois and Michigan Canal—hardly got off the ground before the entire country was plunged into an economic depression caused, in part, by the United States Specie Payment Circular, which went into effect in July 1837. By 1840 Illinois was on the verge of bankruptcy and in debt to the tune of $14,000,000. As a consequence, neither the Belleville spur of the Central Railroad nor the various roads in northern Illinois that would have passed near Galesburg and Ottawa got very far before they were abandoned. The Belleville project collapsed in 1840 after only forty miles of embankment extending north from Cairo were constructed. The Northern Cross venture finally failed in 1842 after some track had been laid between Meredosia and Quincy. No work was ever attempted on the Peoria and Warsaw line. Construction on the Illinois and Michigan Canal slowed to a trickle. The depression in the transportation industry continued for ten long years, and people all over Illinois felt its effects.[2]

Then, as the nation neared and then passed the midpoint of the nineteenth century and economic conditions began to improve, the inhabitants of Illinois were keen to take up their improvement projects where they had left them. "The public prints are full of speculation upon routes for locating, and plans for constructing, rail roads all over the state," wrote the editor of the *Ottawa Free Trader*, William Osman, in January 1851. "And," he continued, "could all the roads which have been projected during [the past year] be constructed, we could have a railroad to nearly every man's door in the country."[3] Osman's words anticipated the most frenzied decade of railroad construction that the people of Illinois and the nation would ever see: the total miles of track laid would more than triple in the United States during the 1850s (from 7,215 miles in 1848 to 32,219 miles in 1858), the largest percentage increase in the country's history. Illinois railroad mileage increased from approximately 100 in 1848 to 2,400 in 1860.[4]

Railroads were not, of course, built to "every man's door," either in Illinois or in the entire United States. But the tremendous changes that railroad construction brought to the Midwest during the 1850s did engender a sense of excitement that touched every city and every small town in the region. In fact, many ambitious entrepreneurs of the 1850s quickly recognized the profits that might be theirs, if, by some chance, their towns were lucky enough to win what editor Osman called the "great railroad lottery" and thus become integrated into the rapidly expanding regional and national economic network.[5] The people of Belleville, Ottawa, and Galesburg were no exception, and businessmen in the three towns quickly began to push their fellow citizens to invest in the new technology. They recognized the necessity of either convincing an established railway company to build through their town or building their own spur to connect with a through railroad. But the most perceptive among the citizens of the three towns realized from the start that their economic futures were not only dependent upon the acquisition of railroad contacts but that they would have to compete with surrounding towns to procure train service; in the 1850s a town would have to find a means of connecting its economic base with the eastern states if it was to remain competitive with its neighbors in the race for urban domination and survival on the Illinois frontier.

The construction of the antebellum American railroad grid has traditionally been studied by historians in either of two ways. First, in the first half of the twentieth century the genealogical histories of particular railroads were written, often lovingly, by devotees of the companies. That is, authors painstakingly traced the descent of their subject lines through generations of mergers among local, independent branch operations that eventually formed huge transportation conglomerates. A second group of historians began in the 1950s to look at railroad construction in the context of general nineteenth-century economic development, highlighting the speculation and corruption that were often the partners of transportation improvements. Recent historians and economists within this wider business-economic tradition have begun to look at railroad-building in order to determine the effects that eastern capital had on western development and to illustrate that the growth of a managerial business class played an important role in the integration of American society in the nineteenth century.[6]

The first (genealogical) approach to railroad history, while often taking into account the effects of human actions on the construction of railroads within a region and into particular towns, was blatantly boosterish and historically progressive; the authors assumed that railroad companies grew from small to large concerns along an inevitable evolutionary path. The other (economic) approach, while much more cynical about railroad developers' roots and motivations, usually sacrificed any local perspective to a much more overarching national view of railway construction. It is ironic that these more modern historians have emphasized human motivation as the primary ingredient in the development of a national railroad network because they have largely abandoned the human approach and have emphasized the importance of local geology or of random chance when they look at the actual location and construction of railways. To them, the "great railroad lottery" was just that, a matter of random chance, when seen from the local level.[7] In other words, viewed from the national level, railroad building has too often been examined as if it were primarily a product of complex social dynamics while, from the local level, it has been explained as if it were mostly the result of natural forces. The midwestern railroad network needs to be studied from a local perspective, taking into account the effects of both social and environmental factors. Doing so shows that unified and fast-acting local leaders could bring advantageous railroad connections to their towns during the 1850s, even if those same towns were located on sites that were initially unattractive to railroad companies. And the reverse could be equally true: divided leaderships could prevent even the most environmentally likely towns from acquiring the best rail connections. In other words, the "great railroad lottery" was not strictly a game of chance after all but a contest in which the odds could be and were readily manipulated by people who had the economic, social, and political wherewithal to participate in the process.

Although the rules and technology of railroad network-building were evolving at the very time that Illinois towns were competing for rail connections, it is clear that local leaders all over the Midwest already held the firm notion that there was a hierarchy of desirable outcomes. First, the worst-case scenario for a town would be to end up with no railroad connections. From the determinist point of view, this would likely be the fate of a town with few or no prerailroad transportation linkages. Second, the least desirable situation for a town that did acquire some railroad connections was to be a dead-end terminus. Again, from the determinist perspective, this would be likely for a town with few or no prerailroad economic linkages. Third, the satisfactory, but not the best, position for a town at the end of the 1850s was to be a stop on a through railroad. This would seem to be the fate of a town with some prerailroad linkages. Finally, the best-case scenario for a town would be a junction for two or more railroad lines. This would seem to be likely for a town with many prerailroad transportation linkages. So, if prerailroad transportation linkages were the most important factors in the acquisition of railroad connections in the three towns, Ottawa's position was clearly more advantageous than those of either Belleville or Galesburg. Belleville was near St. Louis and might have attracted railroad companies that wanted to take advantage of the historical relationship between the two cities. Galesburg, though, was isolated from prerailroad transportation facilities and was certainly not in a position to gain any notice from railroad companies.

It was not long after its founding in 1814 that the citizens of Belleville began to take stock of their position in relation to their neighbors on the banks of the Mississippi River. Even after the United States acquired legal possession of Louisiana from the French in 1803, St. Louis continued to dominate commercially the agricultural hinterland along both sides of the river. The residents of Belleville shared in St. Louis's prosperity during the late 1820s and early 1830s and could hardly complain about the Missouri city's economic hegemony. But then, with the passage of the Illinois Internal Improvement Act of 1837, Bellevillians began to espouse two often contradictory strategies in planning for their town's future. One was to hold even more tightly to St. Louis's economic coattails. Another was to somehow dislodge themselves from the economic orbit of St. Louis and go it alone. Even before the Illinois and Michigan Canal connecting the Great Lakes and Mississippi River watersheds was completed in 1848—indeed, almost before it was started—the proponents of the second strategy realized that railroads would allow them to tap into the northern market and bypass St. Louis when dealing with the East.

By the end of the 1840s proponents of the two contrary strategies began to argue publicly over how the town should go about improving its position vis-à-vis the other towns in southern Illinois. Both groups used the town newspapers to appeal to the entire citizenry. The English language *Belleville Advocate* was nearly a mirror-image of the major German-language newspaper in town, the *Belleviller Zeitung*. Both became the unofficial organs of one group of leaders in Belleville, some of whom were Americans, but most of whom were freethinking German immigrants of the 1830s, led by Frankfurt native Gustave Körner. In the late 1840s, it was this group that began to agitate for direct railroad connections with the East.

However, at the same time that some sought to lessen Belleville's connections with St. Louis, leaders linked to the other English-language newspaper, the *Belleville Times*, were pushing to improve the town's links with the Missouri city. The *Times* was closely associated with William C. Kinney, a member of a long-established St. Clair County family and a driving force behind a move in 1846 to build a macadamized road from Belleville to the ferry crossing to St. Louis at Illinoistown (now East St. Louis). Kinney was joined as an original director of the venture by a board that was overwhelmingly composed of American-born town leaders, many of whom had long-established economic connections with businesses in St. Louis. By the middle of February 1848, the board had convinced business interests to commit to a Belleville-to-St. Louis turnpike by promising to solicit subscriptions. The formerly public venture had been chartered as a private company in September 1847, in part because the public venture had failed to raise enough voluntary subscriptions. All of the original board members were residents of St. Clair County. In March 1848, the new company elected a new board of directors, the majority of whom (four out of seven) were residents of St. Louis. The Belleville members were American-born residents T. A. Harrison and John Reynolds (a long-time Illinoisan from Pennsylvania and Tennessee and former governor of the state) and Bavarian Jacob Knöbel. But some Illinois citizens who had already purchased stock in the company were outraged at the decision to allow the road to be controlled by interests on the west side of the river. By May 1848, work was begun in earnest to complete the turnpike before the next winter. A call went out for an installment of 20 percent on the stock to be payable before the end of the month. The actual construction was going well, but the project's directors and engineer were constantly faced with the difficulty of persuading the stockholders to keep up with their 10 percent per month payment schedule.[8] The turnpike was finally completed to Belleville in 1851 after Illinois residents' continual agitation for the St. Louis-controlled company to finish the job.

Long before the actual completion of the turnpike, which would further assure St. Louis's economic domination of Belleville, and perhaps because of the bitter taste left by what they perceived as second-rate treatment by the St. Louis directors, the other group of town leaders again decided to work to bypass St. Louis. They learned that there were plans to build a railroad between Vincennes, Indiana, and St. Louis. Surely, the leaders thought, such a road would cut through Belleville. But just to be sure, the anti–St. Louis group called for the construction of a local railroad from Illinoistown to Belleville that would then easily connect with the road coming from Vincennes to Belleville (see map 5).[9]

But Belleville's plan to get a jump on the competition by constructing its own railroad was not enough to ensure that the larger railroad would eventually go through the town. The Indiana legislature petitioned the Illinois General Assembly for a right-of-way for the road—the Ohio and Mississippi Railroad—to run from Vincennes across Illinois to Illinoistown, opposite St. Louis. But the request was blocked by representatives from Alton who were upset that the company had not decided to build to their town. Belleville and Alton were the two major competitors for the economic dominance of the Illinois hinterland opposite St. Louis. In 1847 the *New York Tribune* praised Alton as a "place of much business" and as having "very good facilities to St. Louis." The editor of the *Advocate* countered by writing that "the *Tribune* does

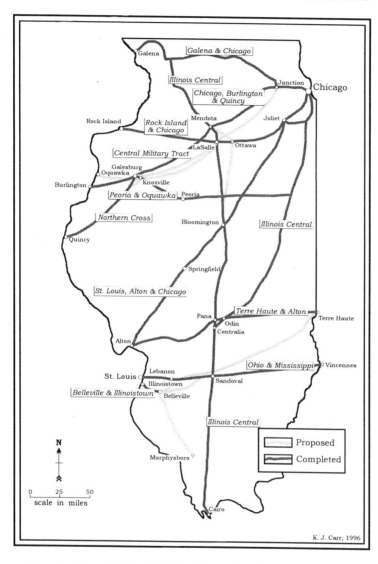

Map 5. Selected Illinois Railroads During the 1850s

not seem to be very well informed about western cities, their positions and advantages." A mass meeting, led by American-born Reynolds, Kinney, James Mitchell, C. Ball, and W. S. Thomas but also including Germans Körner and C. Thiell, was held at the Belleville Courthouse where citizens expressed their outrage at the General Assembly's actions. Convinced that the legislature would eventually give in and that the Ohio and Mississippi or some other railroad would want to build through Belleville, a letter writer to the *Advocate*, calling himself "Vindex," counseled that residents should not be distracted by recent affairs. He wrote that "Belleville would, in a few years, be a city of twenty thousand inhabitants. Why not rival St. Louis?" He suggested that all moneys at the disposal of the town should be put into completing its own railroad to the Mississippi, even if it meant abandoning support for the macadamized road. The General Assembly did finally approve the right-of-way for the railroad, but the place at which it would cross the Mississippi was left open. Belleville representatives, who were adamant supporters of the railroad, voted with the understanding that the road would pass through their town.[10]

The sentiments expressed by Vindex in late 1849 marked a turning point in most Belleville residents' attitudes about their connections with St. Louis. From then on, there was little talk about the town being an adjunct to St. Louis. Public sentiment was now squarely behind those leaders who would make Belleville a powerful city in its own right. However, it was too little, too late because, even though there was now little disagreement over the ultimate aspirations of the town, it was becoming more and more difficult for the residents to agree on particulars and take the type of unified action necessary to attract outside capital and railroads. At the end of 1850, while residents were still waiting to see whether or not the Illinoistown and Vincennes would be given permission to build through Illinois, the news arrived that another railroad company, the St. Louis and Terre Haute (also referred to as the Atlantic and Mississippi) was looking for a route for its tracks. And the news arrived just in time, according to Bellevillians, because in June 1851 citizens had received the bad news that the Illinois town and Vincennes, having finally been given an Illinois charter, would bypass Belleville and locate seven miles to the north and go through Lebanon. Bellevillians were outraged.[11]

Citizens gathered again and voted to send three of their most able residents, including the editor of the *Advocate* (Judge Niles), to talk with the directors of the railroad, but the effort was to no avail. The directors said that they would construct their line in view of the "best interests of the Road." Finally, editor Niles hinted at the possible reason for the town's snubbing by the railroad company when he suggested that the Belleville citizenry, particularly the businessmen, had not bought enough stock in the larger company. Another mass meeting was held, another committee was sent, and another petition was written. Instructions were even sent to Belleville's representative in the General Assembly to push through an amendment to the company's charter that would require the railroad to connect the seats of every county through which it passed, including Belleville. All of the efforts did nothing to change the company's plans. Finally, Belleville's state senator, J. L. D. Morrison, pushed a new measure through the General Assembly that chartered an entirely new railroad, a local Belleville and Illinoistown. The fourteen-mile line would be built solely with Belleville funds. The little railroad was completed in September of 1854 amid joyous celebrations. But the new railroad did nothing more than make the journey between Belleville and St. Louis both a faster and a more comfortable one.[12]

Ottawa had always been a transportation town. As the first western terminus of the Illinois and Michigan Canal and as the designated center of trade in LaSalle County, its economic success seemed forever assured, even after the canal's directors decided in 1836 to build the canal further west to a more navigable position on the Illinois River at LaSalle-Peru.[13] Completed in 1848, the canal was certainly an economic boon for the people along its path. Ottawa benefited immensely and its citizens recognized that their continued prosperity was linked to that of the canal. Such was their total identification with and confidence in the canal, in fact, that Ottawa's leaders did not initially view the new railroad technology as a threat to the canal's or the town's economic prosperity. They did not realize the advantage of railroads in a climate where freezing made water transportation unusable from October until April. Instead, they saw railroads as welcome adjuncts to the canal; they believed that the new technology could be used to link the towns along the artificial waterway with others that lay beside distant lakes and rivers. In other words, Ottawa leaders saw railroads as a means to enhance the town's position as an important transportation node and maybe even to cement forever its position as the economic focus of central Illinois.

Coincidentally, Ottawa's best chance to improve its position in the regional transportation system came at about the same time that it began to reap benefits from the Illinois and Michigan Canal. In February 1850, businessmen in Chicago proposed to build a railroad (the Aurora Branch Line—the parent company of what was later to become the Chicago, Burlington and Quincy) west from Chicago to the Fox River and then south along the Fox to connect with the Illinois River. Ottawa leaders immediately recognized that such a railroad could connect with the Illinois at Ottawa but that it was more likely that its directors would want to build to LaSalle where it could meet not only with the barge traffic of the canal but also with the steamship traffic of the Illinois River. *Free Trader* editor William Osman declared that Ottawans needed to "Improve the River!" from LaSalle to their town so that steamships could make it that far to the east and so that the proposed Fox River Railroad would be built to Ottawa rather than terminate at LaSalle. A group of "leading men of this place" took it upon themselves to travel up the Fox River to negotiate with the owners of the Aurora Branch Line out of Chicago. The Ottawa leaders committed the citizens of their town to pay part of the expenses for conducting a survey along the Fox River for the proposed railway. The same leaders then returned to Ottawa and announced the formation of a company to build a twelve-foot dam on the Illinois just west of Ottawa in order to make the river navigable all the way to Ottawa. The cost of the river improvement project was estimated at $20,000 to $30,000. The leaders were sorely disappointed when, despite their efforts, the Fox River Rail Road Company announced its intention in July 1850 to build to LaSalle-Peru rather than to Ottawa. By November, editor Osman was chastising Ottawa's residents for not acting in time to defeat their rivals down the river. "What is Ottawa doing?" he asked. Ottawa must begin to compete with the other towns of central Illinois, he counseled, by building plank roads and attracting railroad connections or "our water-power and our mineral lands will sleep for ages."[14]

But by the end of 1850, Ottawans were given another chance to connect their water transportation facilities with a railroad. In 1850 the United States government granted a six-mile-wide right-of-way on federal lands for a company to build a railroad between

Chicago and Mobile, Alabama. In February 1851, the Illinois legislature granted a charter to a new Illinois Central Railroad Company. The company would build from Cairo to Chicago and Galena; the specific paths of the routes were left to the company's directors, but they had already decided not to build to Peoria where a railroad bridge over the Illinois River would block steamship traffic. "A Friend" quickly wrote to the *Free Trader* to assure the company that Ottawa "would of course be glad to have the crossing."[15]

The Illinois Central Railroad Company announced in January 1851 that it would, indeed, build to LaSalle, or Ottawa, or Utica—all on the Illinois River—wherever was best for the company. Osman immediately began to write editorials in which he made a case for the company to choose Ottawa. Such a plan would make the most sense, he argued, because it could then build a bridge across the Illinois at the head of navigation; that is, it would if the river were improved to Ottawa. If the railroad built directly to LaSalle, Ottawans realized, a bridge at that town would block any future access to Ottawa by steamships. Osman was careful to point out that the inhabitants of his town were "not desirous of commencing a controversy with the people of Peru or LaSalle upon this subject." Actually, Ottawans knew that a company decision to build to LaSalle would prove disastrous, forever cutting their town off from river traffic and nullifying any reason to improve the river. Ottawa had to court the company, and it was into the river project that the town's leaders began to pour all of their energy. The town's representative to the Illinois House of Representatives, John Hise (a former editor of the *Free Trader*), introduced a bill in the legislature to allow for state support of river improvements. If such a project were completed, wrote Osman, Ottawa would be in "a position where we can compete successfully with all our neighboring towns in the purchase of all kinds of produce, which will open a market here not even surpassed by Chicago." The bill passed in March 1851. If the voters of each town agreed, Ottawa and South Ottawa residents would pay a 4-mill tax; others along the improvements would pay either 2 1/2 or 1 1/4 mills, depending upon their propinquity to the river.[16]

A key provision of the river improvement bill was permission to build the dam on the Illinois River just west of Ottawa in Utica Township. Months before the passage of the improvement bill (in March 1850), eleven of Ottawa's leading citizens, all either lawyers or businessmen, bought the land where a dam would likely be built; they each signed personal notes worth $100. The sale of the land was not revealed to the public until a year after the fact; when the town learned the news of the purchase, the group of men—Lorenzo Leland, William Hickling, William H. H. Cushman, John V. A. Hoes, Joseph Glover, David Sanger, John Armour, William Reddick, George H. Norris, George S. Fisher, and Richard Thorne (all members of the native-born economic leadership of the town except for the Englishman Hickling and the Presbyterian Irish Reddick)—claimed to have been acting for the general benefit of the town. They said that they feared that the land would be "seized by speculators" who would then sell it to the dam builders at a highly inflated price. The eleven purchasers estimated that the value of the land would increase by one to two dollars per acre once the improvement bill was passed. The eleven leaders claimed that they had planned, all along, to turn the deed to the land over to a "River Board" or directors of an improvement company, and that they expected to be reimbursed only their original $100 investments, plus the interest that they had paid on the notes. Indeed, once the bill was passed, the land was turned over to the nine directors appointed by the state, three of whom, Leland, Hickling, and Cushman, were also among the eleven land purchasers. The citizens of Ottawa who lived on the northern side of the Illinois River (closest to the canal) quickly voted to accept their 4-mill tax, but the other towns along the improvement route and Ottawa's residents on the south side of the river balked at the prospect of taxing themselves for a project in which a few investors appeared to have the most interest. Therefore, given the unlikelihood of river improvements to Ottawa, the Illinois Central Railroad Company decided to build to LaSalle-Peru, leaving Ottawa holding the upriver, nonnavigable end of the transportation stick.[17]

Meanwhile a Judge Grant, president of the Rock Island and LaSalle Railroad Company, had visited Ottawa on February 25, 1851. He spoke to a citizens' meeting at the county courthouse about the importance of building a Rock Island to Chicago railroad. He said that eastern capitalists were interested in extending the proposed line eastward to meet up with the Aurora Branch out of Chicago. Would Ottawans, he asked, be willing to put up some money to guarantee that the railroad would build to Ottawa before veering off to the northeast? He said he expected LaSalle

County citizens to pledge $100,000 worth of stock out of the estimated $3,000,000 cost. William Hickling, one of the eleven Ottawa land purchasers, pledged to subscribe $5,000 of his own money to the project. George H. Norris, village trustee, attorney, and another of the eleven, proposed that the town of Ottawa take $25,000 worth of stock in the Rock Island and Chicago. The motion carried with only one "no" vote. Village trustee Joseph Glover, still another of the eleven, asked that the vote be suspended until it could be determined whether such action was permitted under the Ottawa village charter granted by the state in 1839.[18]

Glover's caution was well-founded. He reported to another meeting of the citizenry a week later that the village trustees did not presently have the power to commit the town to such a financial obligation. In order to do so, the town would have to organize and be chartered as a city. Two weeks later the Illinois Central decided not to build through Ottawa. Town leaders now began to see the Rock Island and Chicago line as vital to the town, especially since opposition to the river improvements was growing. In September 1851, the Chicago and Rock Island decided to build straight west from LaSalle to Joliet rather than northeast to Junction (Aurora), guaranteeing that Ottawa would be a stop on the line even if the town did not come up with the $25,000. With Ottawa's position on a railroad assured by default, Osman came out against the notion of incorporation of Ottawa as a city, arguing that the people of Ottawa should not be saddled with a $25,000 bill while the rest of the township escaped unscathed. The citizens voted down the move to incorporate in January 1852.[19]

So Ottawa had lost out to LaSalle-Peru in its bid to become the grand junction of the Illinois Central Railroad, the Illinois and Michigan Canal, and the Illinois River. Its citizens had to be satisfied with their position as a stop on the Rock Island and Chicago, a line that would parallel and essentially make obsolete the Illinois and Michigan Canal. But Ottawans had had their chances: if the Illinois River had been improved, their town could have at least competed with LaSalle-Peru for the Illinois Central line, and they came close to achieving just that. One explanation for their inability to do so can be seen in the way that Ottawans dealt with the residue of the Illinois Central competition. In January 1853, when the yearly tax bills went out across LaSalle County, some Ottawa citizens began to wonder why part of their obligations included the never fully approved river improvement tax. It seems that at the special session of the Illinois legislature in the fall of 1852, an amendment was added to the original river improvement bill authorizing the collection of the tax so that the eleven land purchasers could be reimbursed for their bad investment. When news of the amendment's passage reached Ottawa, the public outcry was so great that the legislature rescinded its amendment and relieved the taxpayers of having to reimburse the Ottawa eleven for the $1,100 debt.[20]

Ottawa's leaders may have had the welfare of the entire town in mind when they worked in private to maximize the town's railroad connections. But their altruism was not appreciated by the town's citizenry. Ottawa taxpayers objected, not to the idea of railroads, but to the fact that economic leaders took the entire matter into their own hands. And this challenge to the leaders' power to make decisions for the whole town made it impossible for them to act quickly enough to attract the Illinois Central, even though their town would seem to have had a better chance to do so than any other town in northern Illinois.

Unlike in Belleville and Ottawa where residents were at least assured of an economic connection with the rest of the nation, Galesburg's early leaders saw that their town was in a potentially fatal position when the railroad age dawned on the Midwest. Its isolated location, partly a result of its late founding in 1835, left the town in a disadvantageous position vis-à-vis the surrounding western Illinois towns. But like Belleville and Ottawa, Galesburg's plunge into the frenzy for railroad connections dates from the late 1840s and early 1850s when the entire state was caught up in the economic euphoria caused by the completion of the Illinois and Michigan Canal. That event made it possible, for the first time, for the southern and western sections of the state to connect with the Chicago and New York marketplaces; and that task could be made even easier if railroads could be built at least to the western terminus of the canal at LaSalle. So in 1851 the citizens of Quincy, on the Mississippi River, obtained a charter to build a new railroad, the Northern Cross, to LaSalle. The new company bought out the old one of the same name at an auction for $21,000 even though the money spent on the original construction totaled $1,850,000. One of the stipulations of the charter of the new company, however, was that the line could not run east of the town of Knoxville in Knox County. Obviously, a deal had been struck with persons representing the interests of Knoxville, since Knoxville lay slightly west of a straight-line course between Quincy and LaSalle.[21] In any case, Galesburg would be left at least five miles west of the right-of-way.

Meanwhile, in 1849 the Illinois General Assembly had granted a charter to the Peoria and Oquawka Railroad to run from Peoria on the Illinois River to Oquawka, a town on the Mississippi ten miles northeast of Burlington, Iowa. This charter did not stipulate any route through Knox County. By the fall of 1849, interests in both Knoxville and Galesburg had pledged to lend financial support to the Peoria and Oquawka if the company would extend their line north through one of the two towns. Merchant Chauncey C. Colton of Galesburg pledged $20,000 to the company if it would build to Galesburg. But lobbyists from Knoxville successfully secured an amendment to the Peoria and Oquawka charter that stated that the line would travel through Knoxville, again leaving Galesburg about five miles off the beaten track. So both the Northern Cross and the Peoria and Oquawka were to meet in Knoxville, making that town, not Galesburg, the superior marketing center in the divide region between the Mississippi and Illinois Rivers.[22]

So in a sense, by the early 1850s Galesburg was left in a similar position to that of Belleville and Ottawa. Leaders from each of the towns had initially been unsuccessful in their efforts to convince the directors of various companies that their towns were the most attractive, and they had lost any rights-of-way to competitors. But unlike in Belleville and Ottawa where divided leaderships and rebellious electorates slowed the reactions of the towns to tenuous economic positions, Galesburg's leaders reacted quickly and decisively to the threat posed by Knoxville's initial lead in the railroad contest. Just five days after the Peoria and Oquawka's charter was amended to favor Knoxville, Galesburg leaders secured a charter for their own railroad on February 15, 1851. The Central Military Tract Railroad was to build northeast from Galesburg to a junction with the Rock Island and Chicago Railroad being built from east to west across the northern part of the state.[23]

Two months later, the ten "corporators" of the Central Military Tract had seen to the election of ten directors (six of whom were also corporators), prepared blank certificates of stock to be sold at

$100 per share, reimbursed seven men with $5 each for expenses incurred in Springfield while they secured the charter, and fanned out along the route of the proposed railroad to solicit subscriptions. By November 1851 the company directors felt financially secure enough to place ads for bids on the grading and masonry work in newspapers in Knoxville, Quincy, Chicago, St. Louis, and Buffalo. Then in March 1852 all work stopped because a hoped-for loan of $50,000 from Knox County had fallen through. All engineering operations and payments were suspended "until after the next harvest." Also in March 1852, Yankee merchant Chauncey Colton left for his annual buying trip to the cities of the East. While in Boston, Colton met Elisha Wadsworth of the Aurora Branch Railroad and James S. Grimes of Burlington, Iowa, who was a director of the Peoria and Oquawka. All three men agreed that the interests of their respective railroads could be better served if they worked to combine the three into a single route from Chicago to Burlington via Galesburg.[24]

On June 22, 1852, the Illinois General Assembly authorized the Aurora Branch to build west to Mendota, fifteen miles north of LaSalle, where it would connect with the Illinois Central and, it was hoped, the Central Military Tract. But having the Central Military Tract under the wings of the Aurora Branch was not enough for Colton and the other local stockholders. The impending construction of the Northern Cross branch line through Knoxville (or, rather, *not* east of Knoxville) to LaSalle meant that it and the Galesburg road would run parallel and would compete for business. Colton met with the Northern Cross directors and convinced them that the plan to join the Aurora branch and the Central Military Tract would leave the Northern Cross at a disadvantage. He suggested that if they would reconsider and build their road through Galesburg, instead of Knoxville, they too could reap the benefits of the combined efforts and, presumably, attract eastern speculative money for the construction of the railroad. The Northern Cross agreed.[25]

Meanwhile, James F. Joy, a representative of the Michigan Central Railroad, who had been scouting Illinois for likely connections for his line that ran from Detroit to Chicago, had visited Springfield. He just happened to be in the capital at the same time that Colton was there to secure an amendment to the Central Military Tract's charter. Joy told Colton that the Michigan Central directors in Boston and New York might be interested in helping to build the Central Military Tract, but only if the control of the board was transferred to the Chicago and Detroit investors in the Michigan Central and if the directors in Galesburg could raise $300,000. The first condition was met on October 14, 1852, when the stockholders of the Central Military Tract gathered for a rare two-session meeting in the First Presbyterian Church in Galesburg. In the morning, the executive committee of the board of directors asked that the stock of the local company be increased to $600,000. In fact, the "stockholders" raised the total to $800,000, the same amount in shares purchased by Joy for sixteen individuals that same morning. Colton owned 129 of 534 shares; merchants Silas Willard and James Bunce (both Yankees) owned 117 and 103 shares, respectively. The only other substantial holder was William Selden Gale (son of the town's founder) who owned 120. That afternoon, the stockholders met again to vote for new directors. When the board was elected, it included only four men from Galesburg and seven from outside.[26]

Even before the October stockholder meeting, the Galesburg board had raised the required $300,000 in local subscriptions. By September, the total had reached only $250,000, but Colton and Willard made up the difference with more of their own funds. The company had met both conditions imposed by Joy and the easterners. Although the Central Military Tract Railroad was now controlled by eastern money, its construction was at least assured. The road from Mendota to Galesburg was completed in December 1854 and was placed under the joint management of the Chicago, Burlington and Quincy in March 1855. The branch to Burlington opened in December 1855 and the Northern Cross reached Quincy in January 1856. The Peoria and Oquawka built to Galesburg and joined the CB&Q in July 1856.[27]

Unlike in Belleville where leaders were initially divided over the proper method of maximizing the town's economic prospects and wavered in their actions, and in Ottawa where leaders were confident and unified but were opposed by a dissatisfied electorate, Galesburg's leaders were not challenged to justify their actions. They were able to act quickly and efficiently and thus were able to acquire the best railroad connections.

Because Belleville's leaders were divided among themselves and pursued competing transportation strategies during the critical railroad-building period, companies bypassed the town and built toward more attractive sites. In Ottawa, the economic leaders were not so much divided as they were limited by a restless public intent on flexing their young political muscles, but they were unable to finance the improvements necessary to attract the Illinois Central and had to settle for the Rock Island and Chicago consolation prize. Galesburg's leaders were challenged neither by another group nor by a contentious citizenry and were able to attract a variety of railroads—despite their town's initial isolation—earning their town the grand prize in the "great railroad lottery." The different decision-making styles that were employed by the leaders of the three towns in their quest for transportation connections would be used again when they faced other problems that would arise in the construction of their frontier communities.

Five The Schools

[The] citizens of Belleville refuse to be taxed . . . to educate their
children. By this vote, Belleville has disgraced herself, most
deeply disgraced herself.

—*Belleville Advocate, 1859*

Can the good citizens of Ottawa afford to see from three to five
hundred of their offspring running in the streets for want of
more school rooms?

—*Ottawa Free Trader, 1859*

The fair name of the "College City" is being tarnished by our
shameful negligence of the interests of our common schools.

—*Galesburg Democrat, 1859*

Displaying differing expectations and decisions about railroad
connections, the people of Belleville, Ottawa, and Galesburg
showed, during the late 1840s and early 1850s, that they could
and would meet the problems of frontier community building on
their own terms and in their own peculiar ways. Each town was
faced with disagreement over the decisions from people of diverse
economic and ethnic backgrounds, and each met the challenge of
possible disruption by acting in a way that would guarantee the
most agreement among the town's leaders. Such would also be the
case with other issues that the people of each town had to settle
during the remainder of the 1850s. One of the most trying and
most important concerns of communities all over Illinois was the
construction of public school systems.

Until recently, the growth of public education in nineteenth-
century America—and Illinois—has been explained as the inevitable fulfillment of democratic idealism. That is, many historians
have looked at the development of public schools merely as evi-
dence that proud Americans could think of themselves as equal to
one another; after all, their offspring could learn their letters
alongside the children of people from all social classes and from
all ethnic backgrounds. Seen in this progressive manner, public
schools were the great equalizers of American society. However, in
the last few decades, educational historians have begun to explore
the local social structures that created varying educational experi-

89

ences in individual communities; these social historians have examined the relationship between the development of free schools and changes within the nation's social order.[1] The different responses of the people of Belleville, Ottawa, and Galesburg to the state's first comprehensive free school act in 1855 provide a dramatic illustration of how the economic, social, and political relationships of a town's occupational, ethnic, and religious groups could affect the formation of public schools.

Before 1855, an entire generation of Illinois citizens had grown to adulthood without the benefit of a mandatory public education. When the Illinois General Assembly passed *An Act to Establish and Maintain a System of Free Schools* in 1855, local boards of education throughout the state were charged with the creation and support of public schools.[2] For the first time in the history of Illinois, the 1855 law effectively required communities to levy property taxes for the maintenance of tuition-free schools. The law also called for the election of three school commissioners in each district, as well as for school conventions, teachers' institutes, and establishment of boards of teacher examiners. It represented a victory for advocates of Illinois public education who had fought for years to force communities to provide at least a basic education to each of their children.

The first attempt by the state to impose taxation for the support of public schools came with the 1825 *Act Providing for the Establishment of Free Schools*. Under the provisions of that law, any township with fifteen families had to supply a free common school for at least three months out of the year for white citizens between the ages of five and twenty-one. The law was effectively nullified, however, by a new law in 1827 stating, "No person shall hereafter be taxed for the support of any free school in this state, unless by his or her own free will and consent." The next attempt to introduce legislation calling for tax-supported education in the form of schools and seminaries came in 1835, but the bill did not pass the General Assembly. A bill encouraging free schools did pass in 1841 but provided for no local taxation. Many thought that the state constitutional convention of 1847 would surely and finally establish public schools, but the final draft of the constitution contained no mention of a statewide system. Pragmatic advocates of education had instead established small, unreliable, often poorly staffed subscription schools, which were financed by parents and by small amounts of money from the state. The state funds were established with the enabling acts of 1802 and 1804 and the state constitution of 1818. The township fund was created by the public ownership and then the sale of one section of land per township; it was eventually controlled by a school commissioner in each county. The seminary fund was a state-controlled account created by the sale of one township of land per county. The state's school and college funds also depended upon the sale of the public domain for their finances, but on a statewide basis. The moneys were to be divided into two parts, five-sixths to an Illinois common school fund and one-sixth into a state college fund. Some communities relied on local state-chartered and partially state-financed private academies, which after 1830 were required to operate elementary schools.[3]

The passage of the 1855 free school act put an end to this quasi-public support of both subscription and academy schools. But it also created a new set of arguments and problems. Voters and boards of education throughout Illinois were faced with decisions about implementing the new law: the arrangement of grades, the length of terms, the content of curricula, and the construction of buildings. And just as communities differed in their solutions to the absence of tax-supported schools before 1855, they reacted variously to the new challenges afterward. The responses of Belleville, Ottawa, and Galesburg are representative of those challenges and responses.

Before the 1855 school law, citizens of the three towns made different provisions for the education of their children. Early Belleville residents supported numerous private academies in the 1820s. The Belleville Academy was chartered by the state in 1821 and thereafter received one-half of the rent proceeds from the township fund. John H. Dennis of Virginia opened another institution, the Aristocratic School, in 1824. Neither the Academy nor Dennis's school seems to have lasted very long. From the 1830s, the nearest colleges or private academies were in St. Louis and in nearby Lebanon, where the Methodist Episcopal church established Lebanon Seminary (now McKendree College) in 1828 and McKendree Female Academy in 1851. Beginning in the 1840s, Belleville residents instead turned to parochial and subscription schools to educate their children. The Presbyterians, for example, operated a school in their church during the 1840s and 1850s. In 1848, German Catholics founded a grammar school. Non-Catholics founded the Belleville School Association, which by 1850 was operating classrooms at the Odd Fellows Hall and elsewhere. By 1852, the School Association was providing education for two hundred students.[4] The association dissolved in 1855 with the passage of the school law.

In the years following the passage of the 1855 school law, progressive educators in Belleville were unable to transform their early initiatives into a unified public school system. As late as 1859, there were no public schoolhouses in town; children attended their classes for only six months a year (the School Association had maintained a ten-month term), meeting in churches, in headquarters of fraternal organizations, and in private homes. As the city's three school directors attempted to create a public high school, they submitted to voters a three-proposition referendum in May 1859 that they hoped would help to rectify some of the deficiencies in the system. Voters approved the directors' proposition to extend the school year to ten months, but by a slim majority of only 33 votes. By a vote of 295 to 131, the electorate resoundingly defeated the proposal to raise taxes for the construction of a schoolhouse. Voters also rejected the emergency purchase of the old Odd Fellows Hall as a public school. Thus, Belleville voters decided that classes would meet for a longer period but that they would be held in inadequate facilities.[5]

By the time that a new group of school directors was to be elected four months later, Belleville's educational situation was desperate. One slate of candidates wanted to expand the school year beyond ten months and also introduce German as a mandatory subject for students of German extraction, beginning in fifth grade. An opposing group of candidates favored using German as the primary language of instruction in the public schools and easing the tax burden by returning to a six-month term. No candidate favored the elimination of German language instruction from the Belleville schools, but there was considerable sentiment for such a move among American-born citizens. The election drew 598 voters—127 more than participated in the May referendum. The candidates who wanted to expand the school term to ten months won by margins greater than 200, supported by a coalition of Protestant Germans and native-born individualist Americans.[6]

Decision making in Belleville between 1855 and 1860 centered around heated arguments over the length of the school term, the actual building of schools, and the proper role of German. But the hotly contested race for school director in September 1859 did not put an end to the "bitter opposition to the Free Schools" that had been expressed in May.[7] The opposition centered around two separate and emotional issues: whether citizens should or should not be involuntarily taxed to support public schools; and whether the German language should be used or even allowed in public schools.

After 1859, the Belleville school system most closely reflected the sentiments of Hessian Germans and progressive American Republicans who wanted strong public schools and a limited use of the German language. But they were stymied by ethnic American voters opposed to any instruction in German and by German Lutherans intent on the use of German as the primary mode of instruction. Both Catholic Germans (who were already supporting a parochial school) and individualist American voters opposed increased taxes for the public schools. The result was indecision and fragmentation that led to the virtual breakdown of and retreat from public education by the German-speaking population of Belleville. Catholics expanded their facilities in 1859 when the School Sisters of Notre Dame opened the Institute of the Immaculate Conception as a young ladies' academy, an addition to the parish graded school. In 1861, Lutherans founded another church, and with it began the Lutheran Church School. The new Lutheran church eventually asked for and received advice on hiring teachers and a minister from the Missouri Synod and then joined the group in 1864. Even freethinking Protestant Germans sought an alternative to public schools in 1860, when they established the short-lived Belleville Institute, for boys twelve to fifteen years who were "interested in a thorough education," and sought a "liberal patronage." At least half of the members of the institute's board of trustees were natives of the central German state of Hesse-Darmstadt, Hesse-Kassel, Frankfurt, or Nassau. The Institute survived only one year, suggesting that if any German children did attend the public schools, they were probably those whose parents were from Hesse. But it is clear that many children in Belleville were not taking advantage of the free schools. Belleville Township's 1859–60 public school attendance rate was 40 percent of the five- to twenty-one-year-old population; that figure compares with 49 percent for St. Clair County as a whole and 61 percent for the state. Less than one-fourth of the 898 pupils in the city's public schools were studying German in 1861; in a last-ditch effort to lure more German students into the schools, high school German-language study was made compulsory in 1874. The high school dissolved in 1878 and did not reopen until 1890.[8]

Once again, this time over the construction of a public school system, Belleville's residents split themselves along ethnic lines. As with the railroads, the town's influential ethnic Americans and the early arriving Hessians could not force the majority population of Catholic and Lutheran Germans to conform. Instead, the town's children were also divided into ethnic and religious groups when their parents sent them off to school in the morning.

As in Belleville, early Ottawa residents had provided for the education of their children with small subscription schools. Horace Sprague, a man from Massachusetts who moved to Illinois with his brother George, opened a school in South Ottawa in 1825 in the home of Henry Allen. Sprague eventually moved on and was followed at the school by a Mr. Kirkpatrick and then by Henry Allen himself. Alonzo Sawyer opened a private school in the Ottawa Mechanics' Hall and taught there until 1845. Thaddeus Hampton succeeded Sawyer and taught in the small school until 1852 when he began editing the town's Republican newspaper. Sprague and Hampton apparently received some money from the township fund. In 1844, a private "select school for young ladies and gentlemen" was opened in Ottawa but did not survive for very long. In 1848 a new District School was opened in town; it was designated the "public school" of Ottawa and students received one-third of their tuition from the common school fund. The eighty District School pupils were all taught, in one room over the Freemasons' Hall, by Mary Lee. However, the school and teacher had competition from Hampton, a Miss Haver, a Miss Cody, and a Miss Mortimer, all of whom operated private schools. Two hundred students attended Ottawa's five schools in 1849, but none of the institutions offered courses at the high school level.[9]

Even before the passage of the 1855 state school law, Ottawans began to agitate for a unified public system. *Ottawa Free Trader* editor William Osman suggested as early as 1849 that all of the town's children ought to be enrolled in the District School and that, if the numbers warranted, citizens ought to create an entire school system. His reasons were entirely financial. Because the district teacher was charged with so many pupils, she could demand a salary of $600 a year; each of the four private school teachers had thirty children a year and earned $300. The town was spending a total of $1,800 to educate two hundred students. Osman argued that if the town distributed its educational money more frugally, it could provide schooling for twice as many students at a lower price. He proposed that Ottawa adopt a public school system; the townspeople could build a large school for $1,500 that would hold four hundred students, hire a "man of experience" to be principal and teach language and science for $600, hire an assistant principal to teach geography and arithmetic for $400, and hire a "competent female" to teach primary students for $300. He further reasoned that since many of Ottawa's leading Yankee families were sending their offspring to private schools in the East, a public school would allow them to keep their children at home where they could be educated with the rest of the town's children. The editor pointed to Chicago as an example of a community in which the "public school system is patronized by all classes . . . [and where] no man's child . . . is too good to go to the district school." Ottawa, Osman argued, could do just as well.[10]

Ottawa's citizens did not act upon Osman's suggestions, however, even though he kept up his barrage of editorials that castigated the town's leaders for their negligence. "There has never been any backwardness on the part of the masses to provide all the necessary means of education, when they have had suitable leaders to direct them," he wrote in the fall of 1849. "Year after year, there is the same neglect and indifference," he continued. He lamented that "youngsters are growing up to be a nuisance. . . . It is high time this was stopped." But the editor's suggestions reached only deaf ears; nothing was done about the District School and the poorer children of the town continued to languish in its inadequate facilities. In the meantime, the wealthy children enjoyed the privileges of private schools, both abroad and at home in Ottawa.[11]

Wholesale grocers George E. Walker and William Hickling took up Osman's call for better public schools when they organized a public meeting of Ottawa's citizenry on the subject in January 1851. Walker, an Ottawa resident since 1827, and Hickling, an Englishman who emigrated in 1834 and married Walker's sister Adeline, remained deeply concerned with the well-being of their town throughout the 1850s. Hickling was elected Ottawa's first mayor in 1853 and was reelected in 1854. Walker won the mayoralty in 1857. And even though Hickling had been one of the eleven land purchasers during the Illinois River improvement fiasco of 1850, he had offered to subscribe $5,000 of his own money to get the Rock Island and Chicago Railroad to build through Ottawa. Both men were Democrats and were known for their support of public improvements. They were also clearly disgusted with the apathy toward the public schools that was displayed by the other economic leaders of Ottawa; only four people showed up at the courthouse to discuss the issue at the public meeting.[12]

Nothing was done for another two years. Then, in April 1853, the former schoolteacher and editor of the *Ottawa Republican*, Thaddeus Hampton, began to champion the public school cause. He argued that Ottawa would have to establish a viable school system soon—beginning with a building for the District School—or it would have to pay "with interest, for the support of pauperism and the punishment of crimes which the absence of schools is sure to engender." However, unlike Osman who earlier called for public schools that would give children of all classes the opportunity to rub shoulders and to learn from one another, Hampton wanted schools that would lessen the likelihood of "juvenile depravity which are incident to towns of mixed populations." Some people in the town agreed with Hampton about the dangers of an uneducated working class and called for a $1 per $100 property tax to support the school. However, the city school directors who had been charged with overseeing the District School refused to call a public meeting to discuss any changes.[13]

Both editors feared the consequences to their town if the large Irish population, the members of which could not usually afford to send their children to private schools, continued to grow without the benefits of a basic education. And by 1853, the leaders of Ottawa, whether Democrats or Republicans, knew that they had better act soon. In 1854 the new Ottawa City Council divided the town into nine school districts, each of which was eventually to have its own school building. Editor Hampton ridiculed Mayor Hickling and his administration for laying out too grandiose a plan, however. "This division," he wrote, "made the districts about the size of onion patches, and would have enabled some of them to erect school houses about the capacity of a dry goods box." Hampton supported an alternative plan that would divide the city into three districts with three schools. Each school, he estimated, could accommodate six to eight hundred pupils and would be sufficient for at least three or four years. The argument between the proponents of nine schools and those who called for just three delayed any action for another year.[14]

In 1855 the leaders of Ottawa were forced to act upon the desire of the populace for more schools. Both Hampton at the *Republican* and Osman's successors at the *Free Trader*, George and Julius Avery, welcomed the prospect of a state-mandated school system. A public meeting, chaired by the wealthy Irish Presbyterian glass merchant William Reddick, on the matter was held January 13, 1855. A nine-person committee was appointed to prepare a charter of Ottawa's public schools to be submitted for approval by the Illinois General Assembly. The people at the meeting also voted to tax themselves at 1 percent of property and called for the erection of a primary school in each of the seven city wards (for $10,000 each) and a central school building for advanced scholars (also for $10,000). The charter was written and was approved by the legislature in February 1855.[15]

Many of the citizens of Ottawa were obviously elated by the news that there was to be, at last, sufficient public schools in town. They must have thought that their work was complete and that the public was satisfied because the election held in March 1855 for the district school board only attracted 216 voters. All of the winning candidates had run unopposed. Five of the new board members, Philo Lindley, George B. Macy, Allen A. Fisher, Giles W. Jackson, and Edwin S. Leland, were Yankees from either New York or New England. Corn dealer Benjamin T. Phelps was a native of Virginia. None of the members of the Ottawa Board of Education was an immigrant. The people of Ottawa did not know that, though they had been given a gift of public schools by the state of Illinois, their own school board was about to take much of it away.[16]

Ground for two primary schools, one in the second ward adjoining the Congregational Church on Madison Street in the center of town and the other in the fifth ward, west of the side cut, was broken in June 1855. By January of the next year when O. P. Perdue had completed his enumeration of the city's population for the school board, the two buildings were still not complete. The 1,391 children between the ages of five and twenty years in town were still without any schools. Finally, in February 1856, the school in the fifth ward was ready for occupancy. But when the students gathered on Monday, February 11, many were turned away because there was not enough room for them all. The same was the case when the second school opened a week later. Six hundred eighteen children were crammed into the two schools, and many more still waited for places. High school students attended classes in the same buildings with the younger children. Despite the overcrowding, the board of education announced that they had divided the city into two school districts and that they had no plans to begin construction of any more buildings.[17]

In the fall of 1856, Professor L. Umlauf of New York opened a female seminary for the young women of Ottawa. However, he charged $180 per year for boarders and $24 per academic course for day students, and only the children of the wealthy could afford to attend. When the public buildings opened for the winter term in January 1857, they were again overcrowded with children; 1,469 pupils attended the two schools. William Osman, recently returned as the editor of the *Free Trader*, asked why so many people were sending their girls to the public schools when Professor Umlauf's seminary was available. When a new school board was to be elected in the spring, none of the sitting members said that they wanted to serve another term. But when the new board of education took over in March, three incumbents, Giles W. Jackson, Edwin S. Leland, and Allen A. Fisher, remained; all of the new members, Oronzo Leavens, Daniel D. Thompson, C. Marshall Van Doren, and Justus Harris, were Yankees.[18]

The new school board was not very different from the old. But, after listening and reading complaints that as many as 500 Ottawa children were not attending school because there was so little room in the two buildings, and after the fifth ward school was damaged by fire in March 1858, the board finally called for bids on the construction of one more school on the north side of town, where many of the wealthier families lived. They also appointed Professor Isaac Stone, principal of the fifth ward school, to be the superintendent of Ottawa Public Schools for $1,000 a year. At the same time, Osman informed the public that Ottawans were spending only $5 per pupil in their schools while other cities spent much more: Springfield residents spent $9, Baltimore spent $22, and New York spent $13 per student. Nevertheless, some Ottawans balked at expending any more money on the public schools and supported "Retrenchment" candidates for the board in 1859. Osman actually supported retrenchment. He argued that the town should "educate the masses for the counter, the machine shop, and for the various branches of commercial business, and make them useful men." He did not like the fact that the "Old Board" had authorized the use of money for the instruction of wealthy high school students in college preparatory classes while many of the city's poorer students still did not have the opportunity to acquire a common school education. Osman was opposed by supporters of the present school system. One "Friend" wrote to the *Free Trader* and asked whether "the cause of education, the welfare of our youth, and the harmony of the community, demand that we should be a little cautious how we disturb the system of our well regulated schools?"[19]

Many Ottawans were apparently less satisfied than "Friend" with the schools; in the election, the Retrenchment candidates won over the Old Board ticket in all five wards that had contested seats. The voting was done at large and the retrenchment ticket consistently tallied two-thirds of the vote. Nearly 1,000 men voted in the elections. It is clear that people on both sides of the issue, those for spending more on schools and those for spending less felt that the issue was an important one. The new board of education, however, was not as stingy with the town's money as their campaign might have predicted. They did reduce the salaries of the teachers in the schools—Principal Stone's was reduced to $900— but they also went on to construct schools in the remaining four wards of the city. Irish immigrant Thomas R. Courtney and longtime Ottawa resident and Virginia native David Walker were members of the new board and were not shy about spending money for schools as long as it was used to give opportunities to the poorer children in town. They did not want to spend any more money on high school classes.[20]

It is clear that the large immigrant population of Ottawa was not satisfied with the public schools but that it was sending its children to the public schools in greater numbers than was the native-born group. There were no parochial schools in town until after 1859 when the Sisters of St. Joseph's Convent was opened in town. The sisters eventually established the Irish Academy of St. Francis Xavier. The German Catholics opened the Dominican St. Francis school and the German Lutherans opened the Evangelical Lutheran school, both in the 1860s. Finally, the French Protestant population opened a school, also in the 1860s. In 1860, 1,469 pupils attended the schools of Ottawa Township, an attendance rate of 87 percent of all children between the ages of 5 and 21. If all of the students of the native population in that age range were attending school, they would have accounted for only 1,100. It is more likely that the immigrants, and particularly the large Irish group, sent their children to the new public schools for a basic education; Catholic grade schools were not opened until late in the century. However, the results of the school board election in 1859 show that they were not very keen on spending much of their hard-earned money on the education of high school students, most of whom came from the wealthier segment of the population.[21]

The Retrenchment board of education did not build a central high school. Instead, higher classes met in the fifth ward school on Columbus Street. High school principal and Ottawa school superintendent Isaac Stone quit the public schools when the new board was elected and opened the Ottawa Literary and Commercial Institute in the fall of 1859. He and five other teachers taught ancient languages and sciences, bookkeeping, French, German, and music along with the rudiments of a common school education. Miss S. J. M. Davis, a graduate of Genessee Wesleyan Seminary of New York and a former teacher at the Columbus Street school, also opened her own school in 1859; she announced that she would offer an "inclusive" curriculum. Both Stone's and Davis's ventures proved to be successful, catering to the children of Ottawa's wealthier families. The two new private schools and the Catholic St. Francis Xavier academy also minimized the need for a separate public high school for years to come. The Ottawa Township High School was not organized until 1878.[22]

When the 1850s came to a close, Ottawa's school system reflected the town's social structure. The Yankee leadership had tried to control the schools after passage of the 1855 state law, but their efforts were rejected by the large immigrant population. The large Irish group eventually took control of the schools and sent their children off to gain a good, but basic, education, but they did not mingle with the offspring of the native-born Yankee leadership.

Galesburg citizens had taken yet another course in educating their children before 1855. In fact, the town founders were content with the absence of common schools because any public system would have provided competition for Galesburg's primary source of education, Knox College and Academy. Grammar schools in Galesburg before 1855 were actually controlled by the college. The schools met for four to six months per year, and the teachers were usually Knox students who needed money to complete their education. Indeed, because students were admitted to the preparatory department of the academy at the age of ten, it made little sense to the leaders of Galesburg to subject taxpayers to the expense of public schools. Knox, like the Belleville Academy and Ottawa's common schools, received money from the rental of the school lands before 1855. A second institution of higher learning, Lombard University, was founded in Galesburg in 1853 by the Spoon River Association of Universalists in response to the "sectarian influence" of their religious opponents. Knox County received $867 in 1855 and $1,016 in 1856 from the seminary and college funds; Knox and Lombard were the only colleges or seminaries in the county at the time.[23]

After the passage of the 1855 school law, Galesburg voters were also faced with making historic decisions about their town's educational facilities. Content with the lack of a publicly financed system, the city delayed its response to the state plan until 1858, when it created the Union Graded School District No. 1. The graded school concept was based on the Prussian model of a primary level for the teaching of the rudiments of reading, writing, and arithmetic; a grammar level for English, geography, and grammar; and a high level for literature and languages. The charter "for the establishment of a system of graded schools in the city of Galesburg" was submitted to the Illinois General Assembly and approved by that body in February 1859. The charter stipulated that it would go into effect upon the approval of a "majority of the legal voters" of the city—that is, the majority of eligible voters rather than a simple electoral majority.[24]

Meanwhile, some prominent citizens were becoming alarmed at the harm that an inadequate school system was doing to the town's reputation. One taxpayer wrote to the *Galesburg Semi-Weekly Democrat* (a Republican newspaper) in April 1859: "I believe I may safely assert, that there is not another town in the State of Illinois, having as large a population as Galesburg, that has done so little, directly, for the improvement of its common schools. In fact, if there is a town, having an equal population to ours, in all the free States of North America, that is more sadly delinquent upon this subject, I would like to peep into it, and see if it is inhabited by white folks." The author, English professor Erastus S. Willcox of Knox College, must have known that he was treading on sacred ground. He and fellow Knox faculty member George Churchill (principal of the Knox Academy) withstood considerable censure for their support of common schools.[25]

The editor of the *Democrat,* C. J. Sellon, also favored change in the school system. He reminded moral members of the community that Galesburg might experience the same sort of problems seen in Chicago if school reform was not achieved. "We have little doubt," he wrote, "that many of the urchins who now daily parade our streets, untaught and uncared for, are candidates, either for the penitentiary or something worse. They are gaining an education, not such as calculated to fit them for life's duties, but rather to exert a pestiferous influence upon all who associate with them." Under pressure to comply with the state law, the Galesburg City Council called a citizens' meeting for May 14 for consideration of the school charter. By a slim majority, those present voted to defer the matter until autumn. In August, proschool forces expressed shame that some citizens would put monetary concerns above the needs of children. "[If] we wish to give our children what is valuable above diamonds, valuable above everything that money can buy, we must make up our minds to pay for it," declared one letter to the editor. "The fair name of the 'College City' is being tarnished by our shameful negligence," said another.[26]

In September, the city's voters elected their three district school directors. To the surprise of some, the proschool slate of candidates won with about 60 percent of the vote. The new directors hurriedly went about the task of implementing the provisions of the school charter—a complete system of graded schools—even though the act had not yet been ratified by the voters. Classes were delayed by two weeks for repairs to makeshift facilities. The schools opened in October 1859, with 648 pupils. In the summer of 1860, the city council called for a referendum on the school charter: 505 people voted "for," and 53 voted "against." Also, the voters agreed that the school term should be extended to more than six months.[27]

The school charter vote signaled a reversal of the attitude among Galesburg's leadership toward public education. The establishment of the Illinois Normal University in 1857 for the training of public school teachers—a genuine threat to Knox's teacher-training program—had finally convinced many local leaders that they should pursue a new course of action. Professor Willcox wrote: "[A] very great change has occurred in the number, the character, and the educational wants of our people, and a change is demanded in our schools that will adapt them to those wants." He outlined the potential economic consequences for a city lacking a decent graded school system: "The establishment of a well-arranged system of free schools will not conflict with the interests of our colleges. . . . [Let] us take a common sense view of this subject. . . . It is hurting every interest we possess; it is detracting from every man's capital who owns a shop, or store, or house and lot in town." He also challenged the Galesburg citizenry to perform its moral duty. "Free schools will not prosper on the merits of their system," he said. "But let true men and true women in the city of Galesburg labor with loving hearts in their behalf, and an intellectual and moral harvest that shall be glorious will be the result."[28]

Professor Willcox initially took a fair amount of ridicule from his colleagues for his stand, but it gradually became obvious that his views were more prescient than ridiculous. When the school director elections took place in the fall of 1859, most of the Knox group had become convinced of the correctness of supporting public schools. At the June 1860 election, the school charter was approved by a vote of 505 to 53. The sudden increase in the number of voters and the small number of votes against the charter appear to have been the result of the sentiment of a new group in Galesburg who had an interest in voting for public schools: the immigrants. A total of 991 students attended the schools in their first year of operation in 1859–60. A census report to the city council counted 1,846 people between ages five and twenty-one. The township ratio of attendance was 53 percent. An analysis of foreign-born children and native-born children indicates that one or both groups greatly exceeded the township average of attendance. If all students were children of the native-born, they would have been attending school at an incredible rate of 92 percent.[29] It is more likely that the foreign-born voted for and sent their children to the new public schools.

Not all of Galesburg's immigrants were equally likely to support public schools, but the Swedes were probably among the converted. One of the most influential members of the Galesburg Swedish community, Lutheran minister T. N. Hasselquist, was a national spokesman for the rapid Americanization of immigrant Swedes. He helped to found the Augustana Synod in 1860 and later urged a close connection between the state churches in Sweden and the churches in the United States. As editor of the *Hemlandet*, a Swedish-language newspaper, from 1855 to 1858, he urged the Swedish Lutheran churches in America to prepare for the eventual use of English. (He sold the newspaper in 1858 to a publisher in Chicago, where it was continued.) So it appeared as if the Swedes of Galesburg at least had the inclination to partici- pate in the establishment of a public school system. Mid-nine- teenth-century Swedish immigrants generally assimilated faster than other groups. They usually had a positive attitude toward American institutions and culture; they were almost all literate and could, therefore, learn English quickly; they were more eager than most to use public schools; and they were generally willing to go through the process of naturalization in order to vote. The attendance figures in the new schools support the possibility that they did so in Galesburg.[30]

But the Swedish voters were simply going along with the domi- nant Yankees associated with Knox College who supported the new system. The low vote against the charter in 1860 indicates that they, too, had finally accepted the public schools, perhaps be- cause they knew that they could maintain their control of them. The final version of the school charter stipulated that the offices of school treasurer and clerk would be held by the town's treasurer and clerk. Galesburg's treasurer and clerk (B. F. Holcomb and W. A. Wood) were both members of the Yankee leadership clique. In fact, the extent to which the college continued to control the schools can be seen in the relationship of public high school graduates to Knox College: of the twenty-one students who gradu- ated from Galesburg High School in the 1860s, twelve went on to graduate from Knox College. Meanwhile, the enrollment of the Knox preparatory department consistently declined.[31]

By 1860, Belleville, Ottawa, and Galesburg had established pub- lic school systems that technically complied with the 1855 Illinois school law. But the differing styles with which the people made and implemented their decisions reflected the cultural priorities of the ethnic, religious, and social groups within the three commu- nities. Belleville residents settled upon a majority-supported solu- tion to their public school problem, but disaffected voters chose to build alternative schools. Theirs was a highly fragmented town in which occupational, ethnic, and religious loyalties were divided and distinct. Loyalties and identities crossed each other in a complex web, and decisions about the educational system were made with difficulty. The result was the formation of at least three mini-school systems that reflected the religious divisions of the city. Ottawa's Yankee leaders initially opposed the establishment of public schools in their town; but when they were forced to construct a system by the 1855 school law, they used it to their own benefit, providing public funds for high school classes for their own children while skimping on the basic schools for the masses, whether immigrant or native-born. Proponents of basic public education, though (and particularly the minority Irish population), were eventually able to wrest the schools away from the wealthy elites, who fled to their own private schools. Ottawans ended up with public schools that provided the entire community with access to primary education but did not provide much in the way of advanced courses. Galesburg citizens needed and finally reached a consensus on the school issue. It was a town in which one ethnic, religious, and economic group, the Knox Yankees, controlled the educational decision making of the community. The minorities of Galesburg had no choice but to assimilate if they were inclined and welcomed, as were the Swedish immigrants, or to separate from the majority and fend for themselves if they were shunned, as were the Irish inhabitants of the town.

Six The Politics

> We hate tyranny in whatever shape we find it; we love freedom
> and the right, honor, and welfare of mankind. And that, we
> think is *true* Americanism.
>
> —*Belleviller Zeitung, 1860*
>
> The Democratic doctrine is . . . what our fathers fought for, and
> let us stand by it now . . . and this mid-night cabal will vanish
> like a mist before the sun beams.
>
> —*Ottawa Free Trader, 1858*
>
> Men may differ widely and vigorously in their views . . . but they
> can hardly stand and persist in acrimonious contention, without
> self-damage.
>
> —*Galesburg Democrat, 1857*

It was not always easy for the people of frontier Belleville, Ottawa,
or Galesburg to decide upon the constitution or upon the goals of
their economic, social, and political institutions. The residents in
each town would often fight over the amount of money that they
should spend to build their infrastructures, and then they would
battle over the control of the completed facilities. In fact, the un-
pleasantness that their different opinions caused sometimes delayed the processes of decision making and the development of
their towns. Such was the case in both Belleville and Ottawa,
where disagreements among the economic leaders and acrimony
between ethnic groups made it difficult for the people to attract
railroad companies to the towns. Likewise, arguments over the
proper involvement of government in the education of Belleville
and Ottawa children slowed the construction of schools. Residents
in these two towns certainly paid a price for their adherence to
the principles of participatory democracy. And such would also be
the case with the local politics of Belleville and Ottawa.

In Galesburg, however, there was very little disagreement among
the leadership, and there was no significant challenge from minorities to hinder the processes of community building during the
1850s. Railways were attracted to Galesburg early and quickly,
chiefly because the town's economic elites were so cohesive. And
106 an entire school system was constructed efficiently, once the

town's leaders had all agreed that the schools would still be controlled by Knox College officials. By 1860, the same process of consensual decision making would be applied to the construction of Galesburg's local governmental system. Residents of Galesburg, though, also paid a price for the method with which they made their community choices: political dissenters were not tolerated, and ethnic minorities who disagreed with majority opinions were virtually eliminated from the decision-making process.

Whether or not they were aware of it, the people of Belleville, Ottawa, and Galesburg, while painstakingly building their own small communities on the Illinois frontier during the 1850s, were also acting out their parts in a wider national political drama. At the beginning of the decade, local Belleville, Ottawa, and Galesburg residents were engaged in political debates that reflected the national realignment of the "Second Party System" that had pitted the Democrats against the Whigs since the 1830s. In the 1840s, the overwhelming majority of the voters of Belleville and Ottawa identified with and cast ballots for Democratic candidates in national and local elections. Most Galesburg voters, however, were more comfortable with the philosophies of the Whig and the short-lived Free-Soil Parties. By the end of the 1850s, however, national political races had become contests between Democrats and Republicans in what has become known as the "Third Party System," and local politics in Belleville and Ottawa had begun to reflect the heated ideological arguments between local Republicans and Democrats. In Galesburg, though, the 1860 presidential election was seen as a forum for local leaders to outdo one another in professing their loyalties only to Abraham Lincoln's Republican Party.[1]

The election of 1860 and the life and administration of the first Republican president are, without a doubt, the most frequently covered aspect of Illinois history. Over the past century, generations of scholars and writers have painstakingly examined every nook and cranny of Abraham Lincoln's personal and political life. One effect of this emphasis upon Lincoln's role in the past has been the tendency of the state's historians to write about individuals, ethnic groups, and towns in order to emphasize their subjects' contributions to Lincoln's career. This has been particularly true of historians of Belleville, Ottawa, and Galesburg. Each of the towns had reputations for radicalism Republicanism during the late 1850s. Belleville was the headquarters of a group of German

Republicans, led by Gustave Körner, Lincoln's eventual ambassa-
dor to Spain. Ottawa was the site of the first Lincoln-Douglas debate of 1858 and was the place where John Hossack and the
"Ottawa Martyrs" challenged the federal fugitive slave act in
1859. Galesburg, another debate site, was a center of "Black Republicanism" (a label that identified particular party members as
abolitionist sympathizers) activities by the people connected with
Knox College.

Another result of the emphasis upon Lincoln's life in Illinois has
been the tendency among historians to examine the politics of
frontier Belleville, Ottawa, and Galesburg primarily from a national perspective.[2] However, if the national political realignment
of the 1850s was also occurring at the local level and if the economic, cultural, and political dynamics within individual communities were contributing to that realignment, it is imperative that
historians also examine town politics from a local perspective.

On the Illinois frontier, a town's economic and cultural leaders
were often also its political leaders. Of course, leaders largely
determined the way in which their towns were perceived by outsiders; they had to be very careful about presenting a positive im-
age of their towns to the wider world so that they could be seen
as places for potential investment and settlement. So it was very
important for the leaders of new Illinois communities to at least
pretend to be in control of their own local political systems. But
developing a core of leaders was often difficult in an environment
in which large portions of the population were transient or in
which investment opportunities came and went with the advanc-
ing frontier. However, each successful town was able to develop
and maintain a core group of people for whom individual achieve-
ment coincided with community institution building. In fact, historians of Illinois towns have often attributed the growth of a
leadership core to the very frontier conditions that often challenged the establishment of authority. Richard S. Alcorn, in his
study of Paris in Edgar County, Illinois, used a "survival of the
fittest" argument in which the competition for success in the local
economy assured a core group of merchants who provided an "island of stability" for the rest of the town. Don H. Doyle credited
longevity as the essential factor for a group to gain social control
and establish institutional and associational networks for maintaining order in his study of Jacksonville, Illinois. Timothy R. Mahoney related the development of local leadership to a town's

changing function in a regional economy in his study of Mississippi River towns, including Galena, Rock Island, Quincy, and Alton.[3]

All of these factors certainly contributed to the formation of leadership cores in frontier towns. And the degree to which leaders did or did not coalesce had a great impact on the types of institutions that they helped to develop. But the development of a core group of leaders, a necessity for the long-term survival of any town, did not mean that the members of the leadership need necessarily have seen eye to eye with one another on all issues of community concern. The differences between the ways in which leaders in Belleville, in Ottawa, and in Galesburg dealt with and felt about one another during the political realignment of the 1850s, therefore, also had a great deal to do with the final local political and governmental institutions that they built in their communities.

Belleville, Ottawa, and Galesburg were incorporated cities by the time of the 1860 presidential election. Belleville had received a charter in 1850, which was rewritten in 1859 when, according to Theodore J. Krafft (the city's first mayor), "the increasing population, business and wants of the city made new ordinances and regulations necessary for the public good." All three cities elected a mayor annually. Belleville had eight aldermen, two for each of four wards, all of whom served one-year terms. There was also a register (clerk), a marshal, a treasurer, an attorney, an assessor, a collector, a surveyor and engineer, a weigher, a market master, and a street inspector, all of whom were appointed by the city council (the mayor and the aldermen). Before receiving its city charter, Belleville was incorporated as a village under a general Illinois town incorporation law in 1819 and was governed by a five-member board of trustees.[4]

Belleville's 1850 city incorporation was motivated by urbanization pressures and did not automatically signal a change in leadership for the town. The village board had traditionally been controlled by the American-born members of the community even though they quickly became outnumbered by immigrant Germans after the European political rebellions of 1848, but not in city hall. Krafft, the first mayor, was German-born, but he was a refugee of earlier European rebellions and had been in America since 1833. In fact, all of the 1850s mayors of Belleville were either ethnic

Americans (John W. Pulliam, Joseph B. Underwood, William C. Davis, James W. Hughes, and Peter Wilding) or early arriving Germans (Krafft and Edward Abend). In addition, three of the four aldermanic posts in 1850 (the city switched from one to two aldermen per ward in 1854) were filled by ethnic Americans John R. Nolen, Peter Wilding, and David W. Hopkins. The fourth ward was represented in the city council by Francis Stoltz, a Bavarian merchant who was also a member of the board of directors of the Belleville and Illinoistown Railroad.[5] Of course, Belleville residents were also governed by the usual slate of elected county officials (clerks, treasurers, coroners, judges, sheriffs, deputies, censors, school commissioners, and notaries), and the city had a great deal of influence over county politics in the 1850s. Bellevillians filled nineteen of St. Clair County positions in 1860; however, half of the Belleville county offices were held by ethnic Americans.[6]

Throughout the 1830s and 1840s, both Belleville and St. Clair County voters overwhelmingly supported Democratic over Whig candidates. The southern native-born American settlers identified closely with the antielitist Democratic politics of the Jackson administration. The early Germans (particularly those who had fled authoritarian regimes in their homelands during the 1850s) also approved of the egalitarian rhetoric of the Democratic Party. The bulk of the Germans who arrived after the 1848 revolutions in Europe also chose to vote for Democrats. But they did so not just because they were in favor of the party's idealism but because they were against the Whig Party, which had a nativist reputation. So both groups of Germans in Belleville, those who arrived in the 1830s and those who immigrated after 1848, supported the same Democratic candidates, but for very different reasons.

At first glance, it looks as if Belleville's reaction to the realignment of party politics during the 1850s closely resembled that of St. Clair County and the rest of Illinois. Before the Republican ascendancy, in the 1848 presidential election, Belleville and the rest of St. Clair voters were twice as likely to be Democrats than Whigs, casting two-thirds of their ballots for Democratic presidential candidate Lewis Cass and one-third for Whig candidate and eventual president Zachary Taylor (see table A-16). In 1856 when the Republicans first fielded a presidential candidate in the person of John C. Frémont, St. Clair and Belleville voters again lined up similarly, casting ballots for the same candidates within three percentage points of the same totals, again for the eventual loser, Frémont. Finally, in 1860, both the county and the city residents voted for winning candidate Lincoln, again by very similar percentages, although Belleville was slightly more Republican than the county as a whole.[7]

Most historians of the party realignment and the Republican ascendency of the 1850s in Illinois give at least some credit to influential German Americans, especially to those of St. Clair County and Belleville. However, St. Clair County in 1860 was not exceptional among southern Illinois counties in voting for Lincoln over Douglas. Four other southern Illinois counties—Madison, Bond, Coles, and Edwards—voted Republican in the 1860 election. All of the remaining forty-two counties south of Springfield voted Democratic. It is surprising, however, that Belleville's touted German Republican leaders were unable to convince more than the slimmest majority of their countrymen to vote for Lincoln in 1860. Given that over three-quarters of Belleville's voters were German-born or first-generation German Americans at the time of the election, it is unusual that their leaders were not able to influence a greater number.[8] Clearly, something was happening on the local political level that did not fit the national picture of Belleville as the center of German Republicanism.

The question of whether or not to ratify the 1848 constitution was the first political issue over which the leaders of Belleville disagreed. In the early 1840s, members of both the Democratic and Whig Parties throughout the state had supported the calling of a convention to write a new Illinois constitution. The original 1818 document was viewed as inadequate after two decades, particularly in regard to the state's banking system and the unchecked powers of the legislature that resulted in the internal improvement schemes and financial disasters of the late 1830s. Illinois voters approved the calling of a convention in 1842, but the General Assembly did not act upon their wishes. Voters again approved the calling of a convention in 1847, and this time the assembly complied.[9]

Election of delegates to the constitutional convention took place on April 19, 1847. Four delegates were elected from St. Clair County. Three of the delegates, George Bunsen, William C. Kinney, and John McCulley, were from Belleville. Bunsen was a German from Frankfurt who had emigrated in 1833. He and Kinney voted against the final constitution. Both had campaigned for election to the convention as opponents of the call to restrict the franchise of Illinois inhabitants who were not citizens. The final 1848 constitution differed from the 1818 document in four major respects. First, it limited the power of the legislature vis-à-vis the executive by reducing the number of members of the General Assembly from 262 to 100. Second, despite Bunsen's and Kinney's protests, suffrage was limited to those residents who were citizens. Third, the General Assembly would be allowed to pass laws for township organization within counties. And fourth, the constitution prohibited state banks but allowed the establishment of "corporations or associations with banking powers." A popular vote on the constitution was taken on March 6, 1848. St. Clair County voters passed the document 1,593 to 948. On the separate "Negro" clause also submitted to the public, which would bar free blacks from settling in the state, 95 percent of St. Clair County voters approved.[10]

Belleville's vote for the constitution was exceptionally close: 540 for and 411 against. The constitution vote was the first in which Belleville residents split their votes down the middle, a trend that was to continue throughout the 1850s and into the 1860 presidential election. It was also the first time that an outside issue had divided the local leadership of Belleville along ideological lines. The most popular German leader in town, state representative Gustave Körner, openly opposed the adoption of the constitution. Some of his objections were pointed toward the more technical aspects of the new document. He did not think that state elections should be moved from August to November because presidential politics would interfere with state politics. He also did not agree that legislative and judicial salaries should be reduced. Körner's major concern, however, was shared by convention delegates Bunsen and Kinney. They did not believe that immigrants should have to become citizens before being allowed to vote. After the adoption of the new constitution, immigrants in Illinois had to wait at least five years until they could acquire American citizenship before they could vote. Belleville's major proponent of the 1848 constitution was William H. Underwood, a young Democratic lawyer who immediately became a candidate for a new circuit judgeship created by the constitution. Körner, Bunsen, and Kinney were also members of the Democratic Party.[11]

So with the 1848 constitutional vote, Belleville's political leaders were already divided over issues that both transcended and reflected political and ethnic loyalties. Almost all of the town's leaders, including Körner, Kinney, Underwood, future United States senator Lyman Trumbull, and future Belleville mayor Edward Abend, were Democrats in 1848.[12] But instead of supporting thé 1848 constitution en masse as did the rest of St. Clair County, Belleville's leaders were divided over the specifics of the document and influenced their followers to split their votes down the middle. In Belleville, it seems, ideological and personal convictions were more important to the town leaders than was party loyalty, a trend that would continue during the time that the entire national political system was being realigned.

The surviving record of Belleville's public political debates of the 1850s on both local and national issues can be found in its local newspapers from the period. Belleville's newspapers, like most in the state before the Civil War, were blatantly political. In fact, many early Illinois papers, including those in Belleville, Ottawa, and Galesburg, were founded as mouthpieces for national political campaigns. Their publishers and editors covered local events and activities, to be sure; but they were also used, more often than not, by local leaders to relate their views on local and wider national political concerns. Of course, Belleville had both English- and German-language papers beginning as early as the 1840s. The *Belleville Advocate*, the acknowledged leading English sheet of the 1850s, began publication as the *Representative and Belleville News* in 1837. It became the *Advocate* in 1840 when it was purchased by James L. Boyd and John T. C. Clark, who bought the newspaper in order to express their support of Democratic presidential candidate Martin Van Buren. From its inception, the *Advocate* often contained gestures of friendship toward the town's German community. It accepted advertisements from German businesses and even called for the publication of a new Democratic statewide newspaper, *The Messenger of Liberty*, in the German language.[13]

In 1844 and again in 1848, the editors of the *Advocate* (R. K. Fleming in 1848) continued to support Democratic candidates for both state and national offices. The newspaper also continued to publish articles of interest to the German element in the community; for example, one complimented the "Industry of Germans," and others praised the thoughts and actions of Gustave Körner. They also gave extensive coverage to the 1848 political revolts in Prussia, Austria, and Bavaria and asked that Belleville's Germans lend financial support to the revolutionary cause. By 1852, the *Advocate*, published by E. H. Fleming and edited by Mr. Niles, was still Democratic, supporting first Stephen A. Douglas, then Franklin Pierce for the presidency. The editors also endorsed Körner for lieutenant governor of Illinois on the Democratic ticket (against Whig candidate J. L. D. Morrison from Quincy) and continued to cater to the German population by publishing articles on "German Social Life," "German Universities," and poetry (in English) about the old country.[14]

But the *Advocate*, by 1852, was beginning to reflect the economic, political, and ethnic dissension that was developing in Belleville. Niles's editorials condemned state senator Morrison for his role in the city's loss of the Illinoistown and Vincennes Railroad. His newspaper supported Democratic state representative Adam Snyder and Belleville businessman F. B. Fouke who tried to convince the railroad company to reconsider their decision not to build to the city. Niles wrote that "our people will not suffer themselves to be trampled upon by a few St. Louis aristocrats, by land speculators, and New York contractors." The reference to aristocrats was aimed toward Whigs in general, while the "land speculators" remark was a none-too-camouflaged attack upon Morrison himself, who owned land north of Belleville where the railroad ultimately located. But Niles was not only anti-Whig. He also lambasted the hierarchy of the Catholic church, calling it a "Religion Against Freedom."[15] So by 1852, the *Belleville Advocate* had been the mouthpiece of the leaders among Belleville's ethnic-American community. Democratic in politics, they were solidly anti-Whig and vehemently anti-Catholic. At the same time, they were supportive of the liberal German community, especially non-Catholics, such as Körner, who supported and participated in Democratic politics and were also anti-Catholic. But their friendship with the German community was tempered by their stand against a religion professed by many of the new immigrants to Belleville.

There were other English-language newspapers in Belleville before 1852, but they were eventually consolidated by the *Advocate*. The *St. Clair Banner*, edited from 1834 to 1847 by D. W. Galwicks and by constitutional convention delegate William C. Kinney, was also Democratic in its politics. It became the *Times* in 1847 and was edited and published by Galwicks and Louis Tramble. The *Banner-Times* differed from the *Advocate* before 1852 in two very important respects. First, it was noticeably less constrained in its political pronouncements against Whiggery than the *Advocate*, attacking Henry Clay and Zachary Taylor for their aristocratic lifestyles. The *Times* was also vehemently opposed to the nativist rhetoric of the Whigs, calling them "Know Nothings" as early as 1848. Thus, it was more populist and potentially more appealing to the working-class German immigrants of Belleville. And it was much less friendly than the *Advocate* toward the successful early German immigrant community, making fun of the "Grey-headed Germans" of Körner's generation, also in 1848.[16]

The *Times* was purchased in 1849 by "Harvey and Walker" and was later edited by G. A. Harvey. The new owner changed the name and the political leanings of the newspaper to the *Illinois Republican*. It became the first Belleville newspaper to support a Whig candidate, endorsing Winfield Scott for president in 1852. The *Republican* also defended Senator Morrison against the attacks from the *Advocate* and supported him for lieutenant governor against Körner in 1852. And just as the *Advocate* began to express its anti-Catholic rhetoric when large numbers of German Catholics arrived in Belleville, the *Republican* expressed dismay at the *Advocate*'s religious stand. An editorial of August 18, 1852, asked that members of both parties "desist from the sinful effort to mix up in indiscriminate and inexplicable confusion, matters sacred and secular."[17] Thus, the Republican became an unusual hybrid: a newspaper that was Whig but also antinativist.

The history of Belleville's early German-language newspapers is much simpler than that of its English-language papers. Before the national political realignment and the wave of German immigration of the 1850s, the German-language publications were published and edited by a small clique of the early immigrants, known as the *Dreissiger*. *Der Freiheitsbote für Illinois* was founded in 1840 by Gustave Körner, who wrote almost all of its articles. Körner openly admitted that the newspaper was published to support the reelection of Democrat Martin Van Buren over Whig William Henry Harrison for president, and he claimed that its issues would cease at the end of the campaign. As promised, the last number was issued on October 28, just before the November elections. Körner's major concern was that he "sharply attack nativism," and he wrote page after page of biting anti-Whig editorials. He also occasionally wrote and solicited articles on nonpartisan subjects, most of which concerned the special interests of Germans; he warned about fake naturalization papers and told about the potentially important "place of Germans in the United States." Körner also published advertisements for German Democratic organizations in St. Clair County in which his fellow émigrés— Joseph Abend, Theodore Engelmann, Johann Mäder, Louis Zöchler—participated.[18]

The *Freiheitsbote* was followed by the *Illinois Beobachter* in 1844. Also a Democratic campaign paper supporting James Knox Polk for president, the *Beobachter* was published by Körner's friend and fellow 1830s revolutionary, Theodore Engelmann. Most of the editorials, however, were probably written by Körner whose concerns were still centered on the evils of nativism. His specific targets were Whig candidate Henry Clay and former Illinois governor and Belleville's candidate for United States representative, John Reynolds. But the *Beobachter* was more concerned with local issues than the *Freiheitsbote* had been. In particular, Körner and Engelmann were troubled over the prospect that so many of their fellow Germans would vote for the Whig Party in the November 1844 elections. Körner's concerns were first expressed as a protest against the method in which the Whig Party was attempting to communicate with the German immigrants in America. He claimed that the biographies of Henry Clay that were circulating among the Germans by the summer of 1844 were translated badly. The August elections for state offices put a real scare into Engelmann and Körner; two of the three winning candidates for Illinois representative from St. Clair County were Democrats (Amos Thompson and Samuel Anderson), but Whig candidate J. L. D. Morrison won the third spot. The vote totals in Belleville—546 for Thompson, 586 for Anderson, and 557 for Morrison—were so close that it was clear that some Germans in the district voted for Morrison even though he was a Whig. And even though Reynolds lost his bid for election to the United States House of Representatives to Alton Democrat Robert Smith, he received more votes than Smith in Belleville (517 to 546). During the next three months, the *Beobachter* ran article after article on what its editor described as the "deceptive nativism" of the Whig Party in Illinois and the nation, emphasizing that the party's representatives wanted to deny Germans the right to vote.[19]

In 1845, Engelmann sold the *Beobachter* to Bartholomew Hauck of Quincy, who renamed it the *Stern des Westens* in that city. Engelmann repurchased one-half of the business from Hauck in 1849, and together they moved the newspaper back to Belleville as the *Belleviller Zeitung*. Hauck was the publisher and Engelmann was the editor. Gustave Körner resumed writing editorials for the newspaper as soon as it was returned to Belleville. In its new incarnation, the *Zeitung* became more a local newspaper than a political mouthpiece. It gave equal coverage to both Catholic and Protestant German activities in town. One of its early missions was to inform the German-American community about the revolutionary activities in Germany and France. In fact, the events of the late 1840s in Germany pulled the immigrant community of Belleville together more quickly than had any of the national political campaigns. Already in January 1849, members of the early arriving group were joining organizations to send moral and material support to the fighters overseas. Men who had had nothing to do with active political campaigns joined groups whose purpose was distinctly prorevolutionary: Francis Stoltz, Jacob Fleischbein, Friedrich Kämpf, Thomas Scholl, Jacob Knöbel, George Leberer, Fritz Bierheller, John Maus, and Theodore Krafft, as well as Körner and Engelmann. By 1852, the *Zeitung*, now owned and edited solely by Hauck, endorsed the candidacy of Democrats for both state and national offices, including Körner for lieutenant governor. Its major concern was, once again, the nativism expressed by the Whig candidate for president, Winfield Scott. In local issues, the newspaper was clearly interested in the liberal causes professed by the *Dreissiger*. Editor Hauck was a leading advocate of improvements in Belleville's schools as early as 1852. And news of the activities of the freethinking *Deutsch-protestantischen Kirchengemeinde* (German Protestant Church) reached the pages of the newspaper much more readily than those of the other church groups.[20]

So before the political realignment of the 1850s, Belleville's newspapers reflected the town's ethnic, political, and religious leadership. Almost all of the leaders of both the American and German communities were Democrats, including Körner, Engelmann, Bunsen, Kinney, Trumbull, Snyder, and Fouke, whose views were expressed by both the *Advocate* and the *Zeitung*. But there were an increasing number of professed Whigs, including Underwood and editor Harvey of the *Republican*. There was also a bridge being built between some members of the American community and the early arriving Germans. But that same group of American-born leaders, represented by the *Advocate*, was also anti-

Catholic, a stand that put them squarely against the new group of German immigrants. At the same time, another group of Americans, this time represented by the *Republican*, was antinativist. The *Zeitung*, of course, was not openly anti-Catholic (it even blamed the Whigs for making religion a question in political campaigns at all), but it was clearly more closely connected with the liberal Protestant church in town than with either the German Lutherans or the German Catholics. Therefore, even before the confusing political battles of the 1850s, the leadership of Belleville was already internally divided. But their political loyalties were not drawn along ethnic or religious lines, making it difficult to predict their moves in the years to come.

By 1856, Belleville's two English newspapers and one German newspaper had been joined by three more papers, one English and two German. The sudden growth in news was a direct result of the changing national and, in this case, local political climate. The *Belleville Advocate*, the only surviving English-language paper after the 1852 campaign, had switched its support to the new Republican Party by 1856. E. H. Fleming, who edited the newspaper in 1849, returned to the *Advocate* along with James S. Coulter, in 1854. They were replaced by Niles in 1856, who stayed until 1857. Then Collins Van Cleve and T. C. Weeden owned and edited the newspaper until 1860. A new paper (the successor to the Whig *Illinois Republican*), the *St. Clair Tribune*, appeared in 1854 under the management of John B. Hay and was edited by William Orr. Orr was replaced by G. A. Harvey (once the editor of the *Republican*), who remained until 1857 when the newspaper was sold to Van Cleve and Weeden of the *Advocate*. The *Tribune* supported Democratic candidates in the 1856 elections. Another Democratic newspaper, the *Belleville Democrat*, was founded in 1857 by W. F. Boyakin and H. L. Fleming. E. R. Stuart and W. H. Shoupe took over ownership in 1859 and hired G. A. Harvey, who began editing his third newspaper in Belleville.[21]

The *Advocate* maintained close ties to the German-language *Zeitung* throughout the 1850s. Both newspapers were accused by their competitors of espousing the views of "Black Republicans."[22] The *Advocate*, like the *Zeitung*, supported the establishment of a large-scale public school system, and they were both connected with other reform movements that their rivals saw as threatening to the local and national society, especially temperance and antislavery. Both newspapers also trumpeted the exploits of Gustave

Körner and had reputations of assumed cultural superiority. The *St. Clair Tribune* editor, in fact, poked fun at the views of the *Zeitung* and the Republicans for being un-American and said that Körner occupied "a sort of 'Wandering Jew' position in politics" for his unwillingness to declare himself officially as a member of the Republican Party in 1856. However, unlike their predecessor, the *Illinois Republican*, the *Tribune* and the *Democrat* were not at all anti-German. In fact, the editor of the *Tribune* praised the editor of the German Democratic newspaper, the *Deutscher Demokrat*, for his "correct views of the true genius of the American Union and its galaxy of States." In another editorial, the *Tribune* editor lambasted the *Monroe Democrat*, a German paper in Waterloo, Illinois, for assuming the failure of the cabbage crop on the American Bottom was of particular concern to German Americans; "the 'son of a Hessian,' " he wrote, "[has] no right to say that the cabbage failure is as bad news for the Dutch, as the potatoe failure is bad news for the Irish!"[23]

By 1860, Belleville's English-language newspapers were representative of the split in the ethnic-American segment of the community. The *Advocate* and its editors (especially Niles) spoke for those in town who were most concerned with the abolition of slavery and the maintenance of a high moral order. The *Tribune* and the *Democrat* represented the views of those Americans in town who had remained with the Democratic Party and were most concerned with the preservation of states' rights and individualism. The *Advocate* was still reaching out to the early arriving Germans, particularly to Körner, who saw the issue of slavery as more important than even nativism. The *Tribune* and the *Democrat*, both edited by G. A. Harvey, however, were the champions of the other segments of the German population—the Catholics and the Lutherans—who were members of those groups that did not possess the economic wherewithal to compete with the Americans or the early Germans.

The developments in Belleville's German-language newspaper story during the 1850s closely resembled that of the English-language sheets. Between 1852 and 1856, the *Belleviller Zeitung* had changed editors five times and had switched from a Democratic to a Republican loyalty. Theodore Engelmann was replaced as editor in 1853 by Franz Grimm, a fiery man who traveled from the editorship of one Belleville paper to another during the 1850s. After four months, Grimm quit the *Zeitung* and went to Tennessee to edit the *Stimme des Volkes* in Memphis. He was succeeded at the *Zeitung* by August Kattman. Owner Bartholomew Hauck then hired Hermann Fiedler to replace Kattmann in 1854. Hannibal Seylern replaced Fiedler, and Dr. F. Wenzel took over in 1855. In March 1856, Wenzel quit to publish the new *Belleviller Volksblatt* (edited by Louis Didier), and Grimm returned to the *Zeitung*. The *Volksblatt* also supported Republican candidates, but only after Didier left to edit the new *Deutscher Demokrat*. In 1857, Grimm took over at the *Volksblatt*, and W. Vollraith replaced him at the *Zeitung*. Hauck sold out to Friedrich Rupp in 1858. Rupp then formed a partnership with Wenzel at the *Volksblatt*. The *Volksblatt* was merged with the *Zeitung*, and Grimm became the editor once again, this time until 1861. Didier had moved from the *Volksblatt* to the *Deutscher Demokrat* in July 1856. The *Demokrat*, published by G. A. Harvey (who had also edited the *Illinois Republican*, the *St. Clair Tribune*, and the *Democrat*), supported Democratic candidates. At the end of 1856, Harvey sold out to August Ruoff and J. Winter. Ruoff replaced Didier as editor. The *Demokrat* ceased publication in 1857.[24] Clearly, there were more than political factors involved in these maneuvers. There appears also to have been concern, especially by Didier, to provide an organ for the nonelite German population.

So by the 1860 elections, the only remaining German-language newspaper in Belleville was, once again, the *Zeitung*. Shortly after the 1856 elections, it had either consolidated with or outlasted its competitors, the *Volksblatt* and the *Demokrat*. But the vote totals in the 1860 elections for president, in which the German residents split between Lincoln and Douglas (as they had on the late 1850s school controversy), prove that the *Zeitung* still did not represent the thoughts of all of the city's German leadership. The arguments surrounding the 1856 election and the acrimony expressed by the publishers and editors of the three newspapers would remain for years to come. The editor and writers of the *Volksblatt*—which began as "a weekly paper, devoted to politics, literature, and agriculture"—were deeply concerned that they not be connected with the anti-immigrant American, or Know-Nothing, Party, as had the national Republicans in 1856.[25]

The *Zeitung* was too mainstream Republican for the likes of Wenzel, Didier, and frequent contributor Dr. Theodore Hilgard (one of the earliest German immigrants of the 1830s), who wanted to show that Germans could indeed vote for Republicans without sacrificing their loyalty to their own people. Didier changed his mind and went to the *Demokrat*. The *Zeitung*, for its part, was apparently oblivious to the charges of nativism by the *Volksblatt*, and later, the *Demokrat*. In fact, the *Zeitung* was practically a German-language version of the *Advocate*, printing articles on the benefits of moderate drinking (although it was officially against the "Maine Law") and the openness of the Republican Party to Germans. The editors were very much influenced by the views of Körner, whose endorsements for local candidates appeared in its pages. But once Wenzel quit and distanced himself from the *Zeitung*, its new editors paid more attention to the charges that there was a connection between the Republicans and the Know-Nothings. In August 1856, editor Grimm tried to recoup the German vote by emphasizing that "Catholics might, with good conscience, support the Republican party."[26]

But the editors of the *Deutscher Demokrat* knew better. Didier launched a continuous barrage of accusations of elitism and nativism against the *Advocate*, the *Zeitung*, the *Volksblatt*, Körner, Friederich Hecker, New England Puritans, and Republicans of all varieties. At one point, the *Demokrat* poked fun at both Körner's and Hecker's "consciences," writing that Hecker was now replacing Körner "as an American martyr."[27] Therefore, even though the *Zeitung* remained as the only German-language newspaper in 1860 Belleville, the sentiments expressed by the other editors in 1856, particularly the *Deutscher Demokrat*, had not diminished. The *Advocate* and the *Zeitung* represented the views of the moralistic Americans and the freethinking Germans. The *Demokrat* spoke for that part of the German population that felt alienated by the Republicans and was becoming closely aligned with the ethnic Americans who were put off by the high tone of both the *Advocate* and the *Zeitung*.

So if its newspapers represented the state of leadership in Belleville, the town must have been a rather acrimonious place in which to live during the 1850s. The leaders' views that were expressed in the newspapers, of course, need not have affected the general population in the city. But an examination of the membership of the parties in Belleville shows that the fractured leadership in the city did affect party loyalty among the inhabitants. Belleville was a politically volatile town during the 1850s with party membership divided along religious and economic lines. City politics were not dominated by either Republicans or Democrats, and city elections were not even supposed to be apolitical. At least four of the town's twenty officeholders in 1860 were members of the Republican Party, and four were Democrats. At least eight of the officeholders were Germans—five from Bavaria, one from Hanover, one from Baden, and one from the Rhineland. At least two of the Democrats were Bavarians.

Two-thirds of Belleville's known Republicans were Germans, but Bavarians and Badenese members were only one-sixth of the party—even though they were more than one-fourth of the city's population in 1860. Ninety-seven percent of the Republicans were either professionals or commercial men, but two-thirds were Germans, with the Hessians and the Prussians making up the majority. Only one laborer could be identified as a member. The six Bavarians and Badenese who were members all had commercial positions. The Democrats held the mayor's office from 1853 until 1860 when incumbent Peter Wilding lost to Republican newspaper editor Franz Grimm. Wilding was an ethnic-American, but at least six of the eight aldermen in 1860 were Bavarians, at least three of whom were also Democrats. The Republican Party in Belleville took great pains to dissociate itself from the national American, or Know-Nothing, Party of the middle of the decade. While certainly nativist, the American Party was particularly anti-Catholic. And since most of Belleville's south Germans were Catholics, they might have been more easily convinced to support the Democratic party in both local and national races.

So Belleville's political structure during the 1850s was similar to its economic and cultural divisions. The town's financially advantaged native-born and *Dreissiger* Hessian minorities were unable to control the political dynamics of the town. Yet numerical superiority itself was not enough to grant control to the other ethnic Germans. The Bavarians and the Badenese were politically separate from the Americans and Hessians and were mostly Democrats. In short, Belleville was as heterogeneous politically as it was economically and demographically. Party membership during the 1850s political realignment was the same as that reflected by the town's leaders in the local newspapers. The town's leaders and their politics divided along economic and religious lines in a city where local government positions were contested with the same competitive fervor as national politics. This competition among the leaders made Belleville's governmental system one that allowed for maximum participation and found room for any and all views along the political spectrum.

Ottawa was incorporated as a city in 1853. As in Belleville and Galesburg, its people elected a mayor annually. The city voters annually elected ten aldermen from five wards until 1855 and, thereafter, four from each of seven wards. Ottawa's remaining city officials—clerk, treasurer, assessor, collector, surveyor, street supervisor, and marshal—were appointed by the city council (the mayor and the aldermen). Before receiving its city charter, Ottawa was incorporated as a village in 1839; and, like Belleville and Galesburg, it was governed by a five-member board of trustees.[28]

Ottawa voters had little influence over LaSalle County politics in the 1850s even though their town was the seat of justice. Only three Ottawans held county offices in 1860, and the town was represented in the Illinois General Assembly by people for whom it did not vote. The town's voters continually rejected the U.S. representative from the Illinois third district, Owen Lovejoy, the abolitionist whose brother Elijah was a martyr to the cause in Alton in 1837. Presidential vote totals in Ottawa would not support the notion that any sort of political realignment took place in the nation; the town electorate backed the Democratic candidates in all of the national elections from 1848 to 1860, even voting for Stephen Douglas over Abraham Lincoln. But in LaSalle County as a whole, voters switched their allegiance from the Democrats of the Second Party System to the Republicans of the Third Party System (see table A-17). Ottawa vote totals show that the town's electorate flirted with the Republican Party, supporting Democrat James Buchanan over John C. Frémont by only eight votes in 1856. However, by 1860, the city had swung decidedly back to the Democrats and to Douglas.[29]

The close presidential votes in Ottawa reflect the fact that the city's leaders were divided over politics during the 1850s. They and the populace of the town argued constantly about both local and national matters, all of which were colored by the political loyalties of the combatants. By the end of the decade, the town's leaders had constructed a local political system that struck a balance between the economic interests of the Democrats and Republicans. They agreed to disagree on political issues while maintaining a united front in support of the town's economic interests.

However, Ottawa's leaders did not capitulate to a purely majoritarian solution to their factionalism as did those in Belleville. In Ottawa, political loyalties did not coincide with the economic or cultural divisions within the town. Political allegiances among the leaders were more often determined by ideological concerns than by economic or cultural ones. As a result, the leaders were both incredibly acrimonious during campaigns and amazingly conciliatory when elections were concluded. The editor of the Democratic *Ottawa Free Trader*, William Osman, for example, called the local Republicans "Lincolnpoops" in one 1858 tirade against his political opponents and then, in 1860, recommended that the public patronize the new grain and lumber warehouse of the town's leading abolitionist (and supporter of Lincoln), John Hossack, because he considered Hossack "one of our most liberal and enterprising citizens." And Thaddeus Hampton, the editor of the *Ottawa Republican*, the town's Republican paper, could be just as mean-spirited and then friendly toward the Democrats. He called the supporters of losing Democratic mayoral candidate, John V. A. Hoes, "Nebraskals" in 1856 but later wrote that he was "sorry to see [Hoes] beaten." Elections in Ottawa were usually closely contested and, more often than not, the local political parties alternated terms in the town's offices.[30]

The editorial leanings of Ottawa's early newspapers reflected the development of political sensibilities in the city, just as they did in Belleville. The earliest paper, the *Republican*, was published in 1836 by John V. A. Hoes (the mayoral candidate in 1856) for the presidential campaign of Democrat Martin Van Buren. The first permanent newspaper, the *Illinois Free Trader*, was founded in 1840 by George F. Weaver and John Hise. Like the *Republican*, it was a Democratic paper in which the editors supported "internal improvements" that would "add to our commercial greatness." Weaver and Hise were opposed to a national bank, abolition, the tariff, and "monopolies of all kinds." From its first issue, the *Illinois Free Trader* published regional and national news of particular concern to Ottawans; it was an early opponent of stricter rules for the enfranchisement of immigrants and paid special attention to the needs of the local Irish population—including news about LaSalle County's St. Patrick's Day celebrations. In 1841 the *Free Trader* editors changed the name of their newspaper to the *Illinois Free Trader and LaSalle County Commercial Advertiser*, perhaps in an attempt to attract more readers and business from outside Ottawa.

Weaver and Hise continued to print news for the residents of the town, paying added heed to the progress of the Illinois and Michigan Canal and the early efforts to build a railroad near Ottawa. Beginning in 1842, the newspaper ran notices about and praised the actions of members of the temperance movement in the United States and reported a meeting of the LaSalle County Washington Temperance Society in Ottawa. In June 1842, Weaver and Hise dissolved their partnership, and Weaver ran the newspaper on his own; he wrote that while he still supported Democrats for political offices, he would not "blindly support any measure, merely because it originated with the democratic party." Weaver was not specific about his objections but was clearly opposed to the extreme capitalist stance of John C. Calhoun. By the fall of 1842, Weaver was supporting Whig candidates for political offices in Illinois and in the nation.[31]

In August 1842, Weaver was bought out by a new partnership of former owner Hise and William Osman. Both of the new owners were from Pennsylvania and would remain in Ottawa throughout the 1840s and 1850s. The newspaper was renamed the *Ottawa Free Trader* and continued publication until 1916. Osman edited and published the paper with various partners—including his brother Moses—into the 1880s, though he turned over complete control to George and Julius Avery from 1853 until 1856. Osman and his newspaper remained supporters of the Democratic Party throughout his life; he backed local, state, and national Democratic candidates through the political transformation of the 1850s.[32]

The *Free Trader* was joined in Ottawa by another newspaper, the *Constitutionalist* in 1844. Published by James Lowry and H. E. Gedney, the new paper was founded to support the presidential candidacy of Henry Clay, and its editors continued their support of Whig candidates into 1848 when it endorsed Zachary Taylor for president. The *Constitutionalist* was vehemently opposed to John C. Calhoun's call to dissolve the Union in 1850. The Whig paper was succeeded in 1852 by the *Ottawa Republican*, which was published by former schoolteacher Thaddeus Hampton and J. W. Kelley until 1857. Hampton published the *Republican* with H. C. Ruffington from 1857 to 1859 and then ran it by himself until 1864. It supported Whig candidate Winfield Scott for the presidency in 1852, and Republicans John C. Frémont in 1856 and Abraham Lincoln in 1860. The *Republican* would continue until 1890 when it was combined with the *Ottawa Times*. Ottawa's only other newspapers before or during the 1850s were the short-lived *United Irishman* of 1848 and the *Ottawa Zeitung* and the *LaSalle County Demokrat* of 1858. The *Irishman* was run by immigrant Maurice Murphy who published it to advocate the dissolution of the union of England and Ireland, which "has not enriched England, but made Ireland poor indeed." Murphy's newspaper was financed by a consortium of influential Ottawans, John Champlin, Abner Fisher, Joseph Glover, and John V. A. Hoes; none of the backers was Irish except, perhaps, for a man named Ryan. In the fall of 1858, C. H. Froese edited the *Zeitung*, a German-language Republican campaign newspaper. At about the same time, the *Demokrat*, published by P. A. Cramer, moved from Mendota to Ottawa.[33]

Throughout the decade preceding the Civil War the *Ottawa Free Trader* and the *Ottawa Republican* were used by their editors to convey the opposing political views of the city's leaders. Time after time, about issue after issue, the two newspapers used national political arguments to back the proponents of opposing policies for Ottawa's development. In fact, the newspapers clearly connected the city's political leaders with those of the national parties, and the editors connected stands on local decisions with the philosophical underpinnings of national leaders. The *Free Trader*'s editor during most of the 1850s, William Osman, was an ardent defender of Stephen Douglas and of popular sovereignty. While he personally did not believe that slavery was morally defensible, he wrote that people ought not to break the laws of the United States in order to rid the country of the terrible institution. Osman was backed by merchant William Reddick, the Presbyterian immigrant from Ireland who rose to become the town's wealthiest citizen.[34]

Osman and Reddick were called upon to defend their position in 1860 when the eight "Ottawa rescue martyrs" were tried in federal court for breaking the Fugitive Slave Law. In September 1859, three slaves belonging to Richard Phillips of New Madrid, Missouri, fled across the Mississippi River into Illinois. One of them, Jim Gray, was caught and imprisoned in Union County in the southern party of the state. A man named Root applied for a writ of habeas corpus, arguing that the Illinois Fugitive Slave Law had been declared unconstitutional by the state supreme court and that Gray was being held illegally in Jonesboro. Failing to acquire a writ in Union County, Root traveled to Ottawa where he sued and acquired one before Justice John Dean Caton of the Illinois Supreme Court. In response to the writ, the Union County sheriff sent Gray to Ottawa with jailer Isaac Albright. Along his route to the north, Gray was seized by his owner, who had obtained a federal writ, under the United States Fugitive Slave Law. In Springfield, a federal judge told the jailer Albright to carry out both writs and to bring Gray back to Springfield if the escaped slave were set free in Ottawa. In Ottawa, Justice Caton ruled that Gray should be set free under Illinois law, but he ordered Albright to take him to Springfield to carry out the federal writ. Upon hearing Caton's ruling, Ottawa resident James Stout stood up and said, "Darkey, if you want your liberty, run." Albright reportedly seized Gray's arm but was unable to hold on to him when several people pushed him toward the back door of the courthouse. Gray was whisked out the door and into a waiting carriage. He was taken out of town and eventually escaped to Canada.[35]

The federal grand jury in Chicago indicted eight townspeople in the Ottawa case. Abolitionist John Hossack, who would later run for governor of Illinois (on an Abolitionist ticket), was tried, convicted, sentenced to ten days in jail, and fined $100; James Stout also got ten days and paid $50; Claudius B. King was imprisoned for a day and was fined $10; the cases of the others, Joseph Stout, Hervey King, C. B. King, Smith, and Campbell, were either dismissed or were never prosecuted.[36]

The reaction of the people of Ottawa to the case was divided along political lines. Republicans Edwin S. Leland, Burton C. Cook, Oliver C. Gray, and Joseph O. Glover served as volunteer counsel to Jim Gray at the Ottawa hearing. Democrat (and former *Free Trader* publisher) Julius Avery, the mayor at the time of the incident, represented Isaac Albright, the jailer. A week after Gray's escape (or rescue), a public meeting was held at the courthouse in Ottawa; the participants drafted a series of resolutions in which they condemned the incident in Ottawa and John Brown's raid on Harper's Ferry. Among those who attended the meeting were many of the town's leading Democrats: Aaron B. Smith, T. L. Dickey, Levi Mason, Jacob Fry, Jared B. Ford, Jeremiah Strawn, George E. Walker, Moses Osman, Thomas Clancy, George L. Shuler, Albert F. Dow, as well as Mayor Avery and *Free Trader* editor Osman. Two months after the incident, William Reddick, newly elected president of the Ottawa Democratic Club, wrote to the *Republican* to defend the resolutions and to make it clear that he supported their views. "Instead of approving the late Ottawa rescue," he emphasized, "I most distinctly disapprove of it in all its parts. I believe all illegal acts of the kind can do no good, but a great amount of harm." He went on to say, "I believe the doctrine of popular sovereignty, so ably sustained by Judge Douglas . . . is correct in principle, and, when fully established and fairly carried out, will be the means of finally adjusting the slavery question."[37]

Ottawa's local politics were so closely connected with national politics that the newspapers sometimes saw entanglements that probably flattered the town by exaggerating its importance in the wider political world. During the campaign for mayor in May 1856, the editor Hampton at the *Republican* charged that the city's Democrats were spreading false stories among "certain classes of citizens to take votes from the Republican candidate," Edwin S. Leland. Hampton charged that the Democrats were telling the Irish population that the Republicans were anti-immigrant. He also insisted that "Douglas had issued instructions to his favorites . . . here to get him endorsed in Ottawa if possible, in order to help his prospects in the Cincinnati convention" for the Democratic presidential nomination. Leland won the election with 389 votes over his Democratic opponent, John V. A. Hoes (the editor of the original Democratic *Republican* in 1836), who garnered 363.[38]

Actually, local elections in Ottawa had more to do with local issues than with presidential candidates even though the town's politicians gladly identified with their political comrades at the national level. From its incorporation in 1853, the city elections in May were colored by partisan wrangling over local issues. The first two mayors, William Hickling in 1853 and 1854 and George N. Norris in 1855, were both Democrats. Hickling, an emigrant from England and a wealthy wholesale grocer, was elected after a protracted fight among Ottawans over whether or not to incorporate as a city. After losing the Illinois Central Railroad's crossing of the Illinois River to their downriver rival, LaSalle, in 1851 and then finally getting the Rock Island and Chicago Railroad to build through town, Ottawans voted not to incorporate in 1852.[39]

In February 1853, editor Osman at the *Free Trader* reported and supported the Illinois General Assembly's charter of the Illinois River Bridge Company. According to the charter, the ten stockholders in the company (John V. A. Hoes, Lorenzo Leland, David Strawn, Milton H. Swift, Alson Woodruf, Henry F. Eames, the Norris and Fisher law firm, the Walker and Hickling grocery company, Richard Thorne, and John F. Nattinger) would advance

$1,000 to $1,500 apiece toward the construction of a bridge across the Illinois River at Ottawa. In addition, the town of Ottawa would either subscribe $10,000 and become a primary owner of the bridge or lend $10,000 worth of credit (at a lower interest rate than for an individual) to the company toward the construction of a bridge. Either way, the taxpayers would pay $10,000. If the bridge were to be publicly owned (under the first option), the voters of Ottawa would first have to vote to incorporate themselves. But even if the city charter were again rejected, the bridge could be built with credit lent to the company by the village. Temperance advocate Hampton, at the *Ottawa Republican*, went to great pains to point out that the construction of the bridge did not depend upon the incorporation of the city; he was against incorporation because a city government could vote to regulate (but allow) liquor sales, a privilege that he opposed since the village trustees had already voted to prohibit sales of intoxicating beverages. Osman supported incorporation because, even though personally for temperance, he was an advocate of regulated liquor sales in the city. Both editors, however, supported the construction of the bridge. This time the voters approved incorporation by a vote of two to one in April 1853.[40]

While the editors of the *Free Trader* and the *Republican* may have stressed that the city charter vote revolved around the temperance question, the people soon showed that they had had another issue on their minds when they went to the polls; it seems that they wanted a bridge across the Illinois River and they were willing to pay for it. But the public had been confused at the time of the vote. Some later said they thought that approving incorporation meant the new city would contribute $10,000 to the bridge's construction and that the structure would be free for the use of travelers. But the village trustees had already agreed to lend $10,000 worth of credit to the bridge company a week before the incorporation vote so the new charter was not needed to finance construction. The newly elected city council, with Mayor Hickling (a bridge company stockholder) at its head, decided not to reverse the village trustees' decision. Both editors supported the council's action, although Hampton was more leery of the prospect of a private company than was Osman. The public, however, did not agree. A "Southsider" offered an alternative plan. He suggested that Ottawa take $10,000 in stock and that the towns south of the Illinois River subscribe $1,000 each. He argued that the people ought to be the stockholders. Instead, the company took the town's $10,000, built the bridge and began deriving profits from tolls after two years.[41]

The question of the bridge's ownership, however, would not go away. The structure was destroyed by a spring freshet in 1857. Osman, at the *Free Trader*, suggested that the city ought to help the company repair it. But the company did not want the city to lend any more money for the bridge. Instead, it repaired the bridge on its own and raised tolls to pay for the work. This brought another round of protest from the public. "South Side" wrote to the *Free Trader* and suggested that the people of Ottawa ought to build a free bridge—this time on the east side of the Fox River—that would compete with the company's structure. Hampton, at the *Republican*, suggested that the city buy the company bridge rather than build a new one. Osman claimed to be neutral on the subject. Despite the agitation and complaints, chiefly from those who lived south of the river, to make the Illinois River bridge free, the company held on to it for another decade.[42]

Finally, in January 1869, a committee appointed by the Ottawa City Council recommended that the council apply to the General Assembly for permission to levy a tax to purchase one-half of the Illinois River bridge; three of the five committee members were either members of the Ottawa eleven or were stockholders in the Illinois bridge. But the committee also reported to the council that the principal stockholders in the bridge were not willing to sell to the populace. The council voted in January 1869 to ask the General Assembly for permission to buy the bridge anyway. Ottawans agreed to pay $31,200 for the Illinois River bridge, but only if the surrounding townships would pay an additional $11,000. Voters in the other townships would not pay so the company refused to sell. In 1871, the city of Ottawa contracted with the Canton Bridge Company to build an iron bridge across the Illinois, which the city purchased in 1878. The owners of the original bridge were left with a wooden white elephant.[43]

Even though the bridge question began as a political issue and resulted in the election of William Hickling to the mayor's office in 1853, it did not divide the leaders of Ottawa in a way that prevented them from working with one another. In fact, the ten stockholders in the Illinois River Bridge Company were from both of the town's political parties: Hoes, Leland, Norris, Walker, and Hickling were all Democrats; Strawn, Woodruf, and Thorne were

Republicans. Norris and Fisher, whose law firm was a stockholder, split their political loyalties; Norris was a Democrat and Fisher was a Republican. The final stockholder, John F. Nattinger, did not reveal his political leanings.

The largely Yankee ethnic makeup of the bridge company is reflective of the way in which Ottawa's leaders were politically divided, yet economically united. They did not let their political differences stand in the way of social and financial friendships, even though their various philosophical stands caused some nasty public bickering. However, the split between the Democrats and the Republicans among Ottawa's leadership caused a volatility in local government from which the city would suffer. Beginning with the election of George N. Norris on an anti-Know-Nothing platform in 1855 and continuing until the end of the decade, control of the city's government swung back and forth between the two parties. In the process, the public's patience was tried again and again.[44]

In 1856, when Democrat John V. A. Hoes ran for mayor against Republican Edwin S. Leland, the populace was divided over the issue of liquor licenses. In September 1855, the city council passed a liquor law that prohibited the sale of alcohol in Ottawa, even though the state's voters had rejected prohibition in June. By the city elections the following May, some citizens had agitated to repeal the ordinance. Leland and editor Hampton, at the *Republican*, advocated the repeal of only that part of the law that prohibited beer sales. Hoes and Osman, at the *Free Trader*, opposed a "lager beer" ordinance because, they argued, the entire liquor law ought to have been eliminated. "It is the opinion of many of the best of Temperance men," wrote Hampton, "that the prohibition of beer is unnecessary." Osman accused the Republicans of "hypocritically recommending lager beer in public." Leland won the mayor's race, but only by a 389 to 363 count. At the first meeting of the city council after the election, "Free Beer" became the law in Ottawa. Hampton explained that the "Nebraska minority [on the council was] against it." Osman countered that "if beer [is] free, let gin and rum be free also."[45]

By the fall of 1856, the Republicans had lost their slim majority in the city. Democrat James Buchanan polled eight more votes for president than Republican John C. Frémont in Ottawa. Hampton tried to explain the outcome by charging that there were a "large number of illegal votes . . . in the city." He also intimated that the Democratic win was possible because, unlike the "masses of intel-

ligent, industrious freemen" and "the Germans [in town who] did
nobly [vote] for freedom," most of the Irish voters were not able
to break "loose from the party that has so long cajoled them." It
was not the first or the last time that the *Republican* bemoaned the
votes and the political strength of the Irish of Ottawa.[46]

In May 1857, Democrat George E. Walker was elected mayor;
he defeated William Cogswell, another Democrat who ran as an
independent candidate. When Walker and the Democrats won, the
city council promptly repealed the ordinance that prohibited liquor and voted to license alcohol sales. Osman was pleased; however, he opposed licensing because he thought that "moral sua-
sion" was the best way to convince Ottawans not to drink.
Hampton opposed the council's repeal of the ordinance and also
opposed licensing because, he argued, "with a license law, drinking assumes more the air of respectability." Both editors had arrived at the same position on the licensing issue, but they had
come from very different directions.[47]

The 1858 city elections centered on the public perception that
Ottawa's taxes were too high. The Republicans accused Walker's
Democratic administration of cronyism and bad fiscal management. They pointed to the promised purchase of new equipment
for the fire companies as one case in which the Democrats had
tried to buy adherents to their party. The Republicans must have
been persuasive; their mayoral candidate, Joseph O. Glover, beat
Democrat N. B. Bristol by an unprecedented 230 votes. Hampton
was surprised at Glover's margin of victory and admitted that
"party lines were disregarded, especially among the Irish citizens." He went on to say that he did not believe "our adopted citizens will ever have cause to regret the course they took. . . . This
time, they let their better judgment take precedence."[48]

The Republicans did not have long to savor their victory or to
persuade many Irishmen to stay with the party. Mayor Glover sat
on the platform in support of Abraham Lincoln at the debate with
Douglas in Ottawa in August, but his presence was not enough to
assure Lincoln's victory in town. Ottawans voted by more than
200 votes for Democratic candidates—Ottawa's William Cogswell
and S. C. Collins from Grundy County—for the Illinois House of
Representatives. However, the Republican candidates for the General Assembly—A. Campbell and R. S. Hick—won in the whole
of LaSalle County. (The representatives would, in turn, vote in the
United States senatorial race for Stephen Douglas.) The vote in

Ottawa, 1,483 strong, was the largest turnout in the town's history. The election was not a good sign for the Republicans of Ottawa. When the city elections were held the next year, the electorate continued to flex its political muscles in large numbers. The school board elections in March brought out an unprecedented 978 voters and put an end to increased spending on the high school courses in Ottawa. Hampton, at the *Republican*, opined that the "Retrenchment" ticket had won the school election because the Democrats had promised that "Irish 'Schoolmarms' would be employed in the schools." That and other promises by the opposing party, he wrote, accounted for the "unusually heavy vote from a class of voters who have hitherto kept away from school elections." Editor Osman, at the *Free Trader*, applauded the outcome of the election.[49]

Hampton correctly identified the growing strength of the Irish voters in Ottawa, and he did not like what he saw. He intimated that the Democratic leaders in town were also unhappy with the changing profile of their party. When the Democrats met to nominate a candidate for mayor in April, they adopted a new procedure. Instead of voting as a whole for hopefuls as they had in the past, the new candidate was to be nominated by a meeting of delegates from each of the seven wards. This, according to Hampton, was to prevent the nomination of William Cogswell, "the choice of the Irish population." The Democrats, of course, denied the accusations but chose Julius Avery (the former publisher of the *Free Trader*) as their nominee. Hampton called Avery "a very fine young man though his political associations are bad." Despite his questionable political judgment, Avery ran unopposed and was elected mayor with 964 votes. Various write-ins garnered 8 votes.[50]

After the 1859 city elections, the Republicans of Ottawa gave up any hope of regaining political control of the city. In the 1860 mayoral race, Democrat David Walker beat Republican John Armour, 688 to 449. In the fall, Douglas carried the town over Lincoln in the presidential race by a substantial majority, 740 to 597, even though the rest of LaSalle County voted for Lincoln. The Democrats, now largely a party of the Irish population of Ottawa, went on to dominate local politics for the next decade. The frontier leaders of the town continued to run for office and to dominate the economic life of the town, but they would soon fade into the political background.[51]

Ottawa's leadership during the crucial decade of the 1850s created a governmental system that allowed, and even encouraged, lively debates between people with differing political ideas and philosophies. Political disagreement among the Yankee elite, however, did not hamper the vitality of their economic and social relationships. And neither did cultural identity determine political affiliations. The leadership was willing to subjugate the importance of local political disagreements to their other interests in town. To the elites, politics was a matter of philosophy alone; philosophies were based upon wider questions than city ordinances and school board elections. Local political concerns were connected with national issues to such an extent that it was impossible for the town's officials to develop a coherent local political agenda. But the philosophies of the leadership were so evenly divided between the Democrats and the Republicans that neither party could control the city long enough to implement its ideological agenda; the leaders spent more time campaigning to defeat their opposite numbers than actually governing the city and developing its institutions.

The mass of Ottawa's citizenry during the 1850s, however, did not appreciate the philosophical games that its leaders were playing with the local government. Fed up with the inefficiency of the Yankee system, the voters, and especially the large Irish population, went to the polls and seized control of city hall for the Democrats. And the Democratic leadership, in their turn, built an infrastructure that met the demands of the Irish, to whom they had become politically beholden.

Prior to becoming a city, Galesburg received a town (village) charter and was governed by a five-member board of trustees in 1842; before then Galesburg officially existed as an adjunct to Knox College, which received its charter from the state in 1837. The incorporation of the Town of Galesburg was simply a housekeeping maneuver on the part of the college leadership; college officials immediately became town trustees, and college rules and ordinances dealing with individual behavior were transferred wholesale to the town.[52] Galesburg received its city charter in 1857. As in Belleville and Ottawa, voters in the city elected a mayor for a yearlong term. However, there were only six aldermen, one for each ward, also elected annually. All of Galesburg's city officers—clerk, treasurer, assessor, attorney, police magistrate, marshal, surveyor, engineer, and street commissioner—were elected in the annual April polling. The switch to city government again did not signal a drastic change in political leadership since many of the same men who operated Knox College also ran for and won seats in the new city government. Harry Sanderson, the first mayor of the city of Galesburg, was a Knox College graduate.

The town and the city of Galesburg had many fewer sympathizers and much less influence in Knox County politics and government than Belleville and Ottawa had in St. Clair County and LaSalle County, respectively. Galesburgers held only three county offices in 1860. Likewise, Galesburg voters did not participate in the 1850s political transformation in the United States to the same degree as those in Belleville and Ottawa. They gave lukewarm support to Whigs in 1848, split their votes between Democrats, Whigs, and Free-Soilers in 1852, and then switched to overwhelming support of Republicans in 1856 and 1860 (see table A-18). Galesburg voters were eventually more adamant in their support of Republicanism than the rest of the Knox County; in 1856, three-quarters of the city's electorate voted for Republicans. And while no figures are available for the 1860 election in Galesburg, the confidence expressed by the editor of the *Galesburg Democrat*, C. J. Sellon, just before the election hints that Lincoln received at least three-quarters of the city's vote. The rest of Knox County was less supportive of Lincoln and might easily have swung the county into the Democratic column if not for the number of Galesburg voters. The city's Yankee leadership was able to use its numerical strength within the area to affect both the political climate and the county's economic and cultural aspirations. However, Galesburg's reputation as a center of radical Republicanism was not always appreciated by the people in surrounding towns and drew criticism from the editors of nearby newspapers. For example, the editor of the *Monmouth Review* in neighboring Warren County labeled members of Galesburg's "Black Republican party" as "desperadoes and blood-thirsty factionalists."[53]

Galesburg's differences with its neighbors may have been a reflection of the attitude with which its leaders approached politics. They did not identify local issues solely in terms of national debates because they assumed that a town's government should exist not only to maintain law and order but also to help shape the moral health of the community. In Galesburg, local politics could be entirely separated from national issues because, according to the leadership, the town's governors and their actions were responsible for the behavior of their own people. Such a patriarchal political view made it possible for people who disagreed strongly on local matters to cooperate fully in securing votes for a single national candidate. And Galesburg's leaders certainly had their fair share of disagreements, particularly over the control of Knox College and the degree to which the college should set the rules for the moral behavior of the townspeople. But instead of channeling the energy of their local arguments into national politics, Galesburg's local leadership structure and, therefore, its local political system encouraged the public airing of disagreements but did not allow them to travel past the city limits.

In Galesburg, leaders may have changed their national party loyalties over time, but they did so en masse and, therefore, brought their followers with them. Galesburg's earliest political leaders, those who were also the leaders of Knox College, were members of the Liberty Party. One hundred sixty-two votes were cast in Knox County in the 1844 election for party candidate James G. Birney. It is likely that the great majority of those votes (10 percent of the county total) were cast in Galesburg since Knox College president Hiram H. Kellogg was a vocal supporter of Birney in 1840. If the 162 Liberty votes cast by Knox County residents in 1844 were all from Galesburgers, then the entire town electorate supported the party (the village contained only 500 people in 1844). By 1848, when Knox County voters cast 20 percent of their votes in the presidential election for Free-Soil candidate Martin Van Buren, most of the Galesburg leadership had switched to that party and had brought most of the town's voters with them. Knox College's second president, Jonathan Blanchard, was an ardent abolitionist and was a supporter of the Free-Soil Party in the late 1840s.[54]

Galesburg's early newspaper history is much simpler than either Belleville's or Ottawa's, but it also reflects the state of leadership in the young community. The earliest sheet (other than the two competing Knox College student newspapers, the *Knox Intelligencer* and the *Northwestern Gazeteer*) was the *News-Letter*, published during the late 1840s and early 1850s. No copies of the *News-Letter* survive, but it was said to reflect the type of leadership structure that existed in Galesburg at the time. It was published by a Mr. Fish, George Lanphere, and W. S. Gale, each of whom wrote about their respective political parties—the Whigs, the Democrats, and the Free-Soilers—all in the same newspaper. (Lanphere remained a Democrat throughout the 1850s and was Stephen Douglas's host when the Lincoln-Douglas debate was held in Galesburg in 1858.) By August 1850, however, the three agreed to avoid mention of political subjects in their newspaper.[55]

Galesburg's first openly political newspaper was the *Western Freeman*, published for a short while in 1853 by W. J. Lane, who used it to further the antislavery cause; it was one of only two Illinois newspapers outside Chicago to be recommended for reading by the American and Foreign Anti-Slavery Society. The *Freeman* was succeeded by the *Galesburg Democrat*, which began publication in January 1854, just one day after Senator Stephen Douglas announced his intention of introducing the Kansas-Nebraska bill. The new paper was published by Southwick Davis, a candidate for Knox County surveyor on the Free-Soil ticket and an 1846 graduate of the college, and W. H. Holcomb, president of the local Free Democratic committee. In its first issue, the editors of the *Democrat* made it clear that they were not running a town newspaper but that they would be the mouthpiece of the "Free Democratic Party of Central Illinois." The newspaper immediately became, however, the local communications medium and published items that were of interest to the Galesburg populace; it reminded readers when their railroad subscriptions were due, printed obituaries of prominent citizens, and announced the times and places for temperance meetings.[56]

Throughout the 1850s, the *Democrat* reported very little acrimony among the residents of Galesburg. And when it did, the issues among the combatants had little to do with disagreements over national political alliances. It was not that the people of Galesburg did not argue with or have prejudices against one another, but the positions expressed by leaders on local disagreements were not dependent on political affiliation. Galesburg's leaders spoke with one voice about basic national issues. They were antislavery and antinativist. Of course, by 1856, the *Democrat* and the Galesburg leadership were squarely supporting Republican presidential candidate John C. Frémont. But while Galesburg's leaders were certain that the new party was not antiforeign or anti-Catholic, they felt obliged to divorce themselves from the American (Know-Nothing) Party. In fact, the editor of the *Democrat*, C. J. Sellon, turned the accusations by opponents of Republicans around and accused the leaders of the American Party in 1856 of claiming to be antiforeign and anti-Catholic so that the Party could lure "honest men into the order," and Sellon claimed that its stand was "a cloak under which to hide its pro-slavery schemes." Obviously, Galesburg's leaders recognized that some of the loyalists of the Republican Party were also susceptible to nativist sentiments. And they had reason to fear that some of the town's Yankee majority might be lured into the Know-Nothing fold. Many of the American-born residents were known to be unsympathetic to the plight of one of the town's foreign elements, the Irish. Even the *Democrat* printed unflattering tidbits and commentaries about the lives and habits of the Irish railroad workers. One article from 1856 told of a "son of Erin" who stopped at a country inn and loudly demanded lodging for the night. "It was evident from his appearance and actions that he and liquor had been jolly companions throughout the day," the article concluded.[57]

Galesburg's dominant Yankees were far less patronizing toward the other large foreign group in town, the Swedish. In April 1856, the *Democrat* welcomed the publication of the *Hemlandet*, the new Swedish-language newspaper, and praised the town's Swedish population as "a very worthy and industrious portion of our community."[58] Apparently, both the editor and the readers of the *Democrat* saw no contradiction between their professed political stand on the question of nativism and their differing treatments of the Irish and the Swedish minorities. Indeed, national politics were so divorced from local concerns that nobody even saw the irony of having a newspaper called the *Democrat* in a Republican town.

Galesburg's local political disputes during the period of national realignment were also nonpartisan. In fact, other than the disagreements over the ultimate shape of the local school system (which was largely an internal struggle among the leaders of Knox College), there was only one major dispute involving a townwide issue during the late 1850s. After receiving its city charter from the General Assembly in February 1857, a rift developed over the mayoralty race to be held in April. Harry Sanderson, the Knox College graduate and town trustee, ran against A. D. Reed. (W. S. Gale, R. H. Whiting, and S. W. Brown had all turned down the chance to run for mayor, an unpaid position.) From its inception, the race was seen as a contest between the

proponents of the licensing of dramshops—Reed's supporters—
and those who would continue the village's prohibition of liquor—Sanderson's followers. In his campaign speeches, however,
Reed did not call for licensing. Instead, he talked about the need
for general "City Improvements," pointing out that there was a
need for a new city hall, a new market house, new sidewalks, and
trees on the city square. However, editor Sellon at the *Democrat*
saw through the ruse and wrote, "We are told . . . that *License* is
not the issue, but that the people are divided on the question of
City Improvements. . . . The people of Galesburg must decide on
Monday next what shall be the future of the city, and we sincerely
hope that every voter will resolve to make it such as every respectable citizen may be proud of at home and abroad." When
they went to the polls, the citizens elected Sanderson mayor with
431 votes to Reed's 217. On a separate ballot on the licensing issue, the people of Galesburg voted to be "respectable," 540 to 104,
and to keep the town dry. There were other disputes among the
leaders of Knox College. One pitted the loyalists of town founder
George Washington Gale against those of the second president of
the college, Blanchard, over the control of the board of trustees.
The internal squabbles were finally resolved in 1860 when Blanchard left town to become president of Wheaton College. Blanchard's antislavery commitment and speeches were apparently so
radical that some members of the Yankee leadership, including
Gale, could not meet his expectations.[59]

So like its newspapers, local Galesburg politics during the na-
tionally turbulent 1850s remained amazingly nonpartisan. The
town's leaders, connected as they were with Knox College, were
some of the most vocal proponents of radical Illinois Republicanism. But their internal squabbles, over either the leadership of the
college or over the morals of the city's residents, did not interfere
with the town's position on national issues. Neither, on the other
hand, did national politics become a factor in city politics. The
pages of the *Galesburg Democrat* reflected this obsession with presenting a unified face to the outside world even though the townspeople often disagreed with one another.

Galesburg's numerically superior Yankee group was able to coalesce around a common political philosophy even though it had
internal religious and cultural dissension. The town's political
structure during the 1850s was simple. It was a stronghold for the
Republican Party, which enjoyed a virtual monopoly in municipal

government. Even though Knox County as a whole fell into Abraham Lincoln's column in the 1860 fall elections, the city was more Republican than the rest of the county. While the county voted for Republicans at a rate of 63 percent—for all offices, president to coroner—the city voted Republican nearly unanimously. During the city elections in April 1860, eight of the eleven successful candidates—mayor, clerk, treasurer, assessor, police magistrate, city marshal, and two of four alderman—ran unopposed in nonpartisan races. But at least nine of the fifteen men who were either elected or were serving terms in city offices in 1860 were vocal members of the national Republican party. They openly participated in the city, county, and state conventions or were members of the "Republican Mechanics," a group of politically concerned artisans. All of the officeholders were from New England, New York, or Illinois except for J. C. Stewart, a baker from Scotland, who was elected mayor, and P. L. Hawkinson, a Swede, who was elected street commissioner. Hawkinson was referred to as a "Swede Republican" in the *Democrat*.[60]

One hundred eighteen of Galesburg's Republicans in the 1850s can be identified by nativity. Eighty-eight percent of the Republicans were native-born, far exceeding the proportion of natives in the town's population. And Yankees made up the bulk of the membership of the party. The foreign-born members of the party—two Scotsmen, four Englishmen, two Canadians, one German, one Irishman, and four Swedes—all followed craft, commercial, or professional occupations. The Irishman in the party, county treasurer George Davis, did not fit the typical profile of an Irish resident in Galesburg; he was a member in good standing of the "Total Abstinence Society," and he was a resident of Illinois for at least fifteen years.[61] Only three Republicans were from the laboring class and all three were native-born. Thirty-four of the Republicans could also be identified as church members; they were overwhelmingly Yankee in their religious leanings. Twenty Republicans were Congregationalists, three were Presbyterians, six were Universalists, one was a Baptist, two were Episcopalians, one was a Lutheran (Commissioner Hawkinson), and two were Swedish Baptists. Information on any of the few Democrats in Galesburg is difficult to find since there was no Democratic newspaper in the city.

Galesburg's local politics, then, were similar to its economic and social structures in that they were controlled by the dominant

Yankees. But the patriarchal leadership system did allow for at least limited participation by minorities who could fit the same economic or cultural profile as the majority group. The Irish population, however, who made up close to 14 percent of Galesburg's population, either did not wish or were not allowed to participate in local politics.

The politics of Belleville, Ottawa, and Galesburg during the 1850s were reflected by the towns' leaders in the local newspapers. Belleville's leaders were divided along economic, ethnic, and religious lines in a city where local government positions were fought over with the same fervor as national politics. Ottawa's leadership was divided politically and philosophically, but the men remained cohesive and friendly in their economic and social relationships. In Galesburg leaders were completely cohesive, and national politics was not allowed to interfere with local government. Belleville's residents developed a competitive political culture that encouraged maximum participation; men from all of the town's groups—ethnic Americans, early arriving Germans, Bavarians, Badenese, and Prussians—could express their views and concerns. In Belleville, politics were wide open and decisions were made according to the will of the majority. Ottawa's frontier political culture was also competitive, but it did not encourage the Yankee leadership to submit readily to the will of the majority. The town's economic elite recognized the necessity of cooperating with one another to secure Ottawa's place as an important trading center in northern Illinois and did not let their political differences stand in the way of economic prosperity. However, almost while the town's leaders were not looking, the large Irish population was able to play an important role in local government by supporting the Democrats in such large numbers that the Yankee leaders were forced to take their economic and social needs into account. Galesburg's political culture allowed for very little dissension. Its leaders discouraged national political disagreement and strove to maintain a method of consensual decision making. But in the process, the Yankees of Galesburg excluded the town's small Irish population while they welcomed the larger Swedish one into the fold.

Seven Conclusion

By 1861, when the nation's political leaders were gearing up for the Civil War, the people of Belleville, Ottawa, and Galesburg had passed through their frontier periods. The rates of population growth in the towns would never again reach the same levels as they had in the 1850s when Belleville grew by 155 percent, Ottawa grew by 192 percent, and Galesburg grew by 519 percent.[1] However, all three young cities continued to grow in population (each had nearly 20,000 inhabitants by 1900) and expanded to many times their original geographic areas. Bellevillians eventually annexed West Belleville, and their city extended all the way to the borders of Illinoistown (now East St. Louis) on the Mississippi River, nearly establishing a geographic link with their former rival city, St. Louis. Ottawa remained a leading economic focus of the Illinois River valley but continues to this day to compete with LaSalle-Peru for the dominant urban influence in the north-central portion of the state. Galesburgers seized the county seat away from Knoxville and went on to become one of the larger towns in western Illinois even though it remains geographically isolated from any metropolitan area.

Despite their continued growth, the residents of all three towns kept on operating within the framework of the economic, cultural, and political institutions that they had established during the 1850s. And the facilities that they built—their railroads, their schools, and the like—and their local methods of political decision making would sustain the communities for many years to come. During their frontier periods, citizens of Belleville, Ottawa, and Galesburg had defined the parameters within which local leaders were permitted to make decisions for their entire populations. And in so doing, they had staked their claims in the regional and national economy and had established cultural institutions that would be used to socialize the next generations into their unique town society.

142   The utter diversity of Belleville's economic, ethnic, and religious

leadership made it impossible for its residents to build and then maintain a political system in which a single group of elites could make uncontested and uncontrolled decisions about the future of the city. Ottawa's more even distribution of ethnic groups may have lulled its Yankee leadership into believing that they could keep control of the town, even while they disagreed with one another on moral and political issues; but the presence of a large minority population also made it impossible for the ethnic American elites to hold on to power in the maturing community. Galesburg's homogeneous population and leadership structure, however, permitted its elite group to maintain their power, and they did.

The people of all three of the frontier cities developed their political systems and built their communities during a time when national politics could not help but affect the outcome of local decision making. In Belleville, where national partisan issues had always dominated local politics, the fervor of the 1850s only served to emphasize and exaggerate the transition from a deferential to a competitive democratic system. Even before the realignment of national politics, Belleville's political leadership were in agreement over ideological issues; and when the demographic profile of the city changed with the immigration of many more Germans, ideology among the elites remained a more important factor in determining political loyalties than did common ethnic background. The sheer number of the new residents made it impossible for the initial leaders to maintain control of the city's politics. In Ottawa, where early national political arguments had both helped and hindered the economic development of the town, the Yankee leaders believed that political allegiances were more important than ethnic ones; they had built their fortunes by remaining loyal to the free trade policies of the early Democratic Party. But during the 1850s, some of those same leaders switched their loyalties to the Republicans and were just as adamant about their politics as those who remained with the Democrats. The entire Ottawa community suffered from the political contentiousness of the town's elites. In Galesburg, leaders had emphasized the need for nonpolitical decision making, even before the 1850s. And when they switched parties to support the Republicans, they did so en masse. They were, ironically, more interested in ideology than in maintaining party loyalty, which facilitated the construction of a deferential local governmental system. But in the charged political atmosphere of the 1850s, when national partisan issues pervaded local politics—as they did in Belleville and Ottawa—the electorate in those communities fractured on both levels and made local government even more competitive.

The histories of frontier Belleville, Ottawa, and Galesburg suggest that the transition from a deferential to a competitive method of decision making in the United States was a complicated phenomenon. It did not occur solely because national political concerns began to permeate the American countryside as a result of nineteenth-century improvements in communication technologies. Nor did the increasing number of immigrants in the country cause people only to vote according to their ethnic, religious, or class loyalties. The experiences of the people in the three towns suggests that a unique set of geographic and social developments in particular settlements was the most important factor in the construction of a local decision-making culture and a mature community.

In fact, the histories of these three Illinois towns suggest a typology of frontier community building throughout the United States. Such a model should take into account the complex web of factors that caused some people to construct towns in which leaders tended to be competitive (as they were in Belleville), or consensual (as they were in Galesburg), or both competitive and cooperative (as they were in Ottawa). Any town under study ought to be analyzed according to three factors that will influence its eventual political development. First, a new frontier settlement should be examined for the degree to which it was either integrated into or isolated from the regional and national economies that surrounded it. Second, each should be analyzed for its ethnic, class, and religious homogeneity or heterogeneity. And third, each community should be studied for the degree of political, economic, and cultural factionalism or cohesiveness among its leaders. Once a frontier settlement is placed along these three axes, it will be possible to make some generalizations about its development based upon a three-dimensional typology scheme.

If a town's structures tended toward one or the other end of all three axes, its people would display the competitive or consensual characteristics of places such as Belleville or Galesburg. That is, if a frontier town was integrated into the regional economy (with easy access to transportation and markets) from the beginning of its settlement period, if it was heterogeneous (with an ethnically diverse population), and if it had a factionalized elite structure (with the power to make political and economic decisions in the hands of different groups of men)—as in Belleville—then it would develop a more competitive decision-making style. If, on the other hand, a town was initially isolated from the regional economy, was fairly homogeneous, and had a leadership structure in which the same group of men made all of the important economic and political decisions—as in Galesburg—then it would keep a more deferential decision-making style during its frontier period. In most cases, however, it does not appear that settlers developed such drastically competitive or neatly consensual structures as they did in Belleville or Galesburg.

Frontier Ottawa did not look like either of the other two towns. Its leaders were certainly the beneficiaries of an immensely favorable economic situation when their town was founded on the Illinois and Michigan Canal in 1830, but that did not make their town completely competitive, as the economic circumstances did in Belleville. And the cultural dominance of the Yankee merchants who settled in Ottawa during the 1830s did not ensure that they would be served by a deferential populace, as it did in Galesburg. The relatively even distribution of the ethnic groups in the town, combined with the ideological factionalism of its leaders, produced a community that was neither competitive nor consensual. The people of frontier Ottawa created a method of democratic decision making that was both competitive and cooperative. And in their own way, they built a community that was the more usual type on the American frontier.

Appendix: Tables

Table A-1 Population Growth of Belleville, Ottawa, and Galesburg

Year	Belleville	St. Clair County	Ottawa	LaSalle County	Galesburg	Knox County
1800		1,225				
1810		5,007				
1820	150	5,248				
1830	200	7,078				274
1840	2,000	13,634	1,006*	9,348	324	7,060
1850	2,941	20,180	2,607*	17,815	672	13,279
1860	7,520	37,694	7,609*	48,332	4,953	28,663
1870	8,146	51,068	7,736	60,729	10,158	39,522

Sources: Margaret Cross Norton, ed., *Illinois Census Returns, 1810, 1818*, Collections of the Illinois State Historical Library, vol. 24 (Springfield: Illinois State Historical Library, 1935); U.S. Department of State, *Abstract of the Fifth Census of the United States, 1830* (Washington, D.C.: Printed at the Globe Office, 1832), pp. 36–37; Records of the Bureau of the Census, Federal Population Schedules, Sixth Census of the United States, 1840, LaSalle County, Illinois, Reel 63, National Archives, Washington, D.C. (microfilm in Newberry Library, Chicago); Records of the Bureau of the Census, Federal Population Schedules, Sixth Census of the United States, 1840, Knox County, Illinois, Reel 62, National Archives, Washington, D.C. (microfilm in Federal Archives and Records Center, Chicago); Records of the Bureau of the Census, Federal Population Schedules, Seventh Census of the United states, 1850, LaSalle County, Illinois, Reel 115, National Archives, Washington, D.C. (microfilm in Newberry Library, Chicago); U.S. Congress, Senate, *Preliminary Report on the Eighth Census, 1860*, 37th Cong., 2d sess., 1862 (Washington, D.C.: Government Printing Office, 1862), pp. 253–54; Records of the Bureau of the Census, Federal Population Schedules, Eighth Census of the United States, 1860, LaSalle County, Illinois, Reel 196, National Archives, Washington, D.C. (microfilm in Newberry Library, Chicago); U.S. Department of Interior, Census Office, *A Compendium of the Ninth Census, 1870* (Washington, D.C.: Government Printing Office, 1872), pp. 38–40; U.S. Department of Interior, Census Office, *The Statistics of the Population of the United States* (Washington, D.C.: Government Printing Office, 1872), pp. 23, 14; Arthur W. Dunn, *An Analysis of the Social Structure of a Western Town* (Chicago: University of Chicago Press, 1896), p. 34; Daniel J. Elazar, *The Politics of Belleville: A Profile of the Civil Community* (Philadelphia: Temple University Press, 1971), p. 70; John Reynolds, "The History of the City of Belleville," in *Revised Ordinances of the City of Belleville,*

149

150   *Appendix: Tables*

with the City Charter and Amendments . . . , pp. 5–33, rev. T. J. Krafft, (Belleville, Illinois: Printed by G. A. Harvey, 1862), p. 19; *History of St. Clair County, Illinois*

(Philadelphia: Brink, McDonough, 1881), p. 185; *Illinois Free Trader,* 19 June 1840, p. 2, col. 1.

*Includes residents of "South Ottawa."

Table A-2 Nativity of Independent Populations, 1850

Birthplace	Belleville #	Belleville %	Ottawa #	Ottawa %	Galesburg #	Galesburg %
Midwestern states	66	8.8	16	2.2	5	2.2
New England states	14	1.9	101	13.7	70	30.6
Middle states	53	7.1	253	34.3	109	47.6
Southern states	88	11.7	25	3.4	9	3.9
Other United States	0	—	0	—	0	—
Norway	0	—	8	1.1	0	—
Sweden	0	—	1	0.1	11	4.8
Ireland	11	1.5	193	26.2	3	1.3
England, Scotland, Wales	15	2.0	40	5.4	11	4.8
Germany	468	62.5	55	7.5	0	—
Switzerland	4	0.5	2	0.3	0	—
France, Alsace	23	3.1	28	3.8	0	—
Austria	0	—	0	—	0	—
Other foreign	0	—	9	1.2	1	0.4
Unknown	7	0.9	6	0.8	10	4.4
Total	749		737		229	

Sources: Records of the Bureau of the Census, Federal Population Schedules, Seventh Census of the United States, 1850, St. Clair County, Illinois, Reel 126, National Archives, Washington, D.C. (microfilm in Newberry Library, Chicago); Records of the Bureau of the Census, Federal Population Schedules, Seventh Census of the United States, 1850, LaSalle County, Illinois, Reel 115, National Archives, Washington, D.C. (microfilm in Southern Illinois University Library, Carbondale); Records of the Bureau of the Census, Federal Population Schedules, Seventh Census of the United States, 1850, Knox County, Illinois, Reel 113, National Archives, Washington, D.C. (microfilm in Newberry Library, Chicago). *Note:* Midwestern states comprise Illinois, Indiana, Iowa, Wisconsin, Michigan, and Minnesota; New England states comprise Maine, New Hampshire, Vermont, Massachusetts, Rhode Island, Connecticut; Middle states comprise New York, Pennsylvania, Ohio, and New Jersey; Southern states comprise Kentucky, Delaware, Virginia, Maryland, Arkansas, South Carolina, North Carolina, Missouri, Alabama, Georgia, Tennessee, Louisiana, Mississippi, Texas, and District of Columbia.

Table A-3 Nativity of Independent Populations, 1860

Birthplace	Belleville #	Belleville %	Ottawa #	Ottawa %	Galesburg #	Galesburg %
Midwestern states	131	6.2	87	4.5	64	4.5
New England states	17	.8	196	10.1	288	20.4
Middle states	101	4.8	577	29.7	521	36.9
Southern states	93	4.4	41	2.1	56	4.0
Other United States	0	—	0	—	2	—
Norway	0	—	19	0.9	1	—
Sweden	0	—	2	0.1	206	14.6
Ireland	45	2.1	535	27.6	122	8.7
England, Scotland, Wales	59	2.8	113	5.8	41	2.9
Germany (total)	1,418	67.5	256	13.2	70	5.0
Prussia	222	10.6				
Saxony	74	3.5				
Bavaria	340	16.2				
Baden	191	9.1				
Hesse	246	11.7				
Nassau	114	5.4				
Hanover	55	2.6				
Württemburg	59	2.8				
Other Germany	117	5.6				
Switzerland	63	3.0	12	0.6	0	—
France, Alsace	92	4.4	65	3.4	0	—
Austria	28	1.3	1	0.1	0	—
Other foreign	25	1.2	25	1.3	36	2.6
Unknown	27	1.5	11	0.6	4	0.4
Total	2,099		1,940		1,411	

Sources: Records of the Bureau of the Census, Federal Population Schedules, Eighth Census of the United States, 1860, St. Clair County, Illinois, Reels 224, 225, National Archives, Washington, D.C. (microfilm in Newberry Library, Chicago); Records of the Bureau of the Census, Federal Population Schedules, Eighth Census of the United States, 1860, LaSalle County, Illinois, Reel 196, National Archives, Washington, D.C. (microfilm in Southern Illinois University Library, Carbondale); Records of the Bureau of the Census, Federal Population Schedules, Eighth Census of the United States, 1860, Knox County, Illinois, Reel 195, National Archives, Washington, D.C. (microfilm in Center for Research Libraries, Chicago).
Note: Midwestern states comprise Illinois, Indiana, Iowa, Wisconsin, Michigan, and Minnesota; New England states comprise Maine, New Hampshire, Vermont, Massachusetts, Rhode Island, Connecticut; Middle states comprise New York, Pennsylvania, Ohio, and New Jersey; Southern states comprise Kentucky, Delaware, Virginia, Maryland, Arkansas, South Carolina, North Carolina, Missouri, Alabama, Georgia, Tennessee, Louisiana, Mississippi, Texas, and District of Columbia.

Table A-4   Nativity of Belleville Population, 1850

Birthplace	Number	Percentage of those given
Midwestern states	1,046	38.70
New England states	25	.90
Middle states	115	4.26
Southern states	182	6.74
Other United States	11	.40
Norway	0	—
Sweden	0	—
Ireland	16	.60
England, Scotland, Wales	26	.90
Germany	1,195	44.20
Switzerland	19	.70
France, Alsace	49	1.80
Austria	0	—
Other foreign	5	.20
Unknown	13	.50
Not given	239	
Total	2,941	

Source: Records of the Bureau of the Census, Federal Population Schedules, Seventh Census of the United States, 1850, St. Clair County, Illinois, Reel 126, National Archives, Washington, D.C. (microfilm in Center for Research Libraries, Chicago). *Note*: Midwestern states comprise Illinois, Indiana, Iowa, Wisconsin, Michigan, and Minnesota; New England states comprise Maine, New Hampshire, Vermont, Massachusetts, Rhode Island, Connecticut; Middle states comprise New York, Pennsylvania, Ohio, and New Jersey; Southern states comprise Kentucky, Delaware, Virginia, Maryland, Arkansas, South Carolina, North Carolina, Missouri, Alabama, Georgia, Tennessee, Louisiana, Mississippi, Texas, and District of Columbia.

Table A-5 Nativity of Belleville Population, 1860

Birthplace	Number	Percentage of those given
Midwestern states	2,891	38.60
New England states	30	0.40
Middle states	261	3.48
Southern states	432	5.76
Other United States	1	0.01
Norway	0	—
Sweden	1	0.01
Ireland	66	0.90
England, Scotland, Wales	136	1.80
Germany (total)	3,214	42.90
Bavaria	762	10.1
Hesse	543	7.2
Prussia	530	7.1
Baden	422	5.6
Nassau	252	3.4
Württemburg	144	1.9
Saxony	140	1.9
Hanover	135	1.8
Other Germany	286	3.8
Switzerland	153	2.00
France, Alsace	217	2.90
Austria	30	0.40
Other foreign	64	0.90
Unknown	0	—
Not given	25	
Total	7,521	

Source: Records of the Bureau of the Census, Federal Population Schedules, Eighth Census of the United States, 1860, St. Clair County, Illinois, Reels 224, 225, National Archives, Washington, D.C. (microfilm in Center for Research Libraries, Chicago).

Note: Midwestern states comprise Illinois, Indiana, Iowa, Wisconsin, Michigan, and Minnesota; New England states comprise Maine, New Hampshire, Vermont, Massachusetts, Rhode Island, Connecticut; Middle states comprise New York, Pennsylvania, Ohio, and New Jersey; Southern states comprise Kentucky, Delaware, Virginia, Maryland, Arkansas, South Carolina, North Carolina, Missouri, Alabama, Georgia, Tennessee, Louisiana, Mississippi, Texas, and District of Columbia.

Table A-6   Occupations of Nativity Groups, Independent Population—
Belleville, 1850

Birthplace	Profes- sional	Commer- cial	Propri- etary	Manu- facturing	Crafts	New/ Tech.	Un- skilled
Midwestern states	4	5	5	2	23	0	0
New England states	2	0	0	3	6	1	0
Middle states	6	4	1	6	18	2	0
Southern states	5	6	3	5	32	3	0
Other United States	0	0	0	0	0	0	0
Norway	0	0	0	0	0	0	0
Sweden	0	0	0	0	0	0	0
Ireland	0	0	0	1	3	0	0
England	1	1	0	0	5	1	0
Germany	18	19	52	47	212	0	3
Switzerland	0	0	1	0	2	0	0
France, Alsace	2	2	2	0	10	0	0
Austria	0	0	0	0	0	0	0
Other foreign	0	0	0	0	0	0	0
Not given	0	0	0	0	2	0	0
Total	38	37	64	64	313	7	3

Source: Records of the Bureau of the Census, Federal Population Schedules, Seventh Census of the United States, 1850, St. Clair County, Illinois, Reel 126, National Archives, Washington, D.C. (microfilm in Newberry Library, Chicago).
Note: Midwestern states comprise Illinois, Indiana, Iowa, Wisconsin, Michigan, and Minnesota; New England states comprise Maine, New Hampshire, Vermont, Massachusetts, Rhode Island, Connecticut; Middle states comprise New York, Pennsylvania, Ohio, and New Jersey; Southern states comprise Kentucky, Delaware, Virginia, Maryland, Arkansas, South Carolina, North Carolina, Missouri, Alabama, Georgia, Tennessee, Louisiana, Mississippi, Texas, and District of Columbia.

Table A-6 cont. on next page

Service	Super-visory	Govern-ment	Transpor-tation	Labor-ing	Miscel-laneous	Unknown	Total
0	0	1	5	12	1	8	66
0	0	0	1	0	0	1	14
0	0	2	5	2	0	7	53
0	0	2	4	4	1	23	88
0	0	0	0	0	0	0	0
0	0	0	0	0	0	0	0
0	0	0	0	3	4	0	11
0	0	2	0	4	0	1	15
0	0	2	13	63	0	39	468
0	0	0	0	1	0	0	4
0	0	1	3	3	0	0	23
0	0	0	0	0	0	0	0
0	0	0	0	0	0	0	0
0	0	0	0	2	2	1	7
0	0	10	31	94	8	80	749

Table A-7 Occupations of Nativity Groups, Independent Population—
Belleville, 1860

Birthplace	Profes-sional	Commer-cial	Propri-etary	Manu-facturing	Crafts	New/Tech.	Un-skilled
Midwestern states	12	22	6	4	31	4	1
New England states	6	0	0	0	4	2	0
Middle states	15	18	4	1	18	2	2
Southern states	6	9	6	3	17	0	1
Other United States	0	0	0	0	0	0	0
Norway	0	0	0	0	0	0	0
Sweden	0	0	0	0	0	0	0
Ireland	2	0	1	1	11	0	6
England	3	5	1	0	29	3	11
Germany (total)	43	74	155	136	416	26	34
Prussia	9	15	15	29	51	8	9
Saxony	4	3	11	11	18	2	0
Bavaria	8	13	38	26	100	2	6
Baden	2	6	24	16	61	1	7
Hesse	8	12	34	27	72	2	4
Nassau	3	7	9	11	36	6	3
Hanover	5	9	1	7	17	0	1
Württemburg	0	3	3	3	22	0	2
Other Germany	4	6	20	6	39	5	2
Switzerland	0	2	2	5	12	1	2
France, Alsace	0	4	12	6	21	2	1
Austria	1	1	2	6	9	1	0
Other foreign	1	0	2	0	4	0	1
Not given	1	1	4	0	1	0	5
Total	90	136	195	162	573	41	64

Source: Records of the Bureau of the Census, Federal Population Schedules, Eighth Census of the United States, 1860, St. Clair County, Illinois, Reels 224, 225, National Archives, Washington, D.C.

Table A-7 cont. on next page

Service	Super-visory	Govern-ment	Transpor-tation	Labor-ing	Miscel-laneous	Unknown	Total
0	2	5	4	13	26	1	131
0	1	1	0	1	2	0	17
3	3	3	4	13	18	0	101
0	0	5	2	17	27	0	93
0	0	0	0	0	0	0	0
0	0	0	0	0	0	0	0
0	0	0	0	0	0	0	0
0	1	0	2	15	6	0	45
0	0	0	0	3	4	0	59
13	3	7	71	304	134	2	1,418
0	0	0	14	55	17	0	222
0	0	0	0	19	6	0	74
6	0	2	18	86	35	0	340
1	2	1	8	50	12	0	191
3	0	1	14	36	32	1	246
1	1	2	8	16	10	1	114
0	0	0	3	8	4	0	55
0	0	0	4	14	8	0	59
2	0	1	2	20	10	0	117
0	0	0	2	28	8	0	63
0	0	0	9	28	8	1	92
1	0	1	0	5	1	0	28
1	0	1	0	5	4	6	25
0	0	0	0	11	1	3	27
15	10	23	95	443	239	13	2,099

(microfilm in Center for Research Libraries, Chicago).

Note: Midwestern states comprise Illinois, Indiana, Iowa, Wisconsin, Michigan, and Minnesota; New England states comprise Maine, New Hampshire, Vermont, Massachusetts, Rhode Island, Connecticut; Middle states comprise New York, Pennsylvania, Ohio, and New Jersey; Southern states comprise Kentucky, Delaware, Virginia, Maryland, Arkansas, South Carolina, North Carolina, Missouri, Alabama, Georgia, Tennessee, Louisiana, Mississippi, Texas, and District of Columbia.

Table A-8 Nativity of Ottawa Population, 1850

Birthplace	Number	Percentage of those given
Midwestern states	666	25.55
New England states	215	8.24
Middle states	763	29.27
Southern states	80	3.07
Other United States	0	—
Norway	35	1.34
Sweden	1	0.04
Ireland	529	20.31
England, Scotland, Wales	87	3.33
Germany	102	3.91
Switzerland	5	0.19
France, Alsace	81	3.11
Austria	0	—
Other foreign	34	1.30
Unknown	9	0.35
Total	2,607	

Source: Records of the Bureau of the Census, Federal Population Schedules, Seventh Census of the United States, 1850, LaSalle County, Illinois, Reel 115, National Archives, Washington, D.C. (microfilm in Newberry Library, Chicago).
Note: Midwestern states comprise Illinois, Indiana, Iowa, Wisconsin, Michigan, and Minnesota; New England states comprise Maine, New Hampshire, Vermont, Massachusetts, Rhode Island, Connecticut; Middle states comprise New York, Pennsylvania, Ohio, and New Jersey; Southern states comprise Kentucky, Delaware, Virginia, Maryland, Arkansas, South Carolina, North Carolina, Missouri, Alabama, Georgia, Tennessee, Louisiana, Mississippi, Texas, and District of Columbia.

Table A-9 Nativity of Ottawa Population, 1860

Birthplace	Number	Percentage of those given
Midwestern states	2,539	33.54
New England states	496	6.55
Middle states	1,824	24.10
Southern states	157	2.07
Other United States	4	0.05
Norway	65	0.86
Sweden	2	0.03
Ireland	1,340	17.70
England, Scotland, Wales	273	3.60
Germany	574	7.58
Switzerland	26	0.34
France, Alsace	179	2.36
Austria	3	0.04
Other foreign	85	1.12
Unknown	2	0.03
Not given	40	
Total	7,609	

Source: Records of the Bureau of the Census, Federal Population Schedules, Eighth Census of the United States, 1860, LaSalle County, Illinois, Reel 196, National Archives, Washington, D.C. (microfilm in Newberry Library, Chicago).
Note: Midwestern states comprise Illinois, Indiana, Iowa, Wisconsin, Michigan, and Minnesota; New England states comprise Maine, New Hampshire, Vermont, Massachusetts, Rhode Island, Connecticut; Middle states comprise New York, Pennsylvania, Ohio, and New Jersey; Southern states comprise Kentucky, Delaware, Virginia, Maryland, Arkansas, South Carolina, North Carolina, Missouri, Alabama, Georgia, Tennessee, Louisiana, Mississippi, Texas, and District of Columbia.

Table A-10   Occupations of Nativity Groups, Independent Populations—Ottawa, 1850

Birthplace	Profes-sional	Commer-cial	Propri-etary	Manu-facturing	Crafts	New/Tech.	Un-skilled
Midwestern states	1	1	0	1	5	0	0
New England states	9	21	2	11	37	7	0
Middle states	31	25	16	22	107	4	4
Southern states	4	6	1	0	7	0	0
Other United States	0	0	0	0	0	0	0
Sweden	0	0	0	1	0	0	0
Norway	0	2	0	0	5	0	0
Ireland	7	5	6	10	48	0	0
England	0	10	1	7	16	0	1
Germany	0	1	12	9	21	1	0
Switzerland	0	0	0	1	0	0	0
France, Alsace	1	0	5	9	5	0	0
Austria	0	0	0	0	0	0	0
Other foreign	1	0	1	0	7	0	0
Not given	0	1	0	0	1	0	0
Total	54	72	44	71	259	12	5

Source: Records of the Bureau of the Census, Federal Population Schedules, Seventh Census of the United States, 1850, LaSalle County, Illinois, Reel 115, National Archives, Washington, D.C. (microfilm in Southern Illinois University Library, Carbondale).

Note: Midwestern states comprise Illinois, Indiana, Iowa, Wisconsin, Michigan, and Minnesota; New England states comprise Maine, New Hampshire, Vermont, Massachusetts, Rhode Island, Connecticut; Middle states comprise New York, Pennsylvania, Ohio, and *New Jersey; Southern states comprise Kentucky, Delaware, Virginia, Maryland, Arkansas, South Carolina, North Carolina, Missouri, Alabama, Georgia, Tennessee, Louisiana, Mississippi, Texas, and District of Columbia.*

Table A-10 cont. on next page

Service	Super-visory	Govern-ment	Transpor-tation	Labor-ing	Miscel-laneous	Unknown	Total
0	0	0	4	2	0	2	16
0	0	2	3	1	1	7	101
0	2	0	9	14	1	18	254
0	0	0	1	3	0	3	25
0	0	0	0	0	0	0	0
0	0	0	0	1	0	0	8
0	0	0	0	0	0	0	1
0	0	0	4	94	0	9	193
0	0	0	0	4	0	1	40
0	0	0	1	8	0	2	55
0	0	0	0	1	0	0	2
0	0	0	0	6	0	2	28
0	0	0	0	0	0	0	0
0	0	0	0	0	0	0	0
0	0	0	0	3	0	1	7
0	2	2	22	137	2	55	737

Table A-11   Occupations of Nativity Groups, Independent Population—
Ottawa, 1860

Birthplace	Profes-sional	Commer-cial	Propri-etary	Manu-facturing	Crafts	New/ Tech.	Un-skilled
Midwestern states	7	12	5	3	32	3	1
New England states	2	24	24	19	77	5	1
Middle states	46	74	64	34	227	10	13
Southern states	5	2	6	1	16	2	0
Other United States	0	0	0	0	0	0	0
Sweden	0	4	0	2	5	0	0
Norway	0	0	0	1	0	0	0
Ireland	4	14	14	21	114	3	21
England	3	9	3	9	54	6	2
Germany	4	9	39	37	98	0	9
Switzerland	0	1	2	2	3	0	0
France, Alsace	2	0	11	3	23	0	3
Austria	0	0	0	1	0	0	0
Other foreign	2	1	2	0	9	0	1
Not given	0	1	0	0	5	0	0
Total	93	151	170	133	663	29	51

Source: Records of the Bureau of the Census, Federal Population Schedules, Eighth Census of the United States, 1860, LaSalle County, Illinois, Reel 196, National Archives, Washington, D.C. (microfilm in Southern Illinois University Library, Carbondale).
Note: Midwestern states comprise Illinois, Indiana, Iowa, Wisconsin, Michigan, and Minnesota; New England states comprise Maine, New Hampshire, Vermont, Massachusetts, Rhode Island, Connecticut; Middle states comprise New York, Pennsylvania, Ohio, and New Jersey; Southern states comprise Kentucky, Delaware, Virginia, Maryland, Arkansas, South Carolina, North Carolina, Missouri, Alabama, Georgia, Tennessee, Louisiana, Mississippi, Texas, and District of Columbia.

Table A-11 cont. on next page

Service	Super-visory	Govern-ment	Transpor-tation	Labor-ing	Miscel-laneous	Unknown	Total
0	0	1	2	15	0	6	87
0	1	7	4	2	0	12	196
0	2	6	33	27	1	40	577
1	0	0	3	1	0	4	41
0	0	0	0	0	0	0	0
0	0	0	4	0	0	4	19
0	0	0	1	0	0	0	2
10	0	1	17	258	0	59	535
1	0	1	2	18	0	5	113
1	0	0	1	47	0	10	256
0	0	0	0	4	0	0	12
1	0	0	0	13	0	9	65
0	0	0	0	0	0	0	1
1	0	0	1	6	0	2	25
0	0	0	0	2	0	3	11
15	3	16	68	393	1	154	1,940

Table A-12 Nativity of Galesburg Population, 1850

Birthplace	Number	Percentage of those given
Midwestern states	224	33.30
New England states	175	26.00
Middle states	150	22.30
Southern states	21	3.10
Other United States	0	—
Norway	0	—
Sweden	44	6.50
Ireland	6	0.90
England, Scotland, Wales	30	4.50
Germany	0	—
Switzerland	0	—
France, Alsace	0	—
Austria	0	—
Other foreign	10	1.50
Unknown	12	1.80
Total	672	

Source: Records of the Bureau of the Census, Federal Population Schedules, Seventh Census of the United States, 1850, Knox County, Illinois, Reel 113, National Archives, Washington, D.C. (microfilm in Center for Research Libraries, Chicago). *Note*: Midwestern states comprise Illinois, Indiana, Iowa, Wisconsin, Michigan, and Minnesota; New England states comprise Maine, New Hampshire, Vermont, Massachusetts, Rhode Island, Connecticut; Middle states comprise New York, Pennsylvania, Ohio, and New Jersey; Southern states comprise Kentucky, Delaware, Virginia, Maryland, Arkansas, South Carolina, North Carolina, Missouri, Alabama, Georgia, Tennessee, Louisiana, Mississippi, Texas, and District of Columbia.

Table A-13 Nativity of Galesburg Population, 1860

Birthplace	Number	Percentage of those given
Midwestern states	1,814	36.90
New England states	687	14.00
Middle states	1,151	23.42
Southern states	119	2.42
Other United States	2	0.04
Norway	4	0.08
Sweden	520	10.60
Ireland	297	6.00
England, Scotland, Wales	99	2.00
Germany	123	2.50
Switzerland	2	0.04
France, Alsace	2	0.04
Austria	2	0.04
Other foreign	71	1.44
Unknown	21	0.40
Not given	39	
Total	4,953	

Source: Records of the Bureau of the Census, Federal Population Schedules, Eighth Census of the United States, 1860, Knox County, Illinois, Reel 195, National Archives, Washington, D.C. (microfilm in Center for Research Libraries, Chicago). *Note*: Midwestern states comprise Illinois, Indiana, Iowa, Wisconsin, Michigan, and Minnesota; New England states comprise Maine, New Hampshire, Vermont, Massachusetts, Rhode Island, Connecticut; Middle states comprise New York, Pennsylvania, Ohio, and New Jersey; Southern states comprise Kentucky, Delaware, Virginia, Maryland, Arkansas, South Carolina, North Carolina, Missouri, Alabama, Georgia, Tennessee, Louisiana, Mississippi, Texas, and District of Columbia.

Table A-14   Occupations of Nativity Groups, Independent Population—
Galesburg, 1850

Birthplace	Profes- sional	Commer- cial	Propri- etary	Manu- facturing	Crafts	New/ Tech.	Un- skilled
Midwestern states	0	1	0	1	3	0	0
New England states	10	10	0	6	31	0	0
Middle states	14	7	2	4	42	2	0
Southern states	1	0	0	0	2	0	0
Other United States	0	0	0	0	0	0	0
Norway	0	0	0	0	0	0	0
Sweden	0	0	0	1	6	0	0
Ireland	0	0	0	1	2	0	0
England	1	0	1	0	4	0	0
Germany	0	0	0	0	0	0	0
Switzerland	0	0	0	0	0	0	0
France, Alsace	0	0	0	0	0	0	0
Austria	0	0	0	0	0	0	0
Other foreign	1	0	0	0	0	0	0
Not given	2	1	0	0	1	0	0
Total	29	19	3	13	91	2	0

Source: Records of the Bureau of the Census, Federal Population Schedules, Seventh Census of the United States, 1850, Knox County, Illinois, Reel 113, National Archives, Washington, D.C. (microfilm in Newberry Library, Chicago).
Note: Midwestern states comprise Illinois, Indiana, Iowa, Wisconsin, Michigan, and Minnesota; New England states comprise Maine, New Hampshire, Vermont, Massachusetts, Rhode Island, Connecticut; Middle states comprise New York, Pennsylvania, Ohio, and New Jersey; Southern states comprise Kentucky, Delaware, Virginia, Maryland, Arkansas, South Carolina, North Carolina, Missouri, Alabama, Georgia, Tennessee, Louisiana, Mississippi, Texas, and District of Columbia.

Table A-14 cont. on next page

Service	Super-visory	Govern-ment	Transpor-tation	Labor-ing	Miscel-laneous	Unknown	Total
0	0	0	0	0	0	0	5
0	0	0	0	1	1	11	70
0	0	0	2	6	1	29	109
0	0	0	0	0	0	6	9
0	0	0	0	0	0	0	0
0	0	0	0	0	0	0	0
0	0	0	0	1	1	2	11
0	0	0	0	0	0	0	3
0	0	0	0	2	0	3	11
0	0	0	0	0	0	0	0
0	0	0	0	0	0	0	0
0	0	0	0	0	0	0	0
0	0	0	0	0	0	0	0
0	0	0	0	0	0	0	1
0	0	0	0	0	0	6	10
0	0	0	2	10	3	57	239

Table A-15 Occupations of Nativity Groups, Independent Population—
Galesburg, 1860

Birthplace	Profes-sional	Commer-cial	Propri-etary	Manu-facturing	Crafts	New/Tech.	Un-skilled
Midwestern states	9	8	5	2	5	3	0
New England states	39	50	30	9	71	15	0
Middle states	47	60	70	29	136	23	5
Southern states	12	3	7	1	12	0	1
Other United States	0	0	1	0	0	0	0
Norway	0	0	0	0	0	0	0
Sweden	5	5	5	12	55	0	3
Ireland	3	2	3	4	22	4	1
England	3	5	2	9	10	4	1
Germany	4	5	8	13	4	6	0
Switzerland	0	0	0	0	0	0	0
France, Alsace	0	0	0	0	0	0	0
Austria	0	0	0	0	0	0	0
Other foreign	3	2	3	1	13	0	0
Not given	0	0	0	0	0	0	0
Total	125	140	134	80	328	55	10

Source: Records of the Bureau of the Census, Federal Population Schedules, Eighth Census of the United States, 1860, Knox County, Illinois, Reel 195, National Archives, Washington, D.C. (microfilm in Center for Research Libraries, Chicago). *Note*: Midwestern states comprise Illinois, Indiana, Iowa, Wisconsin, Michigan, and Minnesota; New England states comprise Maine, New Hampshire, Vermont, Massachusetts, Rhode Island, Connecticut; Middle states comprise New York, Pennsylvania, Ohio, and New Jersey; Southern states comprise Kentucky, Delaware, Virginia, Maryland, Arkansas, South Carolina, North Carolina, Missouri, Alabama, Georgia, Tennessee, Louisiana, Mississippi, Texas, and District of Columbia.

Table A-15 cont. on next page

Service	Super-visory	Govern-ment	Transpor-tation	Labor-ing	Miscel-laneous	Unknown	Total
1	1	1	10	18	1	0	64
0	3	4	19	18	29	1	288
5	4	6	33	57	46	0	521
1	1	0	0	14	4	0	56
0	0	0	0	0	0	1	2
1	0	0	0	0	0	0	1
13	0	1	5	97	4	0	205
4	2	1	10	60	6	1	122
0	1	0	3	4	0	0	41
2	1	0	10	12	5	0	70
0	0	0	0	0	0	0	0
0	0	0	0	0	0	0	0
0	0	0	0	0	0	0	0
0	1	0	3	8	0	2	36
0	0	0	0	0	0	4	4
27	14	13	93	288	95	9	1,411

Table A-16   Votes in Presidential Elections, 1848–1860: St. Clair County and
Belleville

Election Year	St. Clair County	Belleville
1848		
Democrat (Cass)	2,023	727
Whig (Taylor)	1,109	410
Free-Soil (Van Buren)	63	12
(Clay)	0	0
1852		
Democrat (Pierce)	2,571	No
Whig (Scott)	998	total
Free-Soil	0	available
1856		
Democrat (Buchanan)	1,728	445
Republican (Frémont)	1,996	530
American (Fillmore)	973	222
1860		
Democrat (Douglas)	3,014	237
Republican (Lincoln)	3,682	363
Union (Bell)	147	0
Southern Democrat (Breckinridge)	24	0
(Smith)	0	0

Sources: Illinois Election Returns, 1818–1864, from Archives and Ledgers, Reel 30–45A, Archives of the State of Illinois, Springfield, Illinois (microfilm in University of Chicago Regenstein Library, Chicago); *Belleville Times*, 10 November 1848; *Weekly St. Clair Tribune*, 8 November 1856; *Belleviller Zeitung*, 8 November 1860.

Table A-17   Votes in Presidential Elections, 1848–1860: LaSalle County and Ottawa

Election Year	LaSalle County	Ottawa
1848		
Democrat (Cass)	1,238	No
Whig (Taylor)	862	total
Free-Soil (Van Buren)	873	available
(Clay)	0	
1852		
Democrat (Pierce)	1,894	452
Whig (Scott)	1,204	260
Free-Soil	552	?
1856		
Democrat (Buchanan)	2,665	576
Republican (Frémont)	3,721	559
American (Fillmore)	121	22
1860		
Democrat (Douglas)	4,290	740
Republican (Lincoln)	5,342	597
Union (Bell)	35	14
Southern Democrat (Breckinridge)	8	0
(Smith)	7	2

Sources: Howard W. Allen and Vincent A. Lacey, eds., *Illinois Elections, 1818–1990: Candidates and County Returns for President, Governor, Senate, and House of Representatives* (Carbondale: Southern Illinois University Press, 1992), 122, 129, 136, 145; *Ottawa Free Trader*, 8 November (p. 2, col. 1) 1856; 10 November (p. 2, col. 2) 1860; *Ottawa Republican*, 13 November (p. 2, col. 1) 1852.

Table A-18 Votes in Presidential Elections, 1848–1860: Knox County and Galesburg

Election Year	Knox County	Galesburg
1848		
Democrat (Cass)	727	No
Whig (Taylor)	830	total
Free-Soil (Van Buren)	392	available
(Clay)	7	
1852		
Democrat (Pierce)	1,119	No
Whig (Scott)	1,080	total
Free-Soil	391	available
1856		
Democrat (Buchanan)	1,490	160[*]
Republican (Frémont)	2,851	699[*]
American (Fillmore)	277	56[*]
1860		
Democrat (Douglas)	2,208	No
Republican (Lincoln)	3,832	total
Union (Bell)	30	available
Southern Democrat (Breckinridge)	17	
(Smith)	0	

Sources: Illinois Election Returns, 1818–1864, from Archives and Ledgers, Reel 30–45A, Archives of the State of Illinois, Springfield, Illinois (microfilm in University of Chicago Regenstein Library, Chicago); *Galesburg Democrat*, 6 November 1856. *Galesburg Township.

Notes

One Introduction

1. Arthur C. Cole, *The Era of the Civil War, 1848–1870,* vol. 3 of *The Centennial History of Illinois,* ed. Clarence Walworth Alvord (Springfield: Illinois Centennial Commission, 1918), 209–10.

2. *Belleville Advocate,* 13 June 1850; John Reynolds, "The History of the City of Belleville," in *Revised Ordinances of the City of Belleville, with the City Charter and Amendments . . . ,* 5–33, rev. T. J. Krafft (Belleville, Illinois: G. A. Harvey, 1862), 26.

3. *Galesburg Democrat,* 23 April 1857.

4. *Ottawa Republican,* 9, 23 April 1853, 18 August 1855; *Ottawa Free Trader,* 6 June 1857.

5. Bernard Bailyn's important 1967 book, *The Ideological Origins of the American Revolution,* described how the American colonists borrowed ideas from the writings of Revolutionary and opposition Englishmen and then began to accuse the British government of treasonable behavior. In *The Creation of the American Republic, 1776–1787,* published in 1969, Gordon Wood took this ideological argument into the Confederation and Early National periods and showed that the "founding fathers" only turned to democratic decision making out of a frustration with the inefficiencies of classical (Jeffersonian) republicanism. Bernard Bailyn, *The Ideological Origins of the American Revolution* (Cambridge, Massachusetts: Harvard University Press, 1967); Gordon S. Wood, *The Creation of the American Republic, 1776–1787* (New York: W. W. Norton, 1969).

6. In his groundbreaking 1945 work, *The Age of Jackson,* Arthur M. Schlesinger Jr. argued that Andrew Jackson's ascendancy to the presidency in 1828 signaled the political arrival of the working class. By then, he declared, the nation was truly democratic once members of all economic classes could exercise the right to participate in po-

litical decisions. In *Jacksonian America* published in 1969, Edward M. Pessen directly challenged Schlesinger's position and argued, very convincingly, that members of the working class only thought that they controlled national politics under Jackson and his successors; the real power, he theorized, remained in the hands of an elite social and economic group composed of both Democrats and Whigs. Arthur M. Schlesinger Jr., *The Age of Jackson* (Boston: Little, Brown, 1945); Edward Pessen, *Jacksonian America: Society, Personality, and Politics*, rev. ed. (Urbana: University of Illinois Press, 1985).

7.   For extended analyses of the political realignment of the 1850s, see Michael F. Holt, *The Political Crisis of the 1850s* (New York: John Wiley & Sons, 1978), and William E. Gienapp, *The Origins of the Republican Party, 1852–1856* (New York: Oxford University Press, 1987).

8.   The major exception to the usual elitist approach to political affiliation is Paul Kleppner, *The Third Electoral System, 1853–1892: Parties, Voters, and Political Cultures* (Chapel Hill: University of North Carolina Press, 1979).

9.   Frederick Jackson Turner, "The Significance of the Frontier in American History," in *American Historical Association Annual Report for 1893* (1893): 199–227.

10.   Don Harrison Doyle, *The Social Order of a Frontier Community: Jacksonville, Illinois, 1825–70* (Urbana: University of Illinois Press, 1978); Ralph Mann, *After the Gold Rush: Society in Grass Valley and Nevada City, California, 1855–1870* (Stanford, California: Stanford University Press, 1982); Richard Hogan, *Class and Community in Frontier Colorado* (Lawrence: University Press of Kansas, 1990).

11.   Timothy Mahoney and Jon Teaford both examine the development of a regional system of midwestern cities. Mahoney points to the economic status of a town as the primary causal factor in the determination of its social and political structures. Teaford traces the economic, social, and cultural development of the cities of the Midwest to an "interior mentality." Timothy R. Mahoney, *River Towns in the Great West: The Structure of Provincial Urbanization in the American Midwest, 1820–1870* (New York: Cambridge University Press, 1990); Jon C. Teaford, *Cities of the Heartland: The Rise and Fall of the Industrial Midwest* (Bloomington: Indiana University Press, 1993), xi.

12.   See Patricia Nelson Limerick, *The Legacy of Conquest: The Unbroken Past of the American West* (New York: W. W. Nor-

ton, 1987), and Donald Worster, *Rivers of Empire: Water, Aridity, and the Growth of the American West* (New York: Pantheon Books, 1985).

13.   Lewis Atherton, *Main Street on the Middle Border* (Bloomington: Indiana University Press, 1954), xvi.

14.   John Mack Faragher, *Sugar Creek: Life on the Illinois Prairie* (New Haven, Connecticut: Yale University Press, 1986).

Two **The Towns**

1.   Clarence Walworth Alvord, *The Illinois Country, 1673–1818*, vol. 1 of *The Centennial History of Illinois*, ed. Clarence Walworth Alvord (Springfield: Illinois Centennial Commission, 1918); Richard J. Jensen, *Illinois: A Bicentennial History* (New York: W. W. Norton, 1978), 3–31.

2.   Robert P. Howard, *Illinois: A History of the Prairie State* (Grand Rapids, Michigan: William B. Eerdmans, 1972), 26–29, 153; Eaton G. Osman, *The Last of a Great Indian Tribe: A Chapter of Colonial History* (Chicago: A. Flanagan, 1923), 48, 60, 183; Alvord, 88; Jensen, 100; James Scott, *The Illinois Nation: A History of the Illinois Nation of Indians from their Discovery to the Present Day* (Streator, Illinois, 1973), 7; Helen Hornbeck Tanner, ed., *Atlas of Great Lakes Indian History* (Norman: University of Oklahoma Press, 1986), 31.

3.   For an outline of the era in which northern Illinois was settled by Americans, see Theodore Calvin Pease, *The Frontier State, 1818–1848*, vol. 2 of *The Centennial History of Illinois*, ed. Clarence Walworth Alvord (Springfield: Illinois Centennial Commission, 1918).

4.   John Reynolds, "The History of the City of Belleville," in *Revised Ordinances of the City of Belleville, with the City Charter and Amendments . . .*, rev. T. J. Krafft (Belleville, Illinois: G. A. Harvey, 1862), 7; St. Clair County Records, 1798–1817, Supervisors' Record, Reel 30–2695, Illinois Regional Archives Depository, Southern Illinois University, Carbondale, Illinois.

5.   *An Illustrated Historical Atlas of St. Clair County, Illinois* (Chicago: Warner & Beers, 1874), 8; *History of St. Clair County, Illinois* (Philadelphia: Brink, McDonough, 1881), 28–29. Reynolds, "The History of the City of Belleville," 9.

6.   See *An Illustrated Historical Atlas of St. Clair County, Illinois*, 54–55, 60–61, for surveys of the French common fields of Cahokia and Prairie du Pont.

7.   The early families of European American settlers in
       St. Clair County included the Lemens, the Stookeys, and
       the Scotts of Virginia, and the Ogles of Maryland. The
       young, single, male settlers included John Thomas of Vir-
       ginia, John Reynolds of Pennsylvania, and George Wilder-
       man of Maryland. *History of St. Clair County,* 197–99, 201,
       205, 206, 213, 229, 286; J. M. Peck, *A Gazetteer of Illinois
       in Three Parts: Containing a General View of the State, A
       General View of Each County . . .* (Jacksonville, Illinois:
       R. Goudy, 1834), 6.

8.   There was only one sizable group of permanent settlers
       above the bluffs prior to 1814 in St. Clair County. Iso-
       lated Turkey Hill, four miles southeast of the site of
       Belleville, was settled in 1798 by the family of William
       Scott. Peck, 344. Illinois was a county of Virginia until
       the land cessions of 1784. Under Virginia law, members
       of the militia who served with the revolutionary forces
       could locate their bounties anywhere in the state's terri-
       tory. Privates were allowed 100 acres; ensigns, 150; lieu-
       tenants, 200; captains, 300; majors, 400; lieutenant-colo-
       nels, 450; colonels, 500; brigadier generals, 850; and
       major generals, 1,100. The U.S. Ordinance of 1785 de-
       clared that Continental Army bounty lands could only be
       obtained after the official survey of an area; even then
       only one-seventh of the land in each township could be
       set aside for military bounties. The status of Illinois land,
       therefore, was seen as ambiguous, and some Virginia vet-
       erans asserted that they could claim their benefits before
       the survey. The issue was finally settled in 1813 when
       the U.S. Congress passed a special preemption bill author-
       izing prior claims to Illinois property by Virginia militia
       veterans. Benjamin Horace Hibbard, *A History of Public
       Land Policies* (New York: Macmillan Company, 1924),
       118; Payson Jackson Treat, *The National Land System, 1785–
       1820* (New York: E. B. Treat, 1919), 202, 218, 220, 236,
       240, 385; *History of St. Clair County, Illinois,* 27.

9.   Of modern St. Clair's 381,360 acres of land above the
       bluffs, 18,318 acres (4.8%) were preempted before sales
       commenced at the Kaskaskia Land District Office in Au-
       gust 1814. By far the most preempted areas were in
       Township 1 North, Range 8 West of the Third Principal
       Meridian, in which Belleville was located, and in T2S
       R8W, in which members of the Scott settlement of Tur-
       key Hill bought 5,056 acres (21.9%) along Richland
       Creek. There appears to be no direct correlation between
       prairie or timbered land and preemption, but there is a

connection with propinquity to St. Louis, except for the
two settlements around Belleville and Turkey Hill. Board
of Commissioners, Claims for Which Certificates of
Confirmation Granted, 1814–17, Archives of the State of
Illinois, Springfield, Illinois; *An Illustrated Historical Atlas of
St. Clair County, Illinois*, 20–70; Douglas R. McManis, *The
Initial Evaluation and Utilization of the Illinois Prairies, 1815–
1840*, Department of Geography Research Paper, no. 94
(Chicago: Department of Geography, University of Chi-
cago, 1964), 8.

10.   In 1800, St. Clair County held 1,265 people: 729 in Cahokia, 286 in Belle Fountaine, and 250 in L'Aigle Township. There are no figures for the county in 1810. But by
1818, there were about 3,800 people in a county of considerably diminished area. That most of the increase from
1800 to 1818 was due to American immigration is borne
out by the fact that in 1800 there were forty-two slaves
in the county where in 1818 there were eighty-eight.
Since only French Illinoisans were allowed to own slaves
in 1818, it seems likely that if the French accounted for
most of the increase in population, the slave population
would have increased at the same rate, or faster, than the
French themselves. Margaret Cross Norton, ed., *Illinois
Census Returns, 1810, 1818*, Collections of the Illinois State
Historical Library, vol. 24 (Springfield: Illinois State Historical Library, 1935), xxviii, xxx; *An Illustrated Historical
Atlas of St. Clair County, Illinois*, 8; Reynolds, "The History
of the City of Belleville," 17.

11.   There are no surviving examples of booster literature
from the very earliest days of Belleville. The actions and
timing of the town founders, however, show considerable
concern for the successful establishment of an American
city in southern Illinois that could serve as an alternative
to St. Louis. For a discussion of the booster ethos and its
effects on the community of another Illinois town, see
Don H. Doyle, *The Social Order of a Frontier Community:
Jacksonville, Illinois, 1825–70* (Urbana: University of Illinois
Press, 1978), 62–91; Norton, xxx; U.S. Department of
State, *Abstract of the Fifth Census of the United States, 1830*
(Washington, D.C.: The Globe Office, 1832), 36–37; *History of St. Clair County, Illinois*, 185; Reynolds, "The History
of the City of Belleville," 19.

12.   *An Illustrated Historical Atlas of St. Clair County, Illinois*, 8;
Reynolds, "The History of the City of Belleville," 13; *History of St. Clair County, Illinois*, 200, 212, 224.

13.   Reynolds, "The History of the City of Belleville," 20; Peck, 214.

14.   U.S. Department of the Interior, Census Office, *A Compendium of the Ninth Census, 1870* (Washington, D.C.: Government Printing Office, 1872), 38–40; Daniel J. Elazar, *The Politics of Belleville: A Profile of the Civil Community* (Philadelphia: Temple University Press, 1971), 70. There were 2,532 households in St. Clair County in 1840, 1,137 in a "northern" census district and 1,395 in a "southern" district. Five hundred twenty of the heads of household had German surnames, 105 in the north and 425 in the south. Records of the Bureau of the Census, Federal Population Schedules, Sixth Census of the United States, 1840, St. Clair County, Illinois, Reel 70, National Archives, Washington, D.C. (microfilm in Federal Archives and Records Center, Chicago).

15.   McCormack, Thomas J., ed., *Memoirs of Gustave Körner, 1809–1896: Life-Sketches Written at the Suggestion of His Children,* 2 vols. (Cedar Rapids, Iowa: Torch Press, 1909), 1:216–85. For a description of the early German settlements near Belleville, see McCormack, 1:286–310; Peck, 344.

16.   There were thirty-six signatures on the 1838 constitution. Some have been omitted because they are illegible. German Library Association in St. Clair County, Illinois, Vertical Files, Belleville Public Library, Belleville, Illinois. For a description of the economic circumstances in Germany that encouraged emigration, see Mark Wyman, *Immigrants in the Valley: Irish, Germans, and Americans in the Upper Mississippi Country, 1830–1860* (Chicago: Nelson-Hall, 1984), 49–73. For more information about the "Latin Peasants," see Oswald Garrison Villard, "The Latin Peasants of Belleville, Illinois," *Journal of the Illinois State Historical Society* 35 (March 1942): 7–20. Gustave Körner's effort to record the contributions of the 1830s German immigrants to American society can be seen in his *Das Deutsche Element in den Vereinigten Staaten von Nordamerika, 1818–1848* (Cincinnati, Ohio: U. C. Wilde, 1880).

17.   *Belleville Advocate,* 12 December 1846; 15 March 1849; Reynolds, "The History of the City of Belleville," 26, 31.

18.   There was also, of course, the financial distress through which the entire nation suffered from 1818 to 1826. For

the Illinois reaction to the depression, see Pease, *The Frontier State*, 74.

19.   *Illinois Free Trader*, 2 April 1841.

20.   Among the other known early families in the Ottawa area were those of George E. Walker, from Tennessee and the son of Dr. David Walker; John McKernan, from Kentucky; David Strawn, from Ohio; and Josiah E. Shaw, Reuben Reed, Charles Brown, John Hogaboom, Richard Hogaboom, Abel Hogaboom, Daniel F. Hitt, and Henry Brush, all from New York. Elmer Baldwin, *History of LaSalle County, Illinois* (Chicago: Rand, McNally, 1877), 226, 228, 229, 230–31, 255–60; Michael O'Byrne, *History of LaSalle County, Illinois*, 3 vols. (Chicago: Lewis, 1924), 1:39, 63, 138, 141, 231, 233, 240, 257, 407, 417, 3:559; *History of LaSalle County, Illinois, Together With Sketches of Its Cities, Villages and Towns*, 2 vols. (Chicago: Inter-State, 1886), 1:475, 532–33; *The Past and Present of LaSalle County, Illinois, Containing A History of the County— Its Cities, Towns, &c., . . .* (Chicago: H. F. Klett, 1877), 279, 284; W. D., "Old Settler Reminiscences," *Ottawa Free Trader*, 23 January 1858.

21.   Walter A. Howe, comp., *Documentary History of the Illinois and Michigan Canal: Legislation, Litigation, and Titles* (Springfield: Printed by authority of the State of Illinois, 1956), 54.

22.   Howe, 58; *The Past and Present of LaSalle County, Illinois*, 279, 280; Michael P. Conzen, "The Historical and Geographical Development of the Illinois and Michigan Canal National Heritage Corridor," in *The Illinois & Michigan Canal National Heritage Corridor: A Guide to Its History and Sources*, eds. Michael P. Conzen and Kay J. Carr (DeKalb: Northern Illinois University Press, 1988), 7, 9; Pease, *The Frontier State*, 200.

23.   M. Conzen, 7; O'Byrne, 1:116, 141, 195, 201, 228–29, 231, 233, 240, 249, 260; 2:39; 3:560, 583; *The Past and Present of LaSalle County, Illinois*, 283; *Ottawa: Old and New, A Complete History of Ottawa, Illinois, 1823–1914* (Ottawa, Illinois: Republican-Times, 1912–1914), 9; Baldwin, 230– 33, 235, 237–39, 245–46, 251, 253–54, 259–60, 263; *History of LaSalle County, Illinois, Together With Sketches of its Cities, Villages and Towns*, 1:476, 507, 522, 532–33, 537–38, 560, 568–69.

24.   *Ottawa, Old and New*, 169; O'Byrne, 1:257; Wyman, 80–82.

25.   Wyman, 147–48

26.   Baldwin, 199.

27.   *Illinois Free Trader*, 23 May 1840; O'Byrne, 1:136, 265–66, 338; *History of LaSalle County, Illinois, Together With Sketches of its Cities, Villages and Towns*, 1:539; *The Biographical Encyclopedia of Illinois of the Nineteenth Century* (Philadelphia: Galaxy, 1875), 293–95.

28.   Howard, 196, 228–29; Wyman, 83–84; *Ottawa Free Trader*, 19 January 1844.

29.   The "feeder canal" was built by the state to pump more water into the Illinois and Michigan Canal west of Ottawa; the "side cut" was built by the state to provide a power source to the city and to connect the canal with the Illinois River. *Holland's Ottawa City Directory, 1869–70* (Chicago: Western, 1869), 9, 16; *Ottawa Free Trader*, 28 April 1848; *History of LaSalle County, Illinois, Together With Sketches of its Cities, Villages and Towns*, 1:474;

30.   Federal Land Surveyors' Field Notes, vols. 279, 353, Archives of the State of Illinois, Springfield, Illinois.

31.   For information on the United States survey system, see C. Albert White, *A History of the Rectangular Survey System* (Washington, D.C.: Government Printing Office, [1941]). For the most complete description of the processes of settlement in the Military Tract, see Theodore L. Carlson, *The Illinois Military Tract: A Study of Land Occupation, Utilization and Tenure*, Illinois Studies in the Social Sciences, vol. 22 (Urbana: University of Illinois Press, 1951).

32.   The best explanation of the shift in perception regarding prairies is Douglas R. McManis, *The Initial Evaluation and Utilization of the Illinois Prairies, 1815–1840*, Department of Geography Research Paper, no. 94 (Chicago: Department of Geography, University of Chicago, 1964), 30–61. The Galesburg prairie's agricultural potential was recognized by 1834 when J. M. Peck wrote that Knox County's prairies were "large and generally of the best quality. . . . The soil in general is of the first quality." Peck, 138. Everybody agreed that the lowlands were unhealthy, but there were many theories as to the cause of the unhealthiness. Douglas K. Meyer, "Immigrant Clusters in the Illinois Miliary Tract," *Pioneer America: The Journal of Historic American Material Culture* 12 (May 1980): 105; Carlson, *The Illinois Military Tract*, 126; George Washington Gale, *A*

Brief History of Knox College, Situated in Galesburgh, Knox County, Illinois (Cincinnati: C. Clark, 1845), 8; McManis, *The Initial Evaluation,* 44. Geographic studies of land ac-quisition in the Illinois Military Tract have demonstrated this continued preference for timbered land. Siyoung Park, "Perception of Land Quality and the Settlement of Northern Pike County, 1821–1836," *Western Illinois Re-gional Studies* 3 (Spring 1980): 5–21, and Gordana Rezab, "Land Speculation in Fulton County, 1817–1832, *Western Illinois Regional Studies* 3 (Spring 1980): 22–35; William D. Walters Jr. and Floyd Mansberger, "Initial Field Loca-tion in Illinois," *Agricultural History* 57 (July 1983): 289–96. Park and Rezab also found this preference by specula-tors for land near towns. Park, "Perception of Land Quality," 16; Rezab, "Land Speculation," 34. In a group of twenty-four contiguous townships, twelve in Knox County and twelve in its western neighbor Warren County, there were only six instances of settlers purchas-ing land in other than their own counties out of 300 transactions involving Knox and Warren men between 1831 and 1836. Registers' Cash Certificates, Quincy Land Office, 4 vols., Federal Archives and Records Center, Chi-cago, Illinois, vol. 1.

33. The act of Congress of May 6, 1812—appropriating 6,000,000 acres for military bounties—stressed that the lands had to be "fit for cultivation." Therefore, only 3,500,000 acres of the 5,360,000-acre Military Tract were reserved for bounties; the rest of the lands were deemed unfit, were fractions of townships, or contained salt springs or lead mines (both reserved for ownership by the federal government). Richard Peters, ed., *The Pub-lic Statutes at Large of the United States of America, from the Organization of the Government in 1789 to March 3, 1845* (Boston: Little, Brown, 1845), 729–31; *General Public Acts of Congress, Respecting the Sale and Disposition of the Public Lands, with Instructions Issued by the Secretary of Treasury and Commissioner of the General Land Office and Official Opin-ions of the Attorney General on Questions Arising Under the Land Laws,* vol. 2, 808–13; Carlson, *The Illinois Military Tract,* 6. A list of the general instructions for field survey-ors is given in Lowell O. Stewart, *Public Land Surveys: His-tory, Instructions, Methods* (Ames, Iowa: Collegiate Press, 1935), 91–139.

34. Earnest Elmo Calkins, *They Broke the Prairie: Being Some Account of the Settlement of the Upper Mississippi Valley by Re-*

ligious and Educational Pioneers, Told in Terms of One City, Galesburg, and One College, Knox (New York: Charles Scribner's Sons, 1937), 45–46; Gale, *A Brief History*, 5–6.

35.   Membership of the Prudential Committee is unclear: Gale and the Reverend Hiram H. Kellogg were certainly members. The committee probably also included Nehemiah West, a farmer from Oneida County. "Directions for the Exploring Committee," typewritten copy of manuscript, no date, Knox College Archives, Galesburg, Illinois.

36.   Timothy B. Jervis to Hiram H. Kellogg, June 15, 1835, Knox College Archives, Galesburg, Illinois; George Washington Gale, "Report of the Agent," no. 1, 1836, Knox College Archives, Galesburg, Illinois.

37.   The busiest month for land sales was June 1835 when 162,593 acres were sold. Calkins, *They Broke the Prairie*, 55; Registers' Cash Certificates, vol. 1, June 1835; Gale, *A Brief History*, 7.

38.   Gale, "Report of the Agent," no. 1; Registers' Cash Certificates, vol. 1, June 1835.

39.   The story of Barrett's actions is a fine example of the longevity of false history. In his 1845 treatise on the history of Galesburg, Gale stated that Barrett heard of the plans of the Society while the Purchasing Committee was in Knoxville, just east of the township containing the prairie, and that he rushed to Quincy to buy the sections before the committee could make their purchases. In fact, Barrett did not buy the sections until ten days after the committee bought their own land. The sequence of events has been falsely reported in history after history of the settlement of Galesburg. Gale, *A Brief History*, 7; Calkins, *They Broke the Prairie*, 62; Registers' Cash Certificates, vol. 1, 20, 30 October 1835; George Washington Gale, "Report of the Agent," no. 3, no date, Knox College Archives, Galesburg, Illinois.

40.   Federal Township Plats, 22:10. Archives of the State of Illinois, Springfield, Illinois; Gale, *A Brief History*, 7. The difficulty in locating large amounts of land was not unique to Galesburg's settlers but was a general problem for groups. See Morris C. Taber, "The New England Influence in South Central Michigan," *Michigan History Magazine* 45 (December 1961): 305–36; see especially p. 314 for a description of similar problems in Vermontville.

41. The use of modern township names is for the sake of convenience; townships in the area were not politically organized and named until the 1840s.

42. *History of Knox County* (Chicago: Charles C. Chapman, 1878), 106; Albert J. Perry, *History of Knox County, Illinois: Its Cities, Towns, and People* (Chicago: S. J. Clarke, 1912), 36–41. For the founding of Knoxville and the desirability of the site because of its propinquity to prairie and timber land, see *History of Knox County*, 486.

43. The alienation totals in each of the surrounding townships by June 1835 were: Henderson (T12N, R1E), 100%; Sparta (T12N, R2E), 67%; Knox (T11N, R2E), 58%; Orange (T10N, R2E), 42%; and Cedar (T10N, R1E), 47%. Registers' Cash Certificates, vol. 1.

44. "Directions for the Exploring Committee."

45. The names of these town-dwelling families were Ferris (three separate households), Gale, Marsh (two households), Simons, Losee, Waters, West, Churchill, and Gilbert. The township families were Ferris (two more households), West (two more households), Simons (another), and Avery. Records of the Bureau of the Census, Federal Population Schedules, Sixth Census of the United States, 1840, Knox County, Illinois, Reel 62, National Archives, Washington, D.C. (microfilm in Federal Archives and Records Center, Chicago); Earnest Elmo Calkins, "Pioneer Who's Who and Thumb Nail Biographies," unpublished manuscript, Knox College Archives, Galesburg, Illinois; Calkins, *They Broke the Prairie*, 131; Daniel T. Johnson, "Financing the Western Colleges, 1844–1862," *Journal of the Illinois State Historical Society* 65 (Spring 1972): 48–49.

46. Records of the Bureau of the Census, Federal Population Schedules, Seventh Census of the United States, 1850, Knox County, Illinois, Reel 113, National Archives, Washington, D.C. (microfilm in Newberry Library, Chicago); Records of the Bureau of the Census, Federal Population Schedules, Eighth Census of the United States, 1860, Knox County, Illinois, Reel 195, National Archives, Washington, D.C. (microfilm in Center for Research Libraries, Chicago).

Three **The People**

1. Charles Beneulyn Johnson, *Illinois in the Fifties, or, A Decade of Development, 1851–1860*, Illinois Centennial Edition (Champaign, Illinois: Flanigan-Pearson, 1918), 135. For

a fascinating and thorough look at the effects of railroads on the development of Illinois and the Midwest, see William Cronon, *Nature's Metropolis: Chicago and the Great West* (New York: W. W. Norton, 1991), 55–93.

2.   H. D. Estabrook, "The First Train Order by Telegraph," *Baltimore and Ohio Employees Magazine*, 1 (July 1913): 27–29, in Robert Luther Thompson, *Wiring a Continent: The History of the Telegraph Industry in the United States, 1832–1866* (Princeton, New Jersey: Princeton University Press, 1947), 204.

3.   For more information on the transformation of the American family in the nineteenth century, see Nancy F. Cott, *The Bonds of Womanhood: "Women's Sphere" in New England, 1780–1835* (New Haven, Connecticut: Yale University Press, 1977); Mary P. Ryan, *Cradle of the Middle Class: The Family in Oneida County, New York, 1790–1865* (New York: Cambridge University Press, 1981); and Stuart M. Blumin, *The Emergence of the Middle Class: Social Experience in the American City, 1760–1900* (New York: Cambridge University Press, 1989).

4.   More information on the abolitionist movement can be found in James Brewer Stewart, *Holy Warriors: The Abolitionists and American Slavery* (New York: Hill and Wang, 1976). For more information on the national political realignment of the 1850s, see William E. Gienapp, *The Origins of the Republican Party, 1852–1856* (New York: Oxford University Press, 1987); Eric Foner, *Free Soil, Free Labor, Free Men: The Ideology of the Republican Party before the Civil War* (New York: Oxford University Press, 1970); and Michael F. Holt, *The Political Crisis of the 1850s* (New York: Wiley, 1978).

5.   Don Harrison Doyle, *The Social Order of a Frontier Community: Jacksonville, Illinois, 1825–70* (Urbana: University of Illinois Press, 1978), 96.

6.   Doyle, 95; John Mack Faragher, *Sugar Creek: Life on the Illinois Prairie* (New Haven: Yale University Press, 1986), 249; Faragher's figures encompass the entire population, even children. Other studies that include figures on persistence in western communities include James C. Malin, "The Turnover of Farm Population in Kansas," *Kansas Historical Quarterly* 4 (1935): 339–72; Mildred Thorne, "Population Study of an Iowa County in 1850," *Iowa Journal of History* 57 (1959): 305–30; Merle Curti, *The Making of an American Community: A Case Study of Democracy in a Fron-*

tier County (Stanford: Stanford University Press, 1959); and Howard P. Chudacoff, *Mobile Americans: Residential and Social Mobility in Omaha, 1880–1920* (New York: Oxford University Press, 1972).

7. Jack E. Eblen, "An Analysis of Nineteenth-Century Frontier Populations," *Demography* 2 (1965): 405–6.

8. Belleville population information is from the Records of the Bureau of the Census, Federal Population Schedules, Seventh Census of the United States, 1850, St. Clair County, Illinois, Reel 126, National Archives, Washington, D.C. (microfilm in Federal Archives and Records Center, Chicago); Records of the Bureau of the Census, Federal Population Schedules, Eighth Census of the United States, 1860, St. Clair County, Illinois, Reels 224, 225, National Archives, Washington, D.C. (microfilm in center for Research Libraries, Chicago).

9. Eblen, 413; See Stephan Thernstrom and Peter R. Knights, "Men in Motion: Some Data and Speculations About Urban Population Mobility in Nineteenth-Century America," *Journal of Interdisciplinary History* 1 (Summer 1970): 25, for an analysis of the populations of young men in nineteenth-century American towns.

10. The functional occupational categories used here—professional, commercial, proprietary, manufacturing, crafts, new or technical, unskilled, service, supervisory, government, transportation, labor, and miscellaneous—were adapted from Theodore Hershberg and Robert Dockhorn, "Occupational Classification," *Historical Methods Newsletter* 9 (March-June 1976): 78–81.

11. *History of St. Clair County, Illinois* (Philadelphia: Brink, McDonough, 1881), 192–96.

12. Belleville church membership information comes from *History of St. Clair County, Illinois; Belleville, Illinois, City Directory and Business Mirror for 1860* (Bingham & Doughty, 1860); *St. George's Episcopal Church, 1882–1982* (Belleville, Illinois, 1982); *Pilgrims Pressing On, 1837–1974* (Belleville, Illinois, 1974); *Belleville, Illinois, Illustrated* (n.p., n.d.); *St. Peter's Roman Catholic Cathedral* (n.p., n.d.).

13. *Belleville, Illinois, City Directory and Business Mirror for 1860;* Freemasons, Vertical File, Belleville Public Library, Belleville, Illinois.

14. *Statuten und Nebengesetzen des Belleviller Sängerbundes und der Bibliothek Gesellschaft* (Belleville, Illinois, 1870), 13–16.

15.   Ottawa population information is from Records of the Bu-
        reau of the Census, Federal Population Schedules, Sev-
        enth Census of the United States, 1850, LaSalle County,
        Illinois, Reel 115, National Archives, Washington, D.C.
        (microfilm in Newberry Library, Chicago, and Morris Li-
        brary, Carbondale); Records of the Bureau of the Census,
        Federal Population Schedules, Eighth Census of the
        United States, 1860, LaSalle County, Illinois, Reel 196,
        National Archives, Washington, D.C. (microfilm in New-
        berry Library, Chicago, and Morris Library, Carbondale).

16.   *The Past and Present of LaSalle County, Illinois, Containing a
        History of the County—Its Cities, Towns, &c.,* . . . (Chicago:
        H. F. Klett, 1877), 285; *Ottawa Free Trader,* 28 April,
        10 September, 25 February, 31 March 1860; 13 August,
        3 September 1859; Michael O'Byrne, *History of LaSalle
        County, Illinois,* 3 vols. (Chicago: Lewis, 1924), 1:252;
        Elmer Baldwin, *History of LaSalle County, Illinois* (Chicago:
        Rand, McNally, 1877), 543; *Holland's Ottawa City Directory
        for 1869–70* (Chicago: Western, 1869), 16; Philip Devon
        Wolfe, "Ottawa's Economy: Growth and Change in Com-
        merce, Industry, and Government," in *Focus on Ottawa: A
        Historical and Geographical Survey of Ottawa, Illinois, in the
        Twentieth Century,* ed. Michael P. Conzen (Chicago: Com-
        mittee on Geographical Studies, University of Chicago,
        1987), 11.

17.   *History of LaSalle County, Illinois, Together With Sketches of Its
        Cities, Villages and Towns,* 2 vols. (Chicago: Inter-State,
        1886), 1:539.

18.   O'Byrne, 1:265–66, 338; Baldwin, 335.

19.   Ottawa church histories and membership information
        come from Clarence Griggs, comp., *Souvenir, One Hun-
        dredth Anniversary of Christ Episcopal Church, Ottawa, Illi-
        nois,* A.D. 1838–A.D. 1938 (Ottawa: Illinois Office Supply,
        1938), 5, 7, 10; Catherine Schaefer, "A Chronology of
        Missions and Churches in Illinois from 1675 to 1855," *Il-
        linois Catholic Historical Review* (July/October 1918): 107;
        Ruth B. Sapp, *Commemorating the One Hundredth Anniver-
        sary of the First Congregational Church of Ottawa, Illinois*
        (Ottawa: Illinois Office Supply, 1939), 3, 9, 10; *The Past
        and Present of LaSalle County, Illinois,* 291–94; *History of
        LaSalle County, Illinois, Together With Sketches of its Cities, Vil-
        lages and Towns,* 1:497, 501–2; *Ottawa: Old and New, A
        Complete History of Ottawa, Illinois, 1823–1914* (Ottawa, Illi-

nois: Republican-Times, 1912–14), 169–72; *Holland's
Ottawa City Directory*, 21–22.

20. *Holland's Ottawa City Directory*, 23–24; C. C. Tisler, *Story of
Ottawa, Illinois* (Ottawa, Illinois: C. C. Tisler, 1953), 36;
Ottawa Old and New, 156–57, 160; *The Past and Present of
LaSalle County, Illinois*, 283; J. N. Woltz and C. A. Gould,
comps., *Ottawa City Directory and Business Advertiser for
1866–7* (Ottawa, Illinois: Republican Job Printing Office,
1866), 165; *Ottawa Free Trader*, 24 June 1854; 6 January,
26 May 1855; 13 December 1856; 26 December 1857;
16 January, 26 June, 2 July 1858.

21. *By-Laws of Shabbona Chapter, No. 37, Royal Arch Masons,
Ottawa, Illinois, Adopted May 5*, A.D. 1875; A. I. 2405
(Ottawa, Illinois: Osman & Hapeman, 1875), 24–26.

22. Galesburg population information is from Records of the
Bureau of the Census, Federal Population Schedules, Seventh Census of the United States, 1850, Knox County, Illinois, Reel 113, National Archives, Washington, D.C. (microfilm in Newberry Library, Chicago); Records of the
Bureau of the Census, Federal Population Schedules,
Eighth Census of the United States, 1860, Knox County,
Illinois, Reel 195, National Archives, Washington, D.C.
(microfilm in Center for Research Libraries, Chicago).

23. *History of Knox County, Illinois* (Chicago: Charles C. Chapman, 1878), 515–32.

24. Just what they and their fellow keepers—two Irishmen,
one Englishman, one Swede, and two New Yorkers—
were serving in their saloons remains a mystery since the
sale of intoxicating liquors was illegal in Galesburg in
1860. Their saloons may have been outside the city limits.

25. Census real estate totals only give an estimate of wealth
for people residing in the cities; absentee holders are not
included. In Galesburg's case, one must be particularly
leery since the largest city landholder, the mythological
founder, George Washington Gale, lived outside the city
limits and was not counted in the city census. See "Assessor's List for 1859 for the Town of Galesburg in the
County of Knox," Galesburg Public Library, Galesburg, Illinois.

26. Undoubtedly as the result of the ethnic makeup of the
dominant groups, Galesburg's church records are amazingly complete for some denominations but sorely lacking

for others. Galesburg church information is from *History of Knox County, Illinois*; *"That Ye May Tell It To The Generation Following": The First Baptist Church, 1848–1948* (Galesburg, Illinois, 1948); *First Lutheran Church, Ninetieth Anniversary* (Galesburg, Illinois, 1941); *The Manual of the First Universalist Church of Galesburg, Illinois, 1859–1959* (Galesburg, Illinois, 1959); *Brief History of the First Presbyterian Church* (n.p., n.d.); First Methodist Episcopal Church, Ephemera File, Galesburg Public Library, Galesburg, Illinois; St. Patrick's Church, Ephemera File, Galesburg Public Library, Galesburg, Illinois; "Records of the Presbyterian Church in Galesburg, Illinois," Galesburg Public Library, Galesburg, Illinois.

27.   Herman R. Muelder, *Fighters for Freedom: The History of Anti-Slavery Activities of Men and Women Associated With Knox College* (New York: Columbia University Press, 1959), 31; Herman Richard Muelder, *Church History in a Puritan Colony of the Middle West* (Galesburg, Illinois: Central Congregational Church and First Presbyterian Church, 1937), 49.

28.   Muelder, *Church History in a Puritan Colony*, 48–49.

29.   *Galesburg Democrat*, 21 May, 4, 11, 25 June, 6, 13 July, 10, 20 August 1859; 24, 27, 30 January, 7 February, 27 April, 13 November 1860.

30.   "Alpha Lodge, No. 155 of the Galesburg Freemasons," Dues Book, 1862–1878, Galesburg Public Library, Galesburg, Illinois.

Four **The Railroads**

1.   The efforts to build the Central Railroad were connected with a scheme to develop the area of the state where the Ohio River flows into the Mississippi River. The plan was to build a new regional capital of the American "Egypt" called "Cairo." The entire internal improvement act was the result of a complex plan to improve the position of Illinois by changing its economic center from the southern counties, where it had been focused since before statehood, to the newly settled and eastern-capitalized north. The deal, which involved moving the capital from Vandalia to Springfield, compensated the southerners with improvement projects. Carlton J. Corliss, *Main Line of Mid-America: The Story of the Illinois Central* (New York: Creative Age Press, 1950), 6; Theodore Calvin Pease, *The Frontier State, 1818–1848*, vol. 2 of *The Centennial History of*

Illinois, ed. Clarence Walworth Alvord (Springfield: Illinois Centennial Commission, 1918), 194–215, 218–19; Herman R. Lantz, *A Community in Search of Itself: A Case History of Cairo, Illinois* (Carbondale: Southern Illinois University Press, 1972).

2.   *The WPA Guide to Illinois*, written and compiled by the Federal Writers' Project of the Works Progress Administration for the State of Illinois, with a new introduction by Neil Harris and Michael Conzen (New York: Pantheon Books, 1983), 29; Corliss, *Main Line of Mid-America*, 9; Richard C. Overton, *Burlington Route: A History of the Burlington Lines* (New York: Alfred A. Knopf, 1965), 15.

3.   *Ottawa Free Trader*, 11 January 1851.

4.   Carville Earle, "Regional Economic Development West of the Appalachians, 1815–1860," in Robert D. Mitchell and Paul A. Groves, eds., *North America: The Historical Geography of a Changing Continent*, 172–97 (Totowa, New Jersey: Rowman & Littlefield, 1987), 188; Shelton Stromquist, *A Generation of Boomers: The Pattern of Railroad Labor Conflict in Nineteenth-Century America* (Urbana: University of Illinois Press, 1987), 7.

5.   *Ottawa Free Trader*, 1 February 1851.

6.   Examples of the genealogical approach to railroads in Illinois are Carlton J. Corliss, *Main Line of Mid-America*; Richard C. Overton, *Burlington Route*; and Earnest Elmo Calkins, "Genesis of a Railroad," *Transactions of the Illinois State Historical Society* 41 (1935): 43–56. Historians who have written about railroads and their relationship with nineteenth-century economic development are Carter Goodrich, *Government Promotion of American Canals and Railroads, 1800–1890* (New York: Columbia University Press, 1960); John H. Krenkel, *Illinois Internal Improvements, 1818–1848* (Cedar Rapids, Iowa: Torch Press, 1958); Harry N. Scheiber, *Ohio Canal Era: A Case Study of Government and the Economy, 1820–1861* (Athens: Ohio University Press, 1969); and George Rogers Taylor, *The Transportation Revolution, 1815–1860* (New York: Holt, Rinehart and Winston, 1951). Writers of the historical relationship between western development and eastern capital are Arthur M. Johnson and Barry E. Supple, *Boston Capitalists and Western Railroads* (Cambridge, Massachusetts: Harvard University Press, 1967); John Denis Haeger, *The Investment Frontier: New York Businessmen and*

the Economic Development of the Old Northwest (Albany: State University of New York, 1981); Eric J. Hobsbawm, *The Age of Capital* (New York: Charles Scribner's Sons, 1975); John Lauritz Larson, *Bonds of Enterprise: John Murray Forbes and Western Development in America's Railway Age* (Cambridge, Massachusetts: Harvard University Press, 1984); and Albro Martin, *James J. Hill and the Opening of the Northwest* (New York: Oxford University Press, 1978).

7.   The local perspective to railroad building was pioneered by Charles N. Glaab, *Kansas City and the Railroads: Community Policy in the Growth of a Regional Metropolis* (Madison: State Historical Society of Wisconsin, 1962). Also see Don H. Doyle, *The Social Order of a Frontier Community: Jacksonville, Illinois, 1825–70* (Urbana: University of Illinois Press, 1978), 42–46, 79–91, for a local look at railroad building.

8.   *Belleville Advocate*, 3, 25 March; 30 September 1847; 17 February; 24, 30 March 1848; *Belleville Times*, 7 April; 12 May; 9, 30 June 1848; *History of St. Clair County, Illinois* (Philadelphia: Brink, McDonough, 1881), 197, 200–201, 243.

9.   *Belleville Advocate*, 5 October 1848.

10. *Belleville Advocate*, 3 September 1847; 8 February, 5 April, 11 October, 5 November 1849.

11. *Belleville Advocate*, 5, 9 September 1850; 2 October, 5 November 1851.

12. *Belleville Advocate*, 26 November, 17, 24 December 1851; 11, 25 February, 24 March, 23 June 1852; 25 May, 28 September 1853; 17 May, 26 July 1854; *Illinois Republican*, 9, 16 June 1852. See *Illinois Republican*, 7 July 1852, for the complete charter of the Belleville and Illinoistown Railroad Company.

13. *Ottawa: Old and New. A Complete History of Ottawa, Illinois, 1823–1914* (Ottawa, Illinois: Republican Times, 1912–1914), 11; Michael P. Conzen, "The Historical and Geographical Development of the Illinois and Michigan Canal National Heritage Corridor," in Michael P. Conzen and Kay J. Carr, eds., *The Illinois & Michigan Canal National Heritage Corridor: A Guide to Its History and Sources*, 3–25 (Dekalb: Northern Illinois University Press, 1988), 9.

14. *Ottawa Constitutionalist*, 9 March 1850; *Ottawa Free Trader*, 16 February, 2 March, 9 March, 20 July, 30 November 1850.

15.   *Ottawa Free Trader*, 21 December 1850, 8 February 1851;
       Carlton J. Corliss, *Trails to Rails: A Story of Transportation
       Progress in Illinois* (Chicago: Illinois Central System, 1934).

16.   John Hise moved from Pennsylvania to Ottawa in 1839.
       He eventually moved to Chicago where he was also
       elected to the Illinois House of Representatives. Elmer
       Baldwin, *History of LaSalle County, Illinois* (Chicago: Rand,
       McNally, 1877), 254; Michael C. O'Byrne, *History of
       LaSalle County, Illinois* (Chicago: Lewis, 1924), 1:233;
       Ottawa Free Trader, 11 January, 1 February, 8 March
       1851; Howard Gray Brownson, *History of the Illinois Cen-
       tral Railroad to 1870*, University of Illinois Studies in the
       Social Sciences, vol. 4 Urbana: University of Illinois,
       1915).

17.   *Ottawa Free Trader*, 1, 8, 15, 22 March 1851.

18.   *Ottawa Free Trader*, 1 March 1851; *Souvenir Edition, LaSalle
       County Centennial Directory of Former Ottawa Residents, 1831–
       1931* (Ottawa, Illinois: Daily Republican-Times, [1931]),
       7; *Reports of the President, Chief Engineer, and Consulting En-
       gineer of the Chicago & Rock Island Railroad Company, Pre-
       sented to the Board of Directors at Their Meeting at Chicago, De-
       cember 22, 1851* (New York: Wm. C. Bryant, 1852), 2.

19.   Ottawans would vote to incorporate as a city in April
       1853, after a dispute over the village's power to regulate
       liquor sales. *Ottawa Free Trader*, 8, 22 March, 20 Septem-
       ber 1851; 10, 31 January 1852; *Ottawa Republican*,
       9 April 1853.

20.   *Ottawa Free Trader*, 6, 22 January, 12 February 1853.

21.   *The WPA Guide to Illinois*, 29; Illinois General Assembly,
       "An Act to Incorporate the Northern Cross Railroad Com-
       pany," *Private Laws Illinois 1849*, 82, reprinted in *Chicago,
       Burlington & Quincy Railroad Company, Documentary History*,
       570–73, comp. W. W. Baldwin (Chicago: Chicago,
       Burlington & Quincy Railroad, 1928); Overton,
       Burlington Route, 15.

22.   Illinois General Assembly, "An Act to Incorporate the Peo-
       ria and Oquawka Railroad Company," *Private Laws Illinois
       1849*, 99, reprinted in *Chicago, Burlington & Quincy Rail-
       road Company, Documentary History*, 49–53, comp. W. W.
       Baldwin (Chicago: Chicago, Burlington & Quincy Rail-
       road, 1928); Overton, *Burlington Route*, 16.

23.   Illinois General Assembly, "An Act to Incorporate the Cen-
       tral Military Tract Railroad Company," *Private Laws Illi-*

nois 1851, 191, reprinted in *Chicago, Burlington & Quincy Railroad Company, Documentary History*, 37, comp. W. W. Baldwin (Chicago: Chicago, Burlington & Quincy Railroad, 1928).

24.   "A Record of the Proceedings of the Central Military Tract Railroad Co. Chartered February 15th A.D. 1851," 18 April, 27 June, 11 November, 24 December 1851; 13 March 1852, Burlington Archives, Newberry Library, Chicago, Illinois; Overton, *Burlington Route*, 30.

25.   Overton, *Burlington Route*, 32, 34.

26.   Overton, *Burlington Route*, 27–28, 34; "A Record of the Proceedings of the Central Military Tract Railroad Co.," 14 October 1852.

27.   Overton, *Burlington Route*, 34; Larson, *Bonds of Enterprise*, 50.

Five **The Schools**

1.   For an example of the older, progressive approach to school history in Illinois, see Paul E. Belting, "The Development of the Free Public High School in Illinois to 1860," *Journal of the Illinois State Historical Society* 11 (1918–1919): 269–369, 467–565. For two very different modern approaches to the historiography of American public schools, see Michael B. Katz, "The Origins of Public Education: A Reassessment," *History of Education Quarterly* 16 (1976): 381, 407, and Carl F. Kaestle, *Pillars of the Republic: Common Schools and American Society, 1780–1860* (New York: Hill and Wang, 1983), 104–35.

2.   *Laws of Illinois*, 19 G. A. (1855), 51–91, 119–49; "Report of the State Superintendent of Public Instruction," in *Reports Made to the Nineteenth General Assembly of the State of Illinois . . . 1855* (Springfield: Lanphier & Walker, 1855), 65–119.

3.   James E. Herget, "Democracy Revisited: The Law and School Districts in Illinois," *Journal of the Illinois State Historical Society* 72 (1979): 123–36; Robert Gehlmann Bone, "Education in Illinois before 1857," *Journal of the Illinois State Historical Society* 50 (1957): 119–40; Daniel W. Kucera, *Church-State Relationships in Education in Illinois* (Washington, D.C.: Catholic University of America Press, 1955), 22, 32–33.

4.   Kucera, 31; Louis Andrew Butts, "Evolution of Belleville Schools," (thesis, Washington University, 1931), 20; *Laws of Illinois*, 1 G. A. (1820–21), 34–35; *History of St. Clair*

County, Illinois (Philadelphia: Brink, McDonough, 1881), 115–26. Much of the information about early Belleville schools has been gleaned from articles written by an 1850s teacher, county school commissioner, and, later, superintendent of public instruction. Henry Raab, "Teacher's Department," *Belleville Weekly Advocate* (hereafter cited as *Belleville Advocate*), 28 October, 4 November, 11 November, 18 November, 25 November, 2 December 1898. See also George Deeke, "A Picture of Early Belleville," *Journal of the St. Clair County Historical Society* I (1969): 81–96.

5. Butts, 24; *Belleville Advocate*, 11 May, 18 May 1859.

6. *Belleville Advocate*, 2 December 1898; 31 August, 14 September 1859.

7. *Belleville Advocate*, 25 May 1859.

8. Kathleen Neils Conzen, "Germans," in *Harvard Encyclopedia of American Ethnic Groups*, ed. Stephan Thernstrom (Cambridge, Massachusetts: Belknap Press of Harvard University Press, 1980), 405–25; *The History of Cathedral Grade School, 1845–1981* (Belleville, 1981); *Belleville City Directory*, 102; *Historical Review of Belleville, Illinois . . .* (Belleville: Kimball and Taylor, 1870), 58; Reynolds, *Revised Ordinances of the City of Belleville . . .* (Belleville: G. A. Harvey, 1862), 30; *Vierzehnter Synodal-Bericht der Allgemeinen Deutschen Evang.-Luth. Synode von Missouri, Ohio u.a. Staaten abgehatten zu Fort Wayne, Ind., im Jahre 1869* (St. Louis: Concordia, 1869), 4–118; *Belleville Advocate*, 10 February, 13 April 1860; 2 December 1898; Butts, 26; *Third Biennial Report of the Superintendent of Public Instruction . . . 1859–1860* (Springfield, 1860), 6–7, 246.

9. *Holland's Ottawa City Directory, 1869–70* (Chicago: Western, 1869), 18; *Ottawa: Old and New. A Complete History of Ottawa, Illinois, 1823–1914* (Ottawa, Illinois: Republican-Times, 1912–14), 3, 173; *Illinois Free Trader*, 6 June 1840; *Ottawa Free Trader*, 1 November 1844; 8 December 1848; 23 March, 23 November 1849.

10. *Ottawa Free Trader*, 23 March 1849.

11. *Ottawa Free Trader*, 23 November 1849.

12. Elmer Baldwin, *History of LaSalle County, Illinois* (Chicago: Rand, McNally, 1877), 228, 230; *History of LaSalle County, Illinois, Together with Sketches of Its Cities, Villages and Towns*, 2 vols. (Chicago: Inter-State, 1886), 1:475–76; Michael C. O'Byrne, *History of LaSalle County, Illinois*, 3 vols. (Chi-

cago: Lewis, 1924), 1:63, 249; *Ottawa Free Trader*, 25 January 1851.

13.   *Ottawa Republican*, 23 April 1853; 22 April 1854.

14.   *Ottawa Republican*, 17 June 1854.

15.   *Ottawa Republican*, 13 January, 20 January, 10 February, 24 February, 10 March, 1855; *Ottawa Free Trader*, 13, 27 January, 10 March 1855.

16.   *Ottawa Free Trader*, 10 March 1855; *Ottawa Republican*, 10 March 1855; Records of the Bureau of the Census, Federal Population Schedules, Eighth Census of the United States, 1860, LaSalle County, Illinois, Reel 196, National Archives, Washington, D.C. (microfilm in Newberry Library, Chicago, and Morris Library, Carbondale).

17.   *Ottawa: Old and New*, 174; *Ottawa Republican*, 23 June 1855; 25 January, 9 February, 16 February 1856; *Ottawa Free Trader*, 9 February 1856.

18.   *The Past and Present of LaSalle County, Illinois* (Chicago: H. F. Klett, 1877), 285; *Ottawa Free Trader*, 6 September 1856; 24 January, 14 February 1857; Records of the Bureau of the Census, 1860, LaSalle County.

19.   *Ottawa Free Trader*, 23 January, 6 March, 15 May, 26 June, 17 July, 31 July 1858; 19 February, 26 February, 26 1859.

20.   Baldwin, 229; *Ottawa Free Trader*, 5 March, 13 August, 1859; Records of the Bureau of the Census, 1860, LaSalle County.

21.   *Third Biennial Report*, 144; *Ottawa: Old and New*, 177; *Holland's Ottawa City Directory*, 20.

22.   *Ottawa: Old and New*, 174–75; *Ottawa Free Trader*, 23 April, 6 August 1859.

23.   William Lucas Steele, *Galesburg Public Schools: Their History and Work, 1861–1911* (Galesburg: Board of Education, 1911), 217–20, 227. "Report of the State Superintendent of Public Instruction for 1855–56," *Reports Made to the General Assembly of Illinois at its Twentieth Session . . . 1857* (Springfield: Lanphier & Walker, 1857), 259–412 (Knox County figures from p. 381); John Williston Cook, *Educational History of Illinois: Growth and Progress in Educational Affairs of the State from the Earliest Day to the Present* (Chicago: Henry O. Shepard, 1912); *History of Knox County, Illinois* (Chicago: Charles C. Chapman, 1878), 515–32.

24.   *Galesburg Semi-Weekly Democrat* (hereafter cited as *Galesburg Democrat*), 29 June 1859.

25.   *Galesburg Democrat,* 13 April 1859; Hermann R. Muelder, *Missionaries and Muckrakers: The First Hundred Years of Knox College* (Urbana: University of Illinois Press, 1984), 32–33; Albert J. Perry, *History of Knox County, Illinois . . .* (Chicago: S. J. Clarke, 1912), 553.

26.   *Galesburg Democrat,* 16 April, 14 May, 18 May, 3 August, 10 September, 14 September, 17 September 1859.

27.   *Galesburg Democrat,* 17 November 1859; 3 July, 31 August 1860.

28.   *Galesburg Democrat,* 13 April, 23 April 1859.

29.   Steele, 27, 238; *Galesburg Democrat,* 3 July, 16 November 1860; Eighth Census, Knox County Census, Reel 195; *Fourth Biennial Report of the Superintendent of Public Instruction . . . 1861–1862* (Springfield, 1862), 273.

30.   O. Fritiof Ander, "Some Factors in the Americanization of Swedish Immigrants, 1850–1890," *Journal of the Illinois State Historical Society,* 26 (1933): 136–50; Ulf Beijbom, "Swedes," in Thernstrom, ed., 971–81; O. Fritiof Ander, *T. N. Hasselquist: The Career and Influence of a Swedish American Clergyman, Journalist, and Educator* (Rock Island, Illinois: Augustana Historical Society, 1931).

31.   Steele, 21, 242; Muelder, *Missionaries and Muckrakers,* 16, 32–33.

Six **The Politics**

1.   The "First Party System," from the 1790s to the 1820s, saw the Federalists (most often associated with Alexander Hamilton) compete against the Republicans (led by Thomas Jefferson and his successors). The "Second Party System" that took hold in the 1830s pitted Henry Clay's new Whig Party against Andrew Jackson's Democrats (the successor to Jefferson's Republicans). During the 1850s, the Whigs failed to maintain a large following and were replaced by Abraham Lincoln's Republican Party as the major competitor of the Democrats; the origins of the current political system, therefore, can be traced to the 1850s and the "Third Party System." For an analysis of Illinois voting patterns during the shift from the Second to the Third Party System, see Stephen L. Hansen, *The Making of the Third Party System: Voters and Parties in Illinois, 1850–1876,* Studies in American History

and Culture, no. 14 (Ann Arbor: UMI Research Press, 1980).

2. The major exception to this sort of treatment has been Daniel Elazar's work on the political cultures of, among others, the Illinois cities of Belleville, Champaign-Urbana, Decatur, Joliet, Peoria, Rockford, and Springfield. Daniel J. Elazar, *Cities of the Prairie: The Metropolitan Frontier and American Politics* (New York: Basic Books, 1970); Daniel J. Elazar *The Politics of Belleville: A Profile of the Civil Community* (Philadelphia: Temple University Press, 1971).

3. Richard Alcorn, "Leadership and Stability in Mid-Nineteenth Century America: A Case Study of an Illinois Town," *Journal of American History* 61 (1974): 685–702; Don Harrison Doyle, *The Social Order of a Frontier Community: Jacksonville, Illinois, 1825–70* (Urbana: University of Illinois Press, 1978), 92–118; Timothy R. Mahoney, *River Towns in the Great West: The Structure of Provincial Urbanization in the American Midwest, 1820–1870*, (New York: Cambridge University Press, 1990), 273–79.

4. T. J. Krafft, rev., *Revised Ordinances of the City of Belleville, With the City Charter and Amendments* (Belleville, Illinois: G. A. Harvey, 1862), 34, 36; John Reynolds, "The History of the City of Belleville," in *Revised Ordinances of the City of Belleville, with the City Charter and Amendments*, 5–33, rev. T. J. Krafft (Belleville, Illinois: G. A. Harvey, 1862), 17; Elazar, *The Politics of Belleville*, 8.

5. Krafft emigrated from Bavaria. He became a lawyer and practiced in Belleville, where he was also a member of the Library Society; he was naturalized in 1838. Abend, mayor in 1851 and again in 1857–58, emigrated from Bavaria in 1833; he was a lawyer and had been an Illinois state representative in 1849–50. Stoltz eventually became a member of the socially elite Sängerbund und Bibliothek Gesellschaft. *History of St. Clair County, Illinois* (Philadelphia: Brink, McDonough, 1881), 204, 381, 403; *Statuten and Nebengesetzen des Belleviller Sängerbundes und der Bibliothek Gesellschaft* (Belleville, Illinois, 1870), 13–16.

6. Records of the Bureau of the Census, Federal Population Schedules, Eighth Census of the United States, 1860, St. Clair County, Reels 224, 225, National Archives, Washington, D.C. (microfilm in Center for Research Libraries, Chicago); Records of the Bureau of the Census, Federal Population Schedules, Eighth Census of the United States, 1860, Knox County, Reel 195, National Ar-

chives, Washington, D.C. (microfilm in Center for Research Libraries, Chicago).

7.   St. Clair County and Belleville election figures are from "Illinois Election Returns, 1818–1864, From Archives and Ledgers," Reels 30–45A, Archives of the State of Illinois, Springfield, Illinois (microfilm in University of Chicago, Regenstein Library, Chicago); *Belleville Times*, 10 November 1848; *Weekly St. Clair Tribune*, 8 November 1856; *Belleviller Zeitung*, 8 November 1860.

8.   The historical arguments about the influence of German voters in 1860 have swung like a pendulum. Contemporaries placed great emphasis on the role of Germans. Revisionists lessened the importance. More recent historians of Illinois voting, however, have given Germans credit again, especially in Cook and St. Clair Counties. For a review of this literature, see Frederick C. Luebke, introduction to *Ethnic Voters and the Election of Lincoln*, xi–xxxii, ed. Frederick C. Luebke (Lincoln: University of Nebraska Press, 1971). In his work on the Germans of the St. Louis area, Timothy Tucker gives credit to the middle-class German refugees—and especially Gustave Körner— for delivering St. Clair County into the Republican column. Timothy Marlin Tucker, "Political Leadership in the Illinois-Missouri German Community, 1836–1872," (Ph.D. dissertation, University of Illinois, 1968), 3, 117; Arthur C. Cole, ed., *The Constitutional Debates of 1847*, Collections of the Illinois State Historical Library, no. 14 (Springfield: Illinois State Historical Library, 1919), 200.

9.   For an outline of the issues and procedures of the 1847 convention, see Janet Cornelius, *Constitution Making in Illinois, 1818–1970* (Urbana: University of Illinois Press, 1972), 28–42.

10.   Cole, *Constitutional Debates*, 944, 951, 962, 966, 967, 969, 975; George Bunsen, *To the Voters of St. Clair County: Declaration of Candidacy to Amend the Constitution of Illinois* (Belleville, Illinois, [1847]); William C. Kinney, *To My Fellow-Citizens, Declaration of Candidacy to Amend the Constitution of Illinois* (Belleville, Illinois, [1847]); Cornelius, 35–39; Theodore Calvin Pease, *Illinois Election Returns, 1818–1848*, Collections of the Illinois State Historical Library, no. 18 (Springfield: Illinois State Historical Library, 1923), 174–75, 178, 180.

11.   James A. Kettner, *The Development of American Citizenship, 1608–1870* (Chapel Hill: University of North Carolina

Press, 1978), 242–46; *Belleville Times*, 17 March, 25 February 1848; McCormack, Thomas J., ed., *The Memoirs of Gustave Körner, 1809–1896: Life-Sketches Written at the Suggestion of His Children*, vol. 2 (Cedar Rapids, Iowa: Torch Press, 1909), 2:523–24.

12.   The Democrats attended a St. Clair County meeting in Belleville on April 10, 1848. *Belleville Times*, 14 April 1848.

13.   *Belleville Advocate*, 18 April, 19 May 1840.

14.   *Belleville Advocate*, 1 February, 9 March, 9 November, 7 December 1848; 14 January, 16 June, 25 August, 29 September, 6 October, 24 November 1852.

15.   Pease, *Illinois Election Returns*, 549, 573; *Belleville Advocate*, 7 April, 12 May, 23 June 1852.

16.   *St. Clair Banner*, 27 August; 1 November 1844; *Belleville Times*, 28 July; 27 October 1848.

17.   Edmund J. James, *A Bibliography of Newspapers Published in Illinois Prior to 1860*, Publications of the Illinois Historical Library, no. 1 (Springfield, Illinois, 1899), 11; Franklin William Scott, *Newspapers and Periodicals*, Collections of the Illinois State Historical Library, no. 6 (Springfield, Illinois, 1910), 21, 22; Sandra M. Stark, ed., "Illinois Papers," *Illinois Libraries* 64 (March 1962): 210–11; *Illinois Republican*, 30 June, 18 August 1852.

18.   *Der Freiheitsbote für Illinois*, 6 May, 22 July, 26 August 1840.

19.   Carl Wittke, *The German-Language Press in America* (Lexington: University of Kentucky Press, 1957), 54; *Illinois Beobachter*, 25 April, 4, 18 July, 8, 15 August 1844.

20.   Scott, 21–22; *Belleviller Zeitung*, 11, 25 January 1849; 25 March; 22 April, 13 May 1852.

21.   Scott, 20–23.

22.   *St. Clair Tribune*, 23 August 1856.

23.   *St. Clair Tribune*, 2 February, 5 July, 2, 16 August 1856.

24.   Scott, 22–23.

25.   *Belleviller Volksblatt*, 1, 15 March 1856.

26.   *Belleviller Zeitung*, 13, 25 March, 22 April, 12 August 1856.

27.   *Deutscher Demokrat*, 23 August 1856.

28.   *History of LaSalle County, Illinois, Together With Sketches of its Cities, Villages and Towns*, 2 vols. (Chicago: Inter-State, 1886), 1:487–92; *Souvenir Edition, LaSalle County Centennial. Directory of Former Residents, 1831–1931* (Ottawa, Illinois: Daily Republican-Times [1931]), 7.

29.   Robert P. Howard, *Illinois: A History of the Prairie State* (Grand Rapids, Michigan: William B. Eerdmans, 1972), 184–88; Howard W. Allen and Vincent A. Lacey, eds., *Illinois Elections, 1818–1990: Candidates and County Returns for President, Governor, Senate, and House of Representatives* (Carbondale: Southern Illinois University Press, 1992), 122, 129, 136, 145; *Ottawa Free Trader*, 6, 8 November 1856; 6 November 1858; 10 November 1860; *Ottawa Republican*, 13 November 1852.

30.   *Ottawa Free Trader*, 6 November 1858; 31 January, 24 November 1860; *Ottawa Republican*, 17 April, 10 May 1856.

31.   Scott, 270–71; James, 55; *Illinois Free Trader*, 23 May, 6 June, 17 July 1840; 26 March 1841; *Illinois Free Trader and LaSalle County Commercial Advertiser*, 27 August, 22 October, 5, 19 November 1841; 14, 21 January, 4 February, 24 June, 16 September 1842.

32.   "Obituary of William Osman, Printed in the *Daily Free Trader*, January 19, 1909," William Osman Letters, Letter Book, Diary Fragments, 1836–1847, folder 16, item 1, Illinois Historical Survey Library, University of Illinois, Urbana, Illinois; Michael C. O'Byrne, *History of LaSalle County, Illinois*, 3 vols. (Chicago: Lewis, 1924), 1:141, 233; Elmer Baldwin, *History of LaSalle County, Illinois* (Chicago: Rand, McNally, 1877), 253, 254.

33.   Scott, 271; *Ottawa Constitutionalist*, 16 February 1847; 9 March 1850; *Ottawa Republican*, 16 June 1852; 28 1856; 18 September 1858; 19 May 1860; *Ottawa Free Trader*, 13 November 1858.

34.   *Ottawa Free Trader*, 11 February 1860.

35.   *Ottawa Free Trader*, 22 October 1859.

36.   John H. Ryan, "A Chapter from the History of the Underground Railroad in Illinois," *Journal of the Illinois Historical Society* 8 (April 1915): 23–30; *Ottawa Free Trader*, 31 December 1859; 28 April, 3 March, 5 October 1860.

37.   *Ottawa Free Trader*, 22 October, 5 November 1859; 11 February 1860.

38.   *Ottawa Free Trader,* 10 May 1856; *Ottawa Republican,*
        10 May 1856.

39.   *Ottawa Free Trader,* 10, 31 January 1852.

40.   *Ottawa Free Trader,* 26 February, 2 April 1853; *Ottawa Re-
        publican,* 9, 23 April, 14 May 1853.

41.   *Ottawa Free Trader,* 16 April 1853; *Ottawa Republican,*
        26 April 1853; *History of LaSalle County, Illinois, Together
        With Sketches of its Cities, Villages and Towns,* 1:482

42.   *Ottawa Free Trader,* 28 February 1857; *Ottawa Republican,*
        23 May 1857; 20 March, 3 April 1858.

43.   *Ottawa Free Trader,* 8 March 1851; 15 May 1853; *History
        of LaSalle County, Illinois, Together With Sketches of its Cities,
        Villages and Towns,* 1:483–84.

44.   *Ottawa Free Trader,* 12 May 1855.

45.   *Ottawa Free Trader,* 16 June, 15 September 1855; 3 May,
        21 June 1856; *Ottawa Republican,* 21 June 1856.

46.   *Ottawa Free Trader,* 8 November 1856; *Ottawa Republican,*
        8 November 1856.

47.   *Ottawa Republican,* 9 May, 13 June 1857.

48.   *Ottawa Free Trader,* 8 May 1858; *Ottawa Republican,*
        1 May, 8 May 1858.

49.   *Ottawa Free Trader,* 5 March 1859; *Ottawa Republican,*
        5 March 1859.

50.   *Ottawa Republican,* 30 April 1859.

51.   *Ottawa Free Trader,* 12 May, 10 November 1860.

52.   *Galesburg Democrat,* 3 April 1860; "Record of the Proceed-
        ings of the President and Trustees of the Town of Gales-
        burg, From April 21st 1851," MS, Galesburg Public Li-
        brary, Galesburg, Illinois, 149; Earnest Elmo Calkins,
        *They Broke the Prairie: Being Some Account of the Settlement of
        the Upper Mississippi Valley by Religious and Educational Pio-
        neers, Told in Terms of One City, Galesburg, and One College,
        Knox* (New York: Charles Scribner's Sons, 1937), 111,
        137; "Municipal History of Galesburg As Shown by Town
        and City Records: 1841–1933," MS by Fred R. Jeliff,
        Galesburg Public Library, Galesburg, Illinois, [1933].

53.   Knox County and Galesburg election figures are from
        "Illinois Election Returns, 1818–1864, From Archives

and Ledgers," Reels 30–45A; *Galesburg Democrat,*
13 March, 6 November 1856; 6 November 1860.

54.   Pease, *Illinois Election Returns,* 150; Hermann R. Muelder,
*Fighters for Freedom: The History of Anti-Slavery Activities of
Men and Women Associated with Knox College* (New York: Co-
lumbia University Press, 1959), 156–71, 185, 379.

55.   Calkins, *They Broke the Prairie,* 208, 288; Jean C. Lee, *Prairies, Prayers, and Promises: An Illustrated History of Galesburg*
(Northridge, California: Windsor, 1987), 30.

56.   Muelder, *Fighters for Freedom,* 343, 353–54; *Galesburg
Democrat,* 5, 19 January 1854.

57.   *Galesburg Democrat,* 13 March, 17 April 1856.

58.   *Galesburg Democrat,* 14 February 1856.

59.   *Galesburg Democrat,* 12, 24 March, 9, 23 April 1857;
Muelder, *Fighters for Freedom,* 374–94.

60.   *History of Knox County, Illinois* (Galesburg, Illinois: Charles
C. Chapman, 1878), 404–21; *Galesburg Democrat,* 5 Octo-
ber; 10 December, 1859; 31 January; 16, 20 March; 3, 6
April; 20 June; 30 July 1860.

61.   *Galesburg Democrat,* 13 November 1860.

Seven Conclusion

1.   The decade of Belleville's largest growth rate was the
1830s when the town grew by 900 percent from 200 to
2,000 inhabitants.

Bibliography

Unpublished Sources

Belleville

Belleville, Illinois. Belleville Public Library. Vertical Files. Freemasons.
————. Vertical Files. German Library Society in St. Clair County, Illinois.
Carbondale, Illinois. Illinois Regional Archives Depository. Southern Illinois University. St. Clair County Records. Board of Supervisors' Minutes, 1798–1817.
Springfield, Illinois. Archives of the State of Illinois. Board of Commissioners. Claims for Which Certificates of Confirmation Granted, 1814–17.
Washington, D.C. National Archives. Records of the Bureau of the Census. Federal Population Schedules. Sixth Census of the United States. 1840. St. Clair County, Illinois. Reel 70. (Microfilm in Federal Archives and Records Center, Chicago).
————. Federal Population Schedules. Seventh Census of the United States. 1850. St. Clair County, Illinois. Reel 126 (Microfilm in Federal Archives and Records Center, Chicago).
————. Federal Population Schedules. Eighth Census of the United States. 1860. St. Clair County, Illinois. Reels 224, 225 (Microfilm in Center for Research Libraries, Chicago, and Federal Archives and Records Center, Chicago).

Ottawa

Urbana, Illinois. University of Illinois. Illinois Historical Survey Library. William Osman Letters, Letter Book, Diary Fragments, 1836–1847.
Washington, D.C. National Archives. Records of the Bureau of the Census. Federal Population Schedules. Sixth Census of the United States. 1840. LaSalle County, Illinois. Reel 63 (Microfilm in Newberry Library, Chicago).
————. Federal Population Schedules. Seventh Census of the United States. 1850. LaSalle County, Illinois. Reel 115 (Microfilm in Newberry Library, Chicago, and Morris Library, Carbondale).

———. Federal Population Schedules. Eighth Census of the United States. 1860. LaSalle County, Illinois. Reel 196 (Microfilm in Newberry Library, Chicago, and Morris Library, Carbondale).

Galesburg

Chicago, Illinois. General Services Administration. Federal Archives and Records Center. Registers' Cash Certificates. Quincy Land Office. 4 vols. Vol. 1.

Chicago, Illinois. Newberry Library. Manuscripts. Burlington Archives. "A Record of the Proceedings of the Central Military Tract Railroad Company. Chartered February 15th A.D. 1851."

Galesburg, Illinois. Galesburg Public Library. Archives. "Alpha Lodge, No. 155 of the Galesburg Freemasons." Dues Book, 1862–1878.

———. Archives. "Assessor's List for 1859 for the Town of Galesburg in the County of Knox."

———. Archives. "Municipal History of Galesburg As Shown by Town and City Records 1841–1933." MS by Fred R. Jeliff, [1933].

———. Archives. "Record of the Proceedings of the President and Trustees of the Town of Galesburg, From April 21st, 1851."

———. Archives. "Records of the Presbyterian Church in Galesburg, Illinois."

———. Ephemera Files. First Methodist Episcopal Church.

———. Ephemera Files. St. Patrick's Church.

Galesburg, Illinois. Knox College. Archives. "Directions for the Exploring Committee."

———. Archives. George Washington Gale. "Report of the Agent." No. 1, 1836.

———. Archives. George Washington Gale. "Report of the Agent." No. 3, n.d.

———. Archives. Letter from Timothy B. Jervis to Hiram H. Kellogg. Chicago, 15 June 1835.

———. Archives. "Pioneer Who's Who and Thumb Nail Biographies." MS, n.d.

———. Archives. "Town Book of Galesburg, Illinois, 1859–1881." (Microfilm in Galesburg Public Library, Galesburg, Illinois).

Washington, D.C. National Archives. Records of the Bureau of the Census. Federal Population Schedules. Sixth Census of the United States. 1840. Knox County, Illinois. Reel 62 (Microfilm in Federal Archives and Records Center, Chicago).

———. Records of the Bureau of the Census. Federal Population Schedules. Seventh Census of the United States. 1850. Knox County, Illinois. Reel 113 (Microfilm in Newberry Library, Chicago).

———. Records of the Bureau of the Census. Federal Population Schedules. Eighth Census of the United States. 1860. Knox

County, Illinois. Reel 195 (Microfilm in Center for Research Libraries, Chicago).

General

Springfield, Illinois. Archives of the State of Illinois. Federal Land Surveyors' Field Notes.
———. Federal Township Plats.
———. Illinois Election Returns, 1818–1864, From Archives and Ledgers.

Published Primary Sources

Belleville

Abend, Edward. *To the Voters of St. Clair County: Declaration of Candidacy to Amend the Constitution of Illinois.* Belleville Public Library, Belleville, Illinois, 1847.
Belleville Advocate, 18 April 1840–6 April 1860.
Belleville, Illinois, City Directory and Business Mirror for 1860. Belleville, Illinois: Bingham & Doughty, 1860.
Belleville, Illinois, Illustrated. N.p., n.d.
Belleville Times, 21 January–10 November 1848.
Belleviller Volksblatt, 1–15 March 1856.
Belleviller Zeitunq, 25 January 1849–8 November 1860.
Bunsen, George. *To the Voters of St. Clair County: Declaration of Candidacy to Amend the Constitution of Illinois.* Belleville Public Library, Belleville, Illinois, [1847].
Deutscher Demokrat, 23 August 1856.
E. Gest's Report of the Preliminary Surveys, of the Western Division Ohio and Mississippi Rail Road, Chartered by the State of Illinois. Cincinnati: John D. Thorpe, 1851.
Elfter Synodal-Bericht der allgemeinen deutschen evang. Luth. Synode von Missouri, Ohio u. a. Staaten vom Jahre 1863. St. Louis, Missouri, 1864.
Facts and Statements Concerning the Cleveland & St. Louis R. R. from Cleveland, Ohio, by Lebanon, Indiana, to Paris, Illinois. Cleveland: Harris, Fairbanks, Cobb, Herald Office, 1854.
Der Freiheitsbote für Illinois, 16 May–26 August 1840.
Historical Review of Belleville, Illinois. . . . Belleville: Kimball and Taylor, 1870.
Illinois Beobachter, 25 April–15 August 1844.
Illinois General Assembly. "An Act to Legalize the Incorporation of the City of Belleville, and the Official Acts of the City Council of Said City. . . . " In *Private Laws of the State of Illinois, Passed at the*

First Session of the Seventeenth General Assembly . . . 1851, 111–12. Springfield, Illinois: Lanphier & Walker, 1851.

Illinois Republican, 14 January–18 August 1852.

Kinney, William C. *To My Fellow-Citizens: Declaration of Candidacy to Amend the Constitution of Illinois.* Belleville, Illinois, [1847].

Krafft, T. J., rev. *Revised Ordinances of the City of Belleville, with the City Charter and Amendments . . . .* Belleville, Illinois: G. A. Harvey, 1862.

Raab, Henry. "Teacher's Department." *Belleville Advocate*, 28 October– 2 December 1898.

Reynolds, John. "The History of the City of Belleville." In *Revised Ordinances of the City of Belleville, with the City Charter and Amendments . . . ,* 5–33. Revised by T. J. Krafft. Belleville, Illinois: G. A. Harvey, 1862.

Statuten und Nebengesetzen des Belleviller Sängerbundes und der Bibliothek Gesellschaft. Belleville, Illinois, 1870.

St. Clair Banner, 27 August–1 November 1844.

St. Clair Tribune, 2 February–5 November 1856.

Vierzehnter Synodal-Bericht der Allgemeinen Deutschen Evang.-Luth. Synode von Missouri, Ohio u. a. Staaten abgehalten zu Fort Wayne, Ind., im Jahre 1869. St. Louis, Missouri, 1869.

Weekly St. Clair Tribune, 8 November–22 March 1856.

Zwölfter und Dreizehnter Synodal-Bericht der Allgemeinen Deutschen Evang.-Luth. Synode von Missouri, Ohio u. a. Staaten vom Jahre 1864 u. 1866. St. Louis, Missouri, 1867.

Ottawa

"Annual Report of the President and Directors to the Stockholders of the Chicago and Rock Island Rail Road Company. July 1st, 1857." In *Reports of Railroad Companies, 1854–58.* 4 vols. New York: B. F. Corlies, 1857 (Chicago, Newberry Library, Special Collections).

By-Laws and Ordinances of the Town of Ottawa, LaSalle County, Illinois, Adopted May 7th, 1849. Ottawa, Illinois: Printed by Order of the Board of Trustees, 1849.

By-Laws of Shabbona Chapter, No. 37, Royal Arch Masons, Ottawa, Illinois, Adopted May 5, A.D. 1875; A. I. 2405. Ottawa, Illinois: Osman & Hapeman, 1875.

1878–1909: The Ottawa Township High School Thirty-Second Annual Commencement. Graduation Program, June 10, 1909. [Ottawa, Illinois, 1909].

Griggs, Clarence, comp. *Souvenir, One Hundredth Anniversary of Christ Episcopal Church, Ottawa, Illinois,* A.D. 1838–A.D. 1938. Ottawa, Illinois: Illinois Office Supply, 1938.

Holland's Ottawa City Directory, 1869–70. Chicago: Western, 1869.

Illinois Free Trader, 23 May 1840–4 June 1841.

Illinois Free Trader and LaSalle County Commercial Advertiser, 4 June 1841–29 September 1843.

Illinois General Assembly. "An Act to Incorporate the Rock Island and LaSalle Railroad Company." In *Reports of the President, Chief Engineer, and Consulting Engineer of the Chicago & Rock Island Railroad Company*, 27. New York: Wm. C. Bryant, 1852.

Ottawa Constitutionalist, 11 February 1847–12 June 1852.

Ottawa Free Trader, 5 January 1844–15 December 1860.

Ottawa Republican, 19 June 1852–22 September 1860.

[Redfield, Wm. C.]. *Sketch of the Geographical Rout of a Great Railway, By Which it is Proposed to Connect the Canals and Navigable Waters of the States of New-York, Pennsylvania, Ohio, Indiana, Illinois, Missouri, and the Michigan North-West, and Missouri Territories*. New York: G & C & H. Carvill, Ludwig & Tolefree, 1929.

Reports of the President, Chief Engineer, and Consulting Engineer of the Chicago & Rock Island Railroad Company, Presented to the Board of Directors at Their Meeting at Chicago, December 22, 1851. With a Copy of the Charter of Said Company, Granted by the Legislature of the State of Illinois. New York: Wm. C. Bryant, 1852.

Sapp, Ruth B. *Commemorating the One Hundredth Anniversary of the First Congregational Church of Ottawa, Illinois*. Ottawa, Illinois: Illinois Office Supply, 1939.

Woltz, J. N., and C. A. Gould, comps. *Ottawa City Directory and Business Advertiser for 1866–67*. Ottawa, Illinois: Republican Job Printing Office, 1866.

[Wright, John Stephen]. *Grants of Land to Illinois. Plan for Using the Lands Donated by Congress to Illinois Under the "Chicago and Mobile Railroad Bill," and the "Swamp Land Bill."* Chicago: Printed at the Journal Office, 107 Lake Street, 1850.

Galesburg

"Colton Manuscript." Western Historical Collection. Widener Library, Harvard University, Cambridge, Massachusetts. Reprinted in *Burlington West, A Colonization History Of the Burlington Railroad*, 506–15. By Richard C. Overton. Cambridge, Massachusetts: Harvard University Press, 1941.

Galesburg Democrat. 5 January 1854–16 November 1860.

Illinois General Assembly. "An Act to Incorporate the Central Military Tract Railroad Company." In *Private Laws of Illinois, 1851*, 191. Reprinted in *Chicago, Burlington & Quincy Railroad Company, Documentary History*, 37–42. Compiled by W. W. Baldwin. Chicago: Chicago, Burlington & Quincy Railroad, 1928.

———. "An Act to Incorporate the City of Galesburg, in Knox County." In *Private Laws of the State of Illinois, Passed at the Twentieth General Assembly . . . 1857*, 673–705. Springfield, Illinois: Lanphier & Walker, 1857.

————. "An Act to Incorporate the Northern Cross Railroad Company." In *Private Laws of Illinois 1849*, 82. Reprinted in *Chicago, Burlington & Quincy Railroad Company, Documentary History*, 570–73. Compiled by W. W. Baldwin. Chicago: Chicago, Burlington & Quincy Railroad, 1928.

————. "An Act to Incorporate the Peoria and Oquawka Railroad Company." In *Private Laws of Illinois, 1849*, 99. Reprinted in *Chicago, Burlington & Ouincy Railroad Company, Documentary History*, 49–53. Compiled by W. W. Baldwin. Chicago: Chicago, Burlington & Quincy Railroad, 1928.

Litvin, Martin, ed. *Voices of the Prairie Land*. 2 vols. Galesburg, Illinois: Mother Bickerdyke Historical Collection, 1972.

The Manual of the First Universalist Church of Galesburg, Illinois. Galesburg, Illinois, 1860.

Report of the Board of Directors of the Central Military Tract Rail-Road, and of William E. Whittle, Civil Engineer. Galesburg, Illinois: S. Gustavus Cowan's "News-Letter" Book and Job Press Printer, 1851.

General

Fourth Biennial Report of the Superintendent of Public Instruction . . . 1861–1862. Springfield, 1862.

Illinois General Assembly. *Laws of Illinois*. 1st General Assembly. 1820–21.

————. *Laws of Illinois*. 19th General Assembly. 1855.

Peck, J. M. *A Gazetteer of Illinois in Three Parts: Containing a General View of the State, A General View of Each County . . . .* Jacksonville, Illinois: R. Goudy, 1834.

"Report of the State Superintendent of Public Instruction." In *Reports Made to the Nineteenth General Assembly of the State of Illinois . . . 1855*, 65–119. Springfield: Lanphier & Walker, 1855.

"Report of the State Superintendent of Public Instruction for 1855–56." In *Reports Made to the General Assembly of Illinois at Its Twentieth Session . . . 1857*, 259–412. Springfield: Lanphier & Walker, 1857.

Third Biennial Report of the Superintendent of Public Instruction . . . 1859–1860. Springfield, 1860.

U.S. Congress. Senate. *Preliminary Report on the Eighth Census, 1860*. 37th Cong., 2d sess., 1862. Washington, D.C.: Government Printing Office, 1862.

U.S. Department of the Interior. Census Office. *A Compendium of the Ninth Census, 1870*. Washington, D.C.: Government Printing Office, 1872.

————. *The Statistics of the Population of the United States*. Washington, D.C.: Government Printing Office, 1872.

U.S. Department of State. *Abstract of the Fifth Census of the United States, 1830*. Washington, D.C.: Printed at the Globe Office, 1832.

Published Secondary Sources

Belleville

Belcher, Wyatt W. *The Economic Rivalry Between St. Louis and* Chicago. New York: Columbia University Press, 1947.

Bergquist, James M. "People and Politics in Transition: The Illinois Germans, 1850–60." In *Ethnic Voters and the Election of Lincoln,* 190–226. Edited by Frederick C. Luebke. Lincoln: University of Nebraska Press, 1971.

Boylan, Josephine. "The Illinois Railroad and Its Successors." *Journal of the Illinois State Historical Society* 30 (1937): 180–92.

Butts, Louis Andrew. "Evolution of Belleville Schools." Thesis, Washington University, 1931.

Conzen, Kathleen Neils. "Germans." In *Harvard Encyclopedia of American Ethnic Groups,* 405–25. Edited by Stephan Thernstrom. Cambridge, Massachusetts: Harvard University Press, 1980.

Corliss, Carlton J. *Main Line of Mid-America: The Story of the Illinois Central.* New York: Creative Age Press, 1950.

Cross, Jasper W. "The Forty-Eighters and the Election of 1860." *Historical Bulletin* 27 (1949): 78–89.

Deeke, George. "A Picture of Early Belleville." *Journal of the St. Clair Historical Society* 1 (1969): 81–96.

Dorpalen, Andreas. "The German Element and the Issues of the Civil War." *Mississippi Valley Historical Review* 19 (1942–43): 55–76.

Elazar, Daniel J. *The Politics of Belleville: A Profile of the Civil Community.* Philadelphia: Temple University Press, 1971.

Faust, Albert Bernhardt. *The German Element in the United States.* Boston: Houghton Mifflin, 1909.

The History of the Cathedral Grade School, 1845–1981. Belleville, Illinois, 1981.

History of St. Clair County, Illinois. Philadelphia: Brink, McDonough, 1881.

An Illustrated Historical Atlas of St. Clair County, Illinois. Chicago: Warner & Beers, 1874.

Körner, Gustave. *Das Deutsche Element in den Vereinigten Staaten von Nordamerika, 1818–1848.* Cincinnati, Ohio: U. C. Wilde, 1880.

Lantz, Herman R. *A Community in Search of Itself: A Case History of Cairo, Illinois.* Carbondale: Southern Illinois University Press, 1972.

Luebke, Frederick C. Introduction to *Ethnic Voters and the Election of Lincoln,* xl–xxxii. Edited by Frederick C. Luebke. Lincoln: University of Nebraska Press, 1971.

Luthin, Reinhard. "Lincoln Appeals to German Voters." *German-American Review* 25 (1959): 4–15.

McCormack, Thomas J., ed. *The Memoirs of Gustave Körner, 1809–1896: Life-Sketches Written at the Suggestion of His Children.* 2 vols. Cedar Rapids, Iowa: Torch Press, 1909.

Monaghan, Jay. "Did Abraham Lincoln Receive the Illinois German Vote?" In *Ethnic Voters and the Election of Lincoln*, 62–67. Edited by Frederick C. Luebke. Lincoln: University of Nebraska Press, 1971.

Pilgrims Pressing On, 1837–1974. Belleville, Illinois, 1974.

Reflections, 1814–1964. N.p., 1964.

Reynolds, John. *My Own Times*. Chicago: Fergus Printing, 1879.

———. *A Pioneer History of Illinois*. Belleville, Illinois: N. A. Randall, 1852.

St. George's Episcopal Church, 1882–1982. Belleville, Illinois, 1982.

St. Peter's Roman Catholic Cathedral. N.p., n.d.

Tucker, Marlin Timothy. "Political Leadership in the Illinois-Missouri German Community, 1836–1872." Ph.D. dissertation, University of Illinois, 1968.

Villard, Oswald Garrison. "The Latin Peasants of Belleville, Illinois." *Journal of the Illinois State Historical Society* 35 (March 1942): 7–20.

Wittke, Carl. *The German-Language Press in America*. Lexington: University of Kentucky Press, 1957.

Ottawa

Ackerman, William K. *Historical Sketch of the Illinois-Central Railroad with a Brief Biographical Record of Its Incorporators and Some of Its Early Officers*. Chicago: Fergus Printing, 1890.

Agnew, Dwight L. "Beginning of the Rock Island Lines." *Journal of the Illinois State Historical Society* 46 (1953): 407–24.

Baldwin, Elmer. *History of LaSalle County, Illinois . . . A Sketch of the Pioneer Settlers of Each Town to 1840*. Chicago: Rand, McNally, 1877.

Barrionuevo, Carlos J. "From Boat to Boxcar: Railroads Around the Illinois & Michigan Canal, 1850–1880." In *Settling the Upper Illinois Valley: Patterns of Change in the I & M Canal Corridor, 1830–1900*, 23–31. Edited by Michael P. Conzen and Melissa J. Moralee. Studies on the Illinois and Michigan Canal Corridor, no. 3. Chicago: Committee on Geographical Studies, University of Chicago, 1989.

Brownson, Howard Gray. *History of the Illinois Central Railroad to 1870*. University of Illinois Studies in the Social Sciences, vol. 4. Urbana: University of Illinois, 1915.

Conzen, Michael P. "The Historical and Geographical Development of the Illinois and Michigan Canal National Heritage Corridor." In *The Illinois & Michigan Canal Heritage Corridor: A Guide to Its History and Sources*, 3–25. Edited by Michael P. Conzen and Kay J. Carr. DeKalb: Northern Illinois University Press, 1988.

———, ed. *Focus on Ottawa: A Historical and Geographical Survey of Ottawa, Illinois, in the Twentieth Century*. Studies on the Illinois and Michigan Canal Corridor, no. 1. Chicago: Committee on Geographical Studies, University of Chicago, 1987.

Conzen, Michael P., and Melissa J. Moralee, eds. *Settling the Upper Il-*

linois Valley: Patterns of Change in the I & M Canal Corridor, 1830–
1900. Studies on the Illinois and Michigan Canal Corridor, no. 3.
Chicago: Committee on Geographical Studies, University of Chicago, 1989.

Corliss, Carlton J. *Main Line of Mid-America: The Story of the Illinois
Central.* New York: Creative Age Press, 1950.

———. *Trails to Rails: A Story of Transportation Progress in Illinois.* Chicago: Illinois Central System, 1934.

Hayes, William E. *Iron Road to Empire: The History of 100 Years of Progress of the Rock Island Lines.* New York: Summers-Boardman, 1953.

*History of LaSalle County, Illinois, Together with Sketches of Its Cities, Vil-
lages and Towns.* 2 vols. Chicago: Inter-State, 1886.

Howe, Walter A., comp. *Documentary History of the Illinois and Michigan Canal: Legislation, Litigation, and Titles.* Springfield: State of Illinois, 1956.

Lightner, David L. "Construction Labor on the Illinois Central Railroad." *Journal of the Illinois State Historical Society* 66 (1973): 285–
301.

Nannini, Michael. "The Ethnic and Regional Composition of LaSalle
County, 1850–1860." In *Settling the Upper Illinois Valley: Patterns of
Change in the I & M Canal Corridor, 1830–1900,* 77–90. Edited by
Michael P. Conzen and Melissa J. Moralee. Studies on the Illinois
and Michigan Canal Corridor, no. 3. Chicago: Committee on Geo-
graphical Studies, University of Chicago, 1989.

O'Byrne, Michael C. *History of LaSalle County, Illinois.* 3 vols. Chicago: Lewis, 1924.

Osman, Eaton G. *The Last of a Great Indian Tribe: A Chapter of Colonial
History.* Chicago: A. Flanagan, 1923.

Ottawa: Old and New, A Complete History of Ottawa, Illinois, 1823–1914.
Ottawa, Illinois: Republican-Times, 1912–1914.

The Past and Present of LaSalle County, Illinois. Chicago: H. F. Klett,
1877.

Raymond, W. J., and W. F. Tieste. *Ottawa, Illinois: Historical, Biographical, and Commercial.* Ottawa, Illinois: Raymond and Tieste, 1881.

Richardson, Kathleen. "An Analysis of Land Parcel and Landscape
Change in LaSalle County, 1859–1892." In *Settling the Upper Illinois Valley: Patterns of Change in the I & M Canal Corridor, 1830–
1900,* 111–23. Edited by Michael P. Conzen and Melissa J.
Moralee. Studies on the Illinois and Michigan Canal Corridor, no.
3. Chicago: Committee on Geographical Studies, University of
Chicago, 1989.

Ryan, John H. "A Chapter from the History of the Underground
Railroad in Illinois." *Journal of the Illinois State Historical Society* 8
(1915): 23–30.

Schaefer, Catherine. "A Chronology of Missions and Churches in Illinois from 1675 to 1855." *Illinois Catholic Historical Review* (1918):
103–9, 253–56.

Scott, James. *The Illinois Nation: A History of the Illinois Nation of Indians from their Discovery to the Present Day.* Streator, Illinois, 1973.

Souvenir Edition, LaSalle County Centennial, Directory of Former Ottawa Residents, 1831–1931. Ottawa, Illinois: Daily Republican-Times, [1931].

Stromquist, Shelton. *A Generation of Boomers: The Pattern of Railroad Labor Conflict in Nineteenth-Century America.* Urbana: University of Illinois Press, 1987.

Tisler, C. C. *A Short History of the Jordan Hardware Company, Ottawa, Illinois, 1840 to 1953.* Ottawa, Illinois: Illinois Office Supply, 1953.

———. *Story of Ottawa, Illinois.* Ottawa, Illinois: C. C. Tisler, 1953.

Wolfe, Philip Devon. "Ottawa's Economy: Growth and Change in Commerce, Industry, and Government." In *Focus on Ottawa: A Historical and Geographical Survey of Ottawa, Illinois, in the Twentieth Century,* 11–18. Edited by Michael P. Conzen. Studies on the Illinois and Michigan Canal Corridor, no. 1. Chicago: Committee on Geographical Studies, University of Chicago, 1987.

Wyman, Mark. *Immigrants in the Valley: Irish, Germans, and Americans in the Upper Mississippi Country, 1830–1860.* Chicago: Nelson-Hall, 1984.

Yuasa, Shigehiro. "The Commercial Pattern of the Illinois & Michigan Canal, 1848–1860." In *Settling the Upper Illinois Valley: Patterns of Change in the I & M Canal Corridor, 1830–1900,* 9–21. Edited by Michael P. Conzen and Melissa J. Moralee. Studies on the Illinois and Michigan Canal Corridor, no. 3. Chicago: Committee on Geographical Studies, University of Chicago, 1989.

Galesburg

Ander, O. Fritiof. "Some Factors in the Americanization of Swedish Immigrants, 1850–1890." *Journal of the Illinois State Historical Society.* 26 (April-July 1934): 136–50.

———. *T. N. Hasselquist: The Career and Influence of a Swedish American Clergyman, Journalist, and Educator.* Rock Island, Illinois: Augustana Historical Society, 1931.

Baldwin, W. W., comp. *Chicago, Burlington & Quincy Railroad Company, Documentary History.* Chicago: Chicago, Burlington & Quincy Railroad, 1928.

Beijbom, Ulf. "Swedes." In *Harvard Encyclopedia of American Ethnic Groups,* 971–81. Edited by Stephan Thernstrom. Cambridge, Massachusetts: Harvard University Press, 1980.

Brief History of the First Presbyterian Church. N.p., n.d.

Calkins, Earnest Elmo. "Genesis of a Railroad." *Transactions of the Illinois State Historical Society* 42 (1935): 43–56.

———. *They Broke the Prairie: Being Some Account of the Settlement of the Upper Mississippi Valley by Religious and Educational Pioneers, Told in Terms of One City, Galesburg, and One College, Knox.* New York: Charles Scribner's Sons, 1937.

Carlson, Theodore L. *The Illinois Military Tract: A Study of Land Occupation, Utilization and Tenure.* Illinois Studies in the Social Sciences, vol. 22. Urbana: University of Illinois Press, 1951.

Cooley, Verna. "Illinois and the Underground Railroad to Canada." *Transactions of the Illinois State Historical Society* (1917): 76–98.

Cross, Whitney R. *The Burned-Over District: The Social and Intellectual History of Enthusiastic Religion in Western New York, 1800–1850.* Ithaca, New York: Cornell University Press, 1950.

Davis, Grace. *History of the Swedish Baptist Church.* N.p., n.d.

Dunn, Arthur W. *An Analysis of the Social Structure of a Western Town.* Chicago: University of Chicago Press, 1896.

Eastman, Zebina. "History of the Anti-Slavery Agitation and the Growth of the Liberty and Republican Parties in the State of Illinois." In *Discovery and Conquests of the Northwest with the History of Chicago,* 655–77. Edited by Rufus Blanchard. Wheaton, Illinois: R. Blanchard, 1879.

First Lutheran Church, Ninetieth Anniversary. Galesburg, Illinois, 1941.

Fojde, Myron J. "Primitivism and Paternalism." *Western Illinois Regional Studies* 3 (1980): 105–40.

Gale, George Washington. *A Brief History of Knox College, Situated in Galesburgh, Knox County, Illinois.* Cincinnati, Ohio: C. Clark, 1845.

Grace Episcopal Church of Galesburg, Illinois, 1859–1959. Galesburg, Illinois, 1959.

Hildner, Ernest G. "Higher Education in Transition, 1850–1870." *Journal of the Illinois State Historical Society* 61 (Spring 1963): 61–73.

History of Knox County, Illinois. Chicago: Charles C. Chapman, 1878.

Johnson, Daniel T. "Financing the Western Colleges, 1844–1862." *Journal of the Illinois Historical Society* 65 (Spring 1972): 43–53.

Landon, Fred. "Benjamin Lundy in Illinois." *Journal of the Illinois State Historical Society* 30 (1940): 55–67.

Lee, Jean C. *Prairies, Prayers, and Promises: An Illustrated History of Galesburg.* Northridge, California: Windsor, 1987.

Meyer, Douglas K. "Immigrant Clusters in the Illinois Military Tract." *Pioneer America: The Journal of Historic American Material Culture* 12 (May 1980): 97–112.

Muelder, Hermann Richard. *Church History in a Puritan Colony of the Middle West.* Galesburg, Illinois: Central Congregational Church and First Presbyterian Church, 1937.

———. *Fighters for Freedom: The History of Anti-Slavery Activities of Men and Women Associated with Knox College.* New York: Columbia University Press, 1959.

———. *Missionaries and Muckrakers: The First Hundred Years of Knox College.* Urbana: University of Illinois Press, 1984.

Overton, Richard C. *Burlington Route: A History of the Burlington Lines.* New York: Alfred A. Knopf, 1965.

————. *Burlington West: A Colonization History of the Burlington Railroad.* Cambridge, Massachusetts: Harvard University Press, 1941.
————. *The First Ninety Years: An Historical Sketch of the Burlington Railroad, 1850–1940.* Chicago, 1940.

Park, Siyoung. "Perceptions of Land Quality and the Settlement of Northern Pike County, 1821–1836." *Western Illinois Regional Studies* 3 (Spring 1980): 5–21.

Perry, Albert J. *History of Knox County, Illinois: Its Cities, Towns and People.* Chicago: S. J. Clarke, 1912.

Rezab, Gordana. "Land Speculation in Fulton County, 1817–1832." *Western Illinois Regional Studies* 3 (Spring 1980): 22–35.

Steele, William Lucas. *Galesburg Public Schools: Their History and Work, 1861–1911.* Galesburg, Illinois: Board of Education, 1911.

"That Ye May Tell it to the Generation Following": The First Baptist Church, 1848–1948. Galesburg, Illinois, 1948.

U.S. Department of the Interior. Pension Bureau. *A Digest of the Laws of the U.S. Governing the Granting of Army and Navy Pensions and Bounty-Land Warrants* . . . . Washington, D.C.: Government Printing Office, 1881.

General

Alcorn, Richard. "Leadership and Stability in Mid-Nineteenth Century America: A Case Study of an Illinois Town." *Journal of American History* 61 (1974): 685–702.

Allen, Howard W., and Vincent A. Lacey, eds. *Illinois Elections, 1818–1990: Candidates and County Returns for President, Governor, Senate, and House of Representatives.* Carbondale: Southern Illinois University Press, 1992.

Alvord, Clarence Walworth. *The Illinois Country, 1673–1818.* Vol. 1 of *The Centennial History of Illinois.* Edited by Clarence Walworth Alvord. Springfield: Illinois Centennial Commission, 1918.

Atherton, Lewis. *Main Street on the Middle Border.* Bloomington: Indiana University Press, 1954.

Bailyn, Bernard. *The Ideological Origins of the American Revolution.* Cambridge, Massachusetts: Harvard University Press, 1967.

Belting, Paul E. "The Development of the Free Public High School in Illinois to 1960." *Journal of the Illinois State Historical Society* 11 (1918–1919): 269–369, 467–565.

The Biographical Encyclopedia of Illinois of the Nineteenth Century. Philadelphia: Galaxy, 1875.

Blumin, Stuart M. *The Emergence of the Middle Class: Social Experience in the American City, 1760–1900.* New York: Cambridge University Press, 1989.

Bone, Robert Gehlmann. "Education in Illinois before 1857." *Journal of the Illinois State Historical Society* 50 (1957): 119–40.

Carr, Kay J. "Community Dynamics and Educational Decisions: Establishing Public Schools in Belleville and Galesburg." *Illinois Historical Journal* 84 (Spring 1991): 25–38.

Chudacoff, Howard P. *Mobile Americans: Residential and Social Mobility in Omaha, 1880–1920.* New York: Oxford University Press, 1972.

Cole, Arthur C. *The Constitutional Debates of 1847.* Collections of the Illinois State Historical Library, no. 14. Springfield: Illinois State Historical Library, 1919.

———. *The Era of the Civil War, 1848–1870.* Vol. 3 of *The Centennial History of Illinois.* Edited by Clarence Walworth Alvord. Springfield: Illinois Centennial Commission, 1918.

Cook, John Williston. *Educational History of Illinois: Growth and Progress in Educational Affairs of the State from the Earliest Day to the Present.* Chicago: Henry O. Shepard, 1912.

Cornelius, Janet. *Constitution Making in Illinois, 1818–1970.* Urbana: University of Illinois Press, 1972.

Cott, Nancy F. *The Bonds of Womanhood: "Women's Sphere" in New England, 1780–1835.* New Haven, Connecticut: Yale University Press, 1977.

Cronon, William. *Nature's Metropolis: Chicago and the Great West.* New York: W. W. Norton, 1991.

Curti, Merle. *The Making of an American Community: A Case Study of Democracy in a Frontier County.* Stanford, California: Stanford University Press, 1959.

Doyle, Don Harrison. *The Social Order of a Frontier Community: Jacksonville, Illinois, 1825–70.* Urbana: University of Illinois Press, 1978.

Earle, Carville. "Regional Economic Development West of the Appalachians, 1815–1860." In *North America: The Historical Geography of a Changing Continent,* 172–97. Edited by Robert D. Mitchell and Paul A. Groves. Totowa, New Jersey: Rowman & Littlefield, 1987.

Eblen, Jack E. "An Analysis of Nineteenth-Century Frontier Populations." *Demography* 2 (1965): 399–413.

Elazar, Daniel J. *Cities of the Prairie: The Metropolitan Frontier and American Politics.* New York: Basic Books, 1970.

Estabrook, H. D. "The First Train Order by Telegraph." In *Wiring a Continent: The History of the Telegraph Industry in the United States, 1832–1866,* 27–29. By Robert Luther Thompson. Princeton, New Jersey: Princeton University Press, 1947.

Faragher, John Mack. *Sugar Creek: Life on the Illinois Prairie.* New Haven, Connecticut: Yale University Press, 1986.

Foner, Eric. *Free Soil, Free Labor, Free Men: The Ideology of the Republican Party before the Civil War.* New York: Oxford University Press, 1970.

General Public Acts of Congress, Respecting the Sale and Disposition of the Public Lands, with Instructions Issued by the Secretary of Treasury and Commissioner of the General Land Office and Official Opinions of the Attorney General on Questions Arising under the Land Laws. 2 vols. Washington, D.C.: Gales and Seaton, 1838.

Gienapp, William E. *The Origins of the Republican Party, 1852–1856.* New York: Oxford University Press, 1987.

Glaab, Charles N. *Kansas City and the Railroads: Community Policy in the Growth of a Regional Metropolis.* Madison: State Historical Society of Wisconsin, 1962.

Goodrich, Carter. *Government Promotion of American Canals and Railroads, 1800–1890.* New York: Columbia University Press, 1960.

Haeger, John Denis. *The Investment Frontier: New York Businessmen and the Economic Development of the Old Northwest.* Albany: State University of New York, 1981.

Hansen, Stephen L. *The Making of the Third Party System: Voters and Parties in Illinois, 1850–1876.* Studies in American History and Culture, no. 14. Ann Arbor, Michigan: UMI Research Press, 1980.

Herget, James E. "Democracy Revisited: The Law and School Districts in Illinois." *Journal of the Illinois State Historical Society* 72 (1979): 123–36.

Hershberg, Theodore, and Robert Dockhorn. "Occupational Classification." *Historical Methods Newsletter* 9 (March-June 1976): 59–98.

Hibbard, Benjamin Horace. *A History of Public Land Policies.* New York: Macmillan, 1924.

Hobsbawm, Eric J. *The Age of Capital.* New York: Charles Scribner's Sons, 1975.

Hogan, Richard. *Class and Community in Frontier Colorado.* Lawrence: University Press of Kansas, 1990.

Holt, Michael F. *The Political Crisis of the 1850s.* New York: John Wiley & Sons, 1978.

Howard, Robert P. *Illinois: A History of the Prairie State.* Grand Rapids, Michigan: William B. Eerdmans, 1972.

James, Edmund J. *A Bibliography of Newspapers Published in Illinois Prior to 1860.* Publications of the Illinois Historical Library, no. 1. Springfield, Illinois, 1899.

Jensen, Richard J. *Illinois: A Bicentennial History.* New York: W. W. Norton, 1978.

Johnson, Arthur M., and Barry E. Supple. *Boston Capitalists and Western Railroads.* Cambridge, Massachusetts: Harvard University Press, 1967.

Johnson, Charles Beneulyn. *Illinois in the Fifties, or, A Decade of Development, 1851–1860.* Illinois Centennial Edition. Champaign, Illinois: Flanigan-Pearson, 1918.

Kaestle, Carl F. *Pillars of the Republic: Common Schools and American Society, 1780–1860.* New York: Hill and Wang, 1983.

Katz, Michael B. "The Origins of Public Education: A Reassessment." *History of Education Quarterly* 16 (1976): 381–407.

Kettner, James A. *The Development of American Citizenship, 1608–1870.* Chapel Hill: University of North Carolina Press, 1978.

Kleppner, Paul. *The Third Electoral system, 1853–1892: Parties, Voters, and Political Cultures.* Chapel Hill: University of North Carolina Press, 1979.

Krenkel, John H. *Illinois Internal Improvements, 1818–1848.* Cedar Rapids, Iowa: Torch Press, 1958.

Kucera, Daniel W. *Church-State Relationships in Education in Illinois.* Washington, D.C.: Catholic University of America Press, 1955.

Larson, John Lauritz. *Bonds of Enterprise: John Murray Forbes and Western Development in America's Railway Age.* Cambridge, Massachusetts: Harvard University Press, 1984.

Limerick, Patricia Nelson. *The Legacy of Conquest: The Unbroken Past of the American West.* New York: W. W. Norton, 1987.

Mahoney, Timothy R. *River Towns in the Great West: The Structure of Provincial Urbanization in the American Midwest, 1820–1870.* New York: Cambridge University Press, 1990.

Malin, James C. "The Turnover of Farm Population in Kansas." *Kansas Historical Quarterly* 4 (1935): 339–72.

Mann, Ralph. *After the Gold Rush: Society in Grass Valley and Nevada City, California, 1855–1870.* Stanford, California: Stanford University Press, 1982.

Martin, Albro. *James J. Hill and the Opening of the Northwest.* New York: Oxford University Press, 1978.

McManis, Douglas R. *The Initial Evaluation and Utilization of the Illinois Prairies, 1815–1840.* Department of Geography Research Paper, no. 94. Chicago: Department of Geography, University of Chicago, 1964.

Norton, Margaret Cross, ed. *Illinois Census Returns, 1810, 1818.* Collections of the Illinois State Historical Library, vol. 24. Springfield: Illinois State Historical Library, 1935.

Pease, Theodore Calvin. *The Frontier State, 1818–1848.* Vol. 2 of *The Centennial History of Illinois.* Edited by Clarence Walworth Alvord. Springfield: Illinois Centennial Commission, 1918.

————. *Illinois Election Returns, 1818–1848.* Collections of the Illinois State Historical Library, vol. 18. Springfield: Illinois State Historical Library, 1923.

Pessen, Edward. *Jacksonian America: Society, Personality, and Politics.* Rev. ed. Urbana: University of Illinois Press, 1985.

Peters, Richard, ed. *The Public Statutes at Large of the United States of America, from the Organization of the Government in 1789 to March 3, 1845.* Boston: Little, Brown, 1845.

Ryan, Mary P. *Cradle of the Middle Class: The Family in Oneida County, New York, 1790–1865.* New York: Cambridge University Press, 1981.

Schaefer, Catherine. "A Chronology of Missions and Churches in Illinois from 1675 to 1855." *Illinois Catholic Historical Review* (July/October): 103–9, 253–56.

Scheiber, Harry N. *Ohio Canal Era: A Case Study of Government and the Economy, 1820–1861.* Athens: Ohio University Press, 1969.

Schlesinger, Arthur M., Jr. *The Age of Jackson*. Boston: Little, Brown, 1945.

Scott, Franklin William. *Newspapers and Periodicals*. Collections of the Illinois State Historical Library, no. 6. Springfield: Illinois State Historical Library, 1910.

Stark, Sandra M., ed. "Illinois Papers." *Illinois Libraries* 64 (March 1962): 206–76.

Stewart, James Brewer. *Holy Warriors: The Abolitionists and American Slavery*. New York: Hill and Wang, 1976.

Stewart, Lowell O. *Public Land Surveys: History, Instructions, Methods*. Ames, Iowa: Collegiate Press, 1935.

Taber, Morris C. "The New England Influence in South Central Michigan." *Michigan History Magazine* 45 (December 1961): 305–36.

Tanner, Helen Hornbeck, ed. *Atlas of Great Lakes Indian History*. Norman: University of Oklahoma Press, 1986.

Taylor, George Rogers. *The Transportation Revolution, 1815–1860*. New York: Holt, Rinehart and Winston, 1951.

Teaford, Jon C. *Cities of the Heartland: The Rise and Fall of the Industrial Midwest*. Bloomington: Indiana University Press, 1993.

Thernstrom, Stephan, and Peter R. Knights. "Men in Motion: Some Data and Speculations about Urban Population Mobility in Nineteenth-Century America." *Journal of Interdisciplinary History* 1 (Summer 1970): 7–35.

Thorne, Mildred. "Population Study of an Iowa County in 1850." *Iowa Journal of History* 57 (1959): 305–30.

Treat, Payson Jackson. *The National Land System, 1785–1820*. New York: E. B. Treat, 1919.

Turner, Frederick Jackson. "The Significance of the Frontier in American History." In *American Historical Association Annual Report for 1893* (1893): 199–227.

Walters, William D., Jr., and Floyd Mansberger. "Initial Field Location in Illinois." *Agricultural History* 57 (July 1983): 289–96.

White, C. Albert. *A History of the Rectangular Survey System*. Washington, D.C.: Government Printing Office, [1941].

Wood, Gordon S. *The Creation of the American Republic, 1776–1787*. New York: W. W. Norton, 1969.

Worster, Donald. *Rivers of Empire: Water, Aridity, and the Growth of the American West*. New York: Pantheon Books, 1985.

The WPA Guide to Illinois. Written and compiled by the Federal Writers' Project of the Works Progress Administration for the State of Illinois. With a new introduction by Neil Harris and Michael Conzen. New York: Pantheon Books, 1983.

Index

Abend, Edward, 110, 113, 196n. 5
Abend, Joseph, 116
Abend family (Belleville settlers), 21
abolitionism, 126–27, 184n. 4
Achtundvierziger ("Greens"), 22
African Americans, 9, 12, 33; in
  Belleville, 49, 54; in Galesburg, 63–
  65; in Ottawa, 56
Albright, Isaac, 127
Alcorn, Richard S., 108
Allen, Henry, 94
Alton, Illinois, 10, 109, 123
American Bottom, 16, 18
American Party ("Know Nothings"),
  115, 137, 138; in Belleville, 120–22;
  in Ottawa, 131
Anderson, Samuel, 116
Armour, John, 82, 133
Atherton, Lewis, 6
Atlantic and Mississippi Railroad, 78
Augthusen, Hermann, 22
Aurora Branch Line Railroad, 80, 86
Austrians, 55
Avery, George, 97, 125
Avery, Joseph, 27
Avery, Julius, 97, 125, 127, 133
Avery family (Galesburg settlers),
  183n. 45

Bain, Aaron, 24
Ball, C. (Belleville resident), 78
Baptists: in Belleville, 54; in Galesburg,
  34, 65–66, 140; in Ottawa, 61
Barrett, Richard F., 37, 39, 182n. 39
Bassett, G. W. (Ottawa minister), 61
Belleville, Illinois, 10, 16; beer production, 50; churches, 23, 54–58, 185n.
  12; city incorporation, 109; coal
  mining, 16, 20, 23, 49, 50; early history, 19, 20; early industry, 50; elections, 109–23, 170, 197n. 7; ethnic

groups, 23, 47–48, 68, 141, 143,
  150–57; founding, 14–15, 18, 44;
  fraternal organizations, 55; German
  language instruction, 92; government workers, 51; laborers, 50; newspapers, 113–23; occupational structure, 49–52, 154–57; politics,
  109–23; population, 49, 185n. 8;
  population growth, 21, 47, 142,
  149, 201n. 1; property holding, 52–
  53; railroads, 71, 74–79; schools, 91–
  94, 193n. 4; settlement, 6, 11, 14,
  15, 17; wealth structure, 53
Belleville Academy, 91, 101
Belleville Advocate, 23, 70, 75–79, 89,
  113–15, 117, 118, 121
Belleville and Illinoistown Railroad,
  77, 79, 110
Belleville Banner-Times, 114
Belleville Democrat, 118–20
Belleville High School, 92, 94
Belleville Institute, 93
Belleville Library Society, 55
Belleville Republican, 117
Belleville *Sängerbund*, 55
Belleville School Association, 91
*Belleviller Sängerbund and die Bibliothek
  Gesellschaft, Der*, 55
Belleviller Volksblatt, 120, 121
Belleviller Zeitung, 74, 106, 117–21
Belleville Times, 75, 115
Belleville-to-St. Louis Turnpike, 16,
  75–76
Berchelmann, A. (Belleville settler), 22
Bierheller, Fritz, 117
Birney, James G., 136
Black Hawk War, 13, 33
Blair, George, 14, 15
Blanchard, Jonathan, 136, 139
Blunt, Francis, 59
Bornmann, Conrad, 21

219

222 *Index*

Harrison, T. A. (Belleville resident), 76
Harrison, William Henry, 115
Harvey, G. A. (Belleville editor), 115,
117, 118, 119
Hasselquist, T. N. (Galesburg editor),
103
Hauck, Bartholomew, 116, 120
Haver, "Miss" (Ottawa teacher), 94
Hawkinson, P. L. (Galesburg street
commissioner), 64, 140
Hay, John B., 14, 20, 118
Hecker, Friederich, 121
Heimberger, Gustav, 22
Hemlandet (Galesburg newspaper), 104,
138
Hick, R. S. (LaSalle County politician),
132
Hickling, William, 27, 82, 83, 95, 96,
128–30
Hildebrandt, J. C. (Belleville settler), 22
Hilgard, E. (Belleville settler), 22
Hilgard, Fritz, 22
Hilgard, J. (Belleville settler), 22
Hilgard, Theodore, 22, 120
Hilgard, Thomas, 22
Hise, John, 27, 81, 124, 125, 191n. 16
Hitt, Daniel F., 27, 179n. 20
Hoes, John V. A., 27, 82, 124, 126,
128, 130, 131
Hogaboom, Abel, 179n. 20
Hogaboom, John, 179n. 20
Hogaboom, Richard, 179n. 20
Hogan, Richard, 5
Holcomb, B. F. (Galesburg treasurer),
104
Holcomb, W. H. (Galesburg Democrat),
137
Hopkins, David W., 110
Hossack, John, 108, 124, 127
Hughes, James W., 110

Illinois and Michigan Canal, 7, 10, 13,
36, 71, 75, 83, 84; completion, 30;
finances, 29; and Irish laborers, 27,
28; legislation, 27; and Ottawa, 24–
26, 44, 57, 79, 80, 125, 180n. 29
Illinois Beobachter (Belleville newspaper), 116
Illinois Central Railroad, 77, 81, 82,
83, 84, 86, 88, 128

Illinois Constitution of 1818, 19, 112
Illinois Constitution of 1848, 111, 112–
13
Illinois Free School Act (1855), 90
Illinois Free Trader (Ottawa newspaper),
24, 124
*Illinois Free Trader and LaSalle County
Commercial Advertiser* (Ottawa newspaper), 124
Illinois Indian Confederacy, 12
Illinois Internal Improvement Act
(1837), 71, 75
Illinois Military Tract, 10, 33, 36, 40,
181n. 33
Illinois Normal University, 102
Illinois Republican (Belleville newspaper), 115, 118, 119, 120
Illinois River, 10, 30, 31, 81, 85, 129;
site of Fort St. Louis, 13; and
Ottawa, 24
Illinois River Bridge Company, 128,
130
Illinoistown (East St. Louis), Illinois,
10, 75, 142
Illinoistown and Vincennes Railroad,
114
Irish, 46; in Belleville, 48, 51, 52; in
Galesburg, 8, 62, 63, 64, 66, 67,
105, 138, 140, 141; in Ottawa, 1, 8,
27, 28, 56, 58, 62, 82, 99, 105, 124,
132–34

Jackson, Giles W., 97, 98
Jervis, Timothy, 35
Jolliet, Louis, 12
Joy, James F., 86

Kämpf, Friedrich, 117,
Kansas-Nebraska Bill, 137
Kaskaskia Village, Illinois, 13
Kattman, August, 120
Kelley, J. W. (Ottawa editor), 125
Kellogg, Hiram H., 136, 182n. 35
Kerr, Joseph, 20
King, C. B. (Ottawa abolitionist), 127
King, Claudius B., 127
King, Hervey, 127
Kingsbury, S. A. (Galesburg minister),
66

Kay J. Carr is an associate professor of United States history at Southern Illinois University at Carbondale, where she teaches courses on early America, the West, and historical geography. She received her B.A. degree in history from Knox College and her M.A. and Ph.D. degrees in history from the University of Chicago. Previous publications include: *The Illinois and Michigan Canal National Heritage Corridor: A Guide to Its History and Sources* (edited, with Michael P. Conzen); "Illinois in the Early Days: The Life and Times of Christiana Holmes Tillson, 1798–1872" (a new introduction to Tillson's *A Woman's Story of Pioneer Illinois*); and "Community Dynamics and Educational Decisions: Establishing Public Schools in Belleville and Galesburg," which received the Harry E. Pratt Memorial Award as the best article in the *Illinois Historical Journal* in 1991.